# Angelic Troublemakers

# CONTEMPORARY ANARCHIST STUDIES

A series edited by

Laurence Davis, *National University of Ireland, Maynooth*

Uri Gordon, *Arava Institute for Environmental Studies, Israel*

Nathan Jun, *Midwestern State University, USA*

Alex Prichard, *London School of Economics, UK*

**Contemporary Anarchist Studies** promotes the study of anarchism as a framework for understanding and acting on the most pressing problems of our times. The series publishes cutting edge, socially engaged scholarship from around the world—bridging theory and practice, academic rigor and the insights of contemporary activism.

The topical scope of the series encompasses anarchist history and theory broadly construed; individual anarchist thinkers; anarchist-informed analysis of current issues and institutions; and anarchist or anarchist-inspired movements and practices. Contributions informed by anticapitalist, feminist, ecological, indigenous, and non-Western or global South anarchist perspectives are particularly welcome. So, too, are manuscripts that promise to illuminate the relationships between the personal and the political aspects of transformative social change, local and global problems, and anarchism and other movements and ideologies. Above all, we wish to publish books that will help activist scholars and scholar activists think about how to challenge and build real alternatives to existing structures of oppression and injustice.

# Angelic Troublemakers

## Religion and Anarchism in America

*A. Terrance Wiley*

B L O O M S B U R Y
NEW YORK • LONDON • NEW DELHI • SYDNEY

**Bloomsbury Academic**
An imprint of Bloomsbury Publishing Inc

| | |
|---|---|
| 1385 Broadway | 50 Bedford Square |
| New York | London |
| NY 10018 | WC1B 3DP |
| USA | UK |

**www.bloomsbury.com**

**Bloomsbury is a registered trademark of Bloomsbury Publishing Plc**

First published 2014

© A. Terrance Wiley, 2014

**Library of Congress Cataloging-in-Publication Data**
A catalog record for this book is available from the Library of Congress.

ISBN: PB: 978-1-6235-6601-2
HB: 978-1-6235-6813-9
ePub: 978-1-6235-6406-3
ePDF: 978-1-6235-6995-2

Typeset by Newgen Knowledge Works (P) Ltd., Chennai, India
Printed and bound in the United States of America

# CONTENTS

# ACKNOWLEDGMENTS

This project began as a dissertation at Princeton University and it would not have been completed without the many fellowships, mentors, and friendships that came during my years in graduate school. I have a hard time believing that anyone could have a better dissertation committee than I had. I would repeat graduate school three times if they would have me. Eddie Glaude, Eric Gregory, Albert J. Raboteau, Jeffrey Stout, and Cornel West each provided instructions, issued challenges, voiced encouragement in ways that have made me a more thoughtful person, a more careful writer, and this project much stronger than it would have otherwise been, with Glaude and Stout providing especially instructive comments on each draft. Glaude, Stout, and West's respective projects underpin this work at almost every turn and, while they might not recognize it, this is a work in prophetic pragmatism.

Turning the dissertation into a book was hard; but it was much easier with the support that I received from colleagues and students at Carleton College. With this in mind, I would specifically like to thank Dorothy Broom for providing a financial gift to Carleton College that allowed the college to support this project with professional development grants and a much-needed course release during the 2010–11 academic year. Michael McNally's and Bev Nagel's support during my time at Carleton is something that I will always cherish. The same can be said of the exhilarating intellectual exchanges about anarchism, American politics, and religion that I had with students such as Jessie Rothman, Nick Welna, Jaclyn Bovee, Brooke Granowski, Kendall Bills, and Matthew Fitzgerald.

Now that I'm a teacher, it is even clearer how fortunate I am to have studied with Howard Campbell, Alfonso Morales, Maceo Dailey, Pervis Brown, Abraham Smith, Lonnie Kliever, Richard Cogley, Johan Elverskog, Theodore Walker, David Luban, and Robin Lovin. They each shaped my thinking in ways that show up in this book.

Special thanks are due to Robin Lovin, who has probably done more than any other teacher to usher along my academic career. This includes writing recommendation letters at critical points, hosting me during office hours, fielding countless phone calls about this or that, and reading multiple drafts of this manuscript. I will continue to draw from his comments and example as I move forward.

I have

I also benefited immensely from critical suggestions on portions of the manuscript made by Seth Moglen, James Peterson, Lori Pearson, Inese Radzins, Mairaj Syed, David Luban, Anthony Cook, Robert George, Kevin Wolfe, Margaret Mitchell, James Martel, and Joseph Winters. Molly Farneth and Michael Raposa both commented on the entire manuscript in ways that helped me hone my ideas, argument, and prose. These model colleagues humble and inspire.

The same and more could be said about Anthony Pinn. As a practical matter, this book would have never been published without his support. Pinn read an early draft of this manuscript and balanced celebration with constructive criticism; he also forwarded it to an editor at Bloomsbury.

Eventually, the manuscript landed in Uri Gordon's inbox and I am happy that it did. Gordon has provided steady encouragement, edifying advice, and a wonderful example of how to marry philosophical passion with a social justice impulse. My own effort and concern to marry that passion and impluse made Bloomsbury an ideal home for my first book. And I am grateful for Bloomsbury's commitment to engaged scholarship. I also thank editors Ally Jane Grossan and Kaitlin Fontana for their support and patience, and the anonymous readers for the helpful reports written during the proposal process.

And what a process it has been. I have lost and made friends. Thank the gods for friendship. Sharing time with persons such as Davion Chism, Bright Limm, Kimberly Kim, Torry Winn, Kyung Ji Rhee, Alan Borelli, Andrea Jones, Ernest Mitchell, and Molly Farneth has made it easier to keep my head up, to keep on writing when I did not want to, and to smile at that.

Family has been important too. My parents Terry and Alvin Wadley have provided unconditional love and consistent support from the first. Conversations with them during graduate school and the writing of this manuscript kept me hopeful and grounded. Periodic phone calls from my grandma, Helen Wiley, and aunts Lynn, Beverly, Darlene, and Pat were also vital sources of support.

No one has been as supportive as the only person who is as relieved as I am that I have completed this project. Terri Elizabeth Wiley (Lil' Mama) is so good to me. She helped keep me focused. She sometimes exaggerated in the name of love. She edited citations. She proofread drafts, and read and re-read subsequent drafts aloud. She pretended that she was not bored by talk of prima facie duties. But more than helping me with the actual writing, she loves me and is trying to help me gather myself, the tattered pieces. I give thanks to her for this. More than what she does for me, though, is what she represents as an educator and social reformer. She represents well and keeps alive the tradition of Sojourner Truth, Elizabeth Peabody, Anna Cooper, Septima Clark, and other deep-lovers of children. Her devotion to living a life of service to those in need stirs my soul and leaves me (almost!) speechless. The depth of her love for persons helps me believe in possibilities.

This work is in many ways my attempt to come to terms with the lessons on love that I have been taught by family, friends, and the ancestors. Buried in the parts of this text are thoughts and ideas that some will undoubtedly regard as a bit too hopeful about the possibilities for realizing social justice on earth. If I sometimes seem too hopeful, it is merely an effect of the fact that I am the product of a whole lot of love and I have shared space with persons who love freedom and justice and truth.

*So perish all compromises with tyranny.*
WILLIAM LLOYD GARRISON

*Justice is the first virtue of social institutions, as truth is of systems of thought. A theory however elegant and economical must be rejected or revised if it is untrue; likewise laws and institutions no matter how efficient and well-arranged must be reformed or abolished if they are unjust.*
JOHN RAWLS, *A Theory of Justice*

*Every definitional and programmatic approach to justice makes it into a dimension of State action. But the State has nothing to do with justice, for the State is indifferent or hostile to the existence of a politics that touches on truths.*
ALAIN BADIOU, *Metapolitics*

# Introduction

Few political philosophies are as misunderstood as anarchism. The term conjures images of disorder for many, even though only a minority of anarchists has advocated the use of violence of any sort. At least three factors have affected how many imagine anarchism. First, anarchism has often been reduced to the terrorist ethos that marked the political movement (namely anarcho-syndicalism or anarcho-communism) during the late nineteenth and early twentieth centuries, where anarchist labor activists turned to assassination as a method of social change. Second, many anarchists have been "militant atheists," often hostile toward religion. This hostility probably reached its height around the time of the Spanish Civil War, where while controlling Spain's Catalonia ("Anarchist Catalonia") region from 1936 to 1939, a contingent of anarchists demolished Catholic buildings and murdered clerics. And finally, a third factor shaping the perception of anarchism among many is that some anarchists, such as the egoist Max Stirner, have been proponents of nihilism.

This book is about three anarchists of a different sort. The main interpretive chapters, descriptive ethical case studies, are devoted to analyzing the religious ethics, political philosophies, and social activism of Henry David Thoreau, Dorothy Day, and Bayard Rustin in terms of an anarchist conceptual scheme that promises to elucidate the implications of particular varieties of religious radicalism for the modern territorial state and our normative relation to it. By examining them, I hope to shed light on a highly influential strand of religious ethics and radical activist practice in the modern period, as well as on a variety of anarchism that does not conform to the negative stereotypes of the position.

None of the three religious radicals would condone terrorism. None of them is an atheist or a proponent of nihilism. The reasons they offer for anarchist suspicion of modern territorial states are, I will argue, largely religious in character. Analysis of the explicit and implicit arguments for anarchism extant in the social thought of three religiously inclined, amateur intellectual, radical lay activists will facilitate the refinement of anarchist thought proper; and, employing anarchism as a theoretic or conceptual scheme by which to consider the religious ethics and political philosophies of Thoreau, Day, and Rustin provides a means by which to clarify critical aspects of their social and religious thought and practice, which promises to reveal that the category of anarchism is broader than is ordinarily assumed, with deep American roots and strong ties to rich, transnational anti-imperialist and anticolonialist traditions, from Gandhian nonviolence to Zapatista radicalism. In particular, with these three radical American exemplars we will see the way in which theologically sourced compassion, emphases on moral responsibility (for oppression and social suffering), and ethics of noncomplicity (Thoreau) or noncooperation (Day and Rustin) with unjust (racist and imperialist) social practices can commend an anarchist posture or attitude that is thoroughly other-regarding.

This philosophically grounded, historically oriented, social theoretically informed study, then, should furnish a deeper understanding of anarchist philosophy, a fuller appreciation of the anarchist dimensions of radical nonviolent activism, and thus a clearer view of how anarchist commitments have combined with and can cohere with radical religiosity and the transnational nonviolent direct action tradition, a tradition to which the three American figures in question have contributed immensely. When taken as a whole, by carefully tending to the religious visions of three American radicals, this book identifies and explores reasons of various kinds that lend support to a single religious-ethical or sociopolitical practice that is recognizably anarchist in its unwillingness to attribute genuine authority to the legal regimes of modern territorial states and undeniably revolutionary in its commitment to fundamentally transforming standing social institutions and power relations, so as to instantiate more just social conditions.

# I

Given the negative stereotypes in circulation, it is crucial to provide a preliminary conceptual analysis of anarchism as it will be understood in the interpretive chapters. I should say, first, that I am primarily interested in anarchism as a political philosophy or political philosophical orientation taken by agents in the sociopolitical arena. Anarchism as a political philosophical position or practice can be thought of as a set of claims about and an attendant attitude toward coercion and political authority. To discuss these issues in such terms is to emphasize particular political philosophical questions: What is the proper relation of the individual to a given political entity such as the territorial state? What authority does the territorial state have, as a normative matter, over individual persons? What, if anything, do individuals owe to a standing state or political authority? These questions are pertinent to analysis of anarchist thought in that they direct attention to the most basic dimension of anarchist philosophy. For, it is on the basis of the answers that anarchists deliver in response to the above questions that anarchists can be distinguished from proponents of other political theories.

Indeed, while there are varieties of anarchism, as a general matter, anarchist theory and praxis begin with criticism of or opposition to the predominant existing political organization, namely the modern territorial state. In particular, anarchist opposition to certain existing political institutions entails denying that those institutions possess legitimate authority.

To possess legitimate "political" authority is to be entitled to impose obligations on persons designated as political subjects and to enforce compliance or to penalize noncompliance with those obligations. All existing modern territorial states assert that they possess legitimate political authority. Modern territorial states also claim to be sovereign authorities in relation to some territorial space. Following Max Weber, we can say that territorial states are "ruling organizations" that "claim a monopoly on the legitimate use of force."[1] And, more to the point, with Robert Paul Wolff we can say that territorial states *claim* that they *actually* have the right to command and the right to be obeyed.[2] It is precisely this claim that anarchists take issue with, as this kind of claim conflicts with the related ideas of moral autonomy and voluntarism that most anarchists embrace.

To exercise moral autonomy (in the non-Kantian, nonmetaphysical sense) is to act on the basis of reasons that one understands to be the right reasons for action in particular cases. This connects to the idea of voluntarism. Central to the idea of voluntarism in question is the idea that, in certain domains of social and political life, persons can become subjects owing certain moral duties to persons or institutions *only* through voluntary submission or consent. Significantly, anarchists reject nonvoluntarist conceptions of *political* obligation.[3]

This last point is essential and directs attention to one of the most important issues that I will address in this book. It is often assumed that to be an anarchist one must reject all possible forms of political organization or association. And there are in fact anarchists who, a priori or even in theory, deny the possibility of a morally acceptable political organization.[4] Yet there are anarchists who with Proudhon, the first self-declared anarchist, maintain that some form of government is or would be morally acceptable. To that end, anarchists Bakunin, Paul Goodman, and Murray Bookchin, for example, all proposed one form of governmental organization or another. They preferred smaller-scale, local-level political organization, and often described the ideal social situation as one in which there is decentralized power or organization. Such anarchists accept and will only accept (what is often referred to as) unanimous direct democracy as a legitimate political procedure or procedural system. This is because, in practice, only consensus or unanimous direct democracy, where all rules governing a given society are consented to by each person who is to be subject to those rules, is compatible with the idea of moral autonomy that these anarchists endorse. Any other political authority lacks legitimacy from their vantage point.[5] Accordingly, for such anarchists, commitment to voluntarism or the idea of moral autonomy counts as a reason to deny the legitimacy of the modern territorial state.[6] But, once again, a commitment to voluntarism or the idea of moral autonomy does not entail the rejection of political organization as such. Insofar as one *does not* embrace conceptions of moral autonomy or voluntarism that prohibit promising or contracting per se, then one might regard consent-based political organizations as morally acceptable.

Just as it is sometimes assumed that anarchism entails a rejection of political organization as such, persons committed to individual moral autonomy or voluntarism are often characterized as egotistical, selfish, or individualistic in the pejorative sense. My analysis should undermine this assumption by showing the way in which assertions of autonomy—that is, an insistence on moral autonomy—or voluntarism can be and have often been motivated by other-regarding concern about social justice. To put this differently, autonomy has been expressed as morally grounded refusals to participate in the subjugation of oppressed "others," a way to resist doing the dirty work of oppressive agencies and agents.

To understand how assertions of autonomy can function in this manner we only need to consider the issue of promise making from another angle. While the anarchists that I am interested in are not morally opposed to promise making per se, they do maintain that there are certain promises that one must not make. Religiously motivated anarchists such as Thoreau, Day, and Rustin hold that one ought to refrain from making general, that is, open-ended, promises to adhere to decisions of bodies that might prescribe actions that would entail the violation of a given moral principle, rule, or value. That is, they maintain that one must not issue promises when doing so might commit one to the performance of a particular act that from one's own moral vantage constitutes an immoral or wrongful moral act.[7]

Most persons implicitly accept this condition on promise making, yet do not spend that much time reflecting on its political philosophical implications in the context of the territorial state, where persons are expected to promise to comply with laws or commands in advance of knowing what practices they will be required to participate in or support. In the chapters that follow, I will discuss how a commitment to noncomplicity or noncooperation with injustice leads Thoreau, Day, and Rustin to reject the authority of the territorial state on account of territorial states' exclusive decision-making processes and due to the fact that territorial states so often enact laws, implement policies, and engage in practices that are morally problematic. In the light of this, I hope to show that Thoreau, Day, and Rustin offer religious-ethical reasons that support an anarchist ethic and ethos. Anarchists insist that insofar as one has not explicitly consented to the rule of a given territorial state or its officials, then one is under no *moral* obligation to obey the commands of its officials. Those officials lack legitimate authority and their commands lack moral force.

This connects to a final distinction that warrants being mentioned. Throughout this book I will take for granted that one's stance with respect to the legitimacy of the territorial state, and the concomitant issue of whether one bears a moral duty to comply with rules or laws announced by the state, can be separated from the question as to whether one bears duties to defy, withdraw from, or seek the elimination of the state. Consequently, denying the legitimacy of the territorial state does not necessarily entail subscription to the additional duties just mentioned. To that end, while some persons (generally regarded as anarchists) contend that there is a duty to withdraw support from existing states, others (generally regarded as anarchists) do not.[8] In view of this, I will distinguish between these two groups of anarchists as follows: A *weak* anarchist is one who denies the legitimacy of existing territorial states and so holds that individuals do not have moral obligations to obey the laws or commands of territorial states.[9] A *strong* anarchist is one who rejects the idea that there are moral obligations to obey state authorities as such and additionally argues that individual persons have a moral duty to "oppose"[10] and, "so far as is possible," eliminate the state.[11] So both weak and strong anarchists deny the legitimacy of territorial state authorities and reject the idea that there is a moral duty to obey territorial state laws and commands. What differentiates the two is that the strong anarchist (*pace* the weak anarchist) further contends that one ought to oppose or seek to eliminate existent states.

Adopting a stipulated definition of anarchism will put us in a position to appreciate the profound political implications of the radical religious and social thought and praxis of Thoreau, Day, and Rustin, as it will be evident that each of the three commends an attitude toward political authority that is consistent with the principles of anarchism, or one of its varieties, as it has come to be understood in recent decades among theorists and philosophers. One might doubt the significance of the type of principled rejection of political obligation and the state's political authority that I have designated as weak anarchism. But the import of even the weak anarchist's stance will be easier to appreciate if we keep in mind the fact that there is a limited range of normative postures that one can assume in relation to the modern territorial state—especially the state's claims regarding its own sovereignty and authority—meditate intently on what it means to reject that authority, and consider carefully the importance that dissenting activists, carried away by the spirit of weak anarchism, have historically played in major social movements. Weak anarchism represents an attitude toward authority that has fostered vital resistance to domination and my turn to a figure such as Rustin with this language in mind should facilitate a better appreciation of what is necessary for achieving substantive social change, challenging those who would celebrate past radical activism to more candidly assess what we must do to resist the modes of domination that mark our era.

# II

This book is divided into three chapters, with each chapter focusing respectively on Henry David Thoreau, Dorothy Day, and Bayard Rustin.

In Chapter 1, "The Conscience on Fire: Thoreau's Anarchist Ethic," I concentrate on the writings and social action of Henry David Thoreau. What interests me is Thoreau's conscientious struggle to determine how he should relate to his neighbors and to the modern territorial state in the light of what he understood to be the implications of the Protestant Reformation, the European Enlightenment, the English, American, and French revolutions, and the religious-ethical principles to which he was committed. Thoreau reached conclusions about his duties that ruled out his embracing constitutional democracy. By the end of Chapter 1 it should be clear that Thoreau's theologically motivated conception of moral rightness, when combined with his theory of the state, generates an anarchist ethic and situates him among a transnational group of mid-nineteenth-century figures that responded to the emergent territorial state and its racial supremacist, imperialist practices with an anarchist ethic.

This reveals the fact that Thoreau should be distinguished from certain other racial and social justice activists who endorsed political disobedience and nonviolent direct action. Take, for example, Martin Luther King Jr, who Thoreau greatly influenced. Thoreau and King both embraced a rigorous deontological ethic that is incompatible with an idea that an individual ought to comply with the law in virtue of its being the law, even when the source of the law in question is a democratic procedure. In addition, they both maintained that noncooperation with evil or unjust practices represents a viable way to undermine those practices. But carefully analyzing Thoreau's political essays shows that, in contrast to King's ostensibly ameliorative disobedience, Thoreau provides a recipe for eliminating the modern territorial state: he aimed to abolish it rather than reform it. In my chapters on Thoreau, I will endeavor to show that Thoreau is best described as a *strong* anarchist in that he denies the authority of the legal regimes of modern territorial states and argues that individual persons have a duty to withdraw from, to oppose, and to disobey certain laws and commands of territorial states. Emphasizing this point will put on display the grounds that make it appropriate to classify Thoreau's political philosophy as an expression of *strong* anarchism.

Thoreau's political philosophy can be properly understood only if we appreciate the metaphysical-theological-ontological assumptions that undergird it, as Thoreau's conception of moral rightness, the human person, and individual moral responsibility are grounded in his theological commitments. To read Thoreau's work carefully is to see that there is an unmistakable religious aspect to his social and political philosophy and there is a mystical dimension to his spirituality or religious practices. He meditates. He watches nature. He reads religious scripture. He might be a lay monk. And his sojourn at Walden's Pond is as much a spiritual retreat as it is anything else: "*Walden* is a book about spiritual renewal at a sacred place."[12] As Alan D. Hodder notes in *Thoreau's Ecstatic Witness*, Thoreau's contemporaries "generally conceived him in spiritual terms . . . even if as an unorthodox [religious] figure."[13]

And so, in the early sections of Chapter 1, I spell out the terms of Thoreau's religious ethics, focusing on two of Thoreau's classic book-length manuscripts, *A Week on the Concord and Merrimack Rivers* (*A Week*) and *Walden*. Beginning with a consideration of Thoreau's religiosity, and considering his idea of conscience and the doctrine of noncomplicity in relation to his theology, puts up front a component of his thought that is not always discussed in relation to or as a basis for Thoreau's normative political commitments. I then connect his religious vision to his political vision. While the features of Thoreau's religiosity that I will present are not necessarily or inevitably reason(s) for the adoption of an anarchist philosophy, the direction that Thoreau takes these features—the way in which he interprets them—ends up entailing an anarchist ethic.[14] I argue that Thoreau is best regarded as an anarchist in the light of the fact that he rejects the legitimacy of the modern territorial state, and this includes representational/constitutional democracy, for religious-ethical reasons.

In particular, my analysis in Chapter 1 shows that he agrees with anarchists who claim that, empirically speaking, there is hardly reason to suppose that any actual territorial state will have laws which do not themselves become instruments of arbitrarily exercised power. For Thoreau, the actual state is a vehicle of domination and so cannot in good faith be presented as an effective means by which to protect persons from various kinds of domination. To demonstrate all of this, I will give acute attention to Thoreau's explicit references to and criticisms of the territorial state, law, authority, and political action, as these references and criticisms appear in *A Week*, *Walden*, and the essays "Resistance to Civil Government," "Slavery in Massachusetts," and "A Plea for Captain John Brown."

Thoreau's prophetic thought can be summarized as follows. First, Thoreau embraces the idea of divine immanence and asserts that each human being has the divinity or divine power within. Second, implicit in Thoreau's thought is a rejection of the divine right of kings, the idea that God has appointed standing (earthly) authorities to their positions so that they can be said to rule by divine right. Third, Thoreau posits the existence of an objective moral order that is accessible to a human faculty—conscience or reason. Fourth, he calls for a moral awakening, a recovery of the self through self-culture or self-improvement. Fifth, Thoreau claims that certain existing social practices and institutions, particularly the territorial state, impede awakening. Finally, he contends that awakening or recovery of the self will entail noncooperation with and elimination of the evil or unjust practices of the territorial state; this means that self-recovery, when generalized, will, as social movement, entail revolution of a certain sort.

I can restate more concisely this simple prophetic message as I understand Thoreau to present it. God is immanent. Human persons possess a divine power within. We have lost sight of this power. It can and must be recovered. To recover this power would require us to reject many of the practices in which we are currently participants. In particular, we would have to resist contributing to the violence and injustice propagated by the territorial state, or officials of the state. And we most certainly cannot be represented by nor be representatives of the territorial state. Therefore, a recovery of the self or the divine power within the self would mean a revolution. Importantly, Thoreau does not propose that persons committed to justice seize control of the territorial state. Rather, they are charged with becoming the kinds of persons that call into being and make possible the emergence of new institutions. This last point is crucial. Anarchism, as I suggested above, does not, as it is sometimes believed, entail a wholesale rejection of organizations or institutions. To that end, anarchists such as Peter Kropotkin, George Woodcock, and Murray Bookchin have proposed different forms of government to replace the modern territorial state, including its representational democratic emanation. By the end of Chapter 1 we will see that Thoreau advocates for a government that is probably best described as anarchism as government by consent.

In Chapter 2, "Love in Action: Dorothy Day's Christian Anarchism," Thoreau's political philosophy is contrasted with the Christian-motivated anarchism of Dorothy Day, a convert to Roman Catholicism who cofounded the *Catholic Worker* and the Catholic Worker movement. Just as with my analysis of Thoreau, my analysis of Dorothy Day is very much a story about how a person's conception of God can inform a conception of the self and thus shape a person's political ethics. That is to say, similar to the chapters on Thoreau, it is a story about how our political notions are often wrapped up in our notions about God and the self.

Dorothy Day flirted with anarchism as early as 1914, yet she did not fully embrace it until later: "I wavered between my allegiance to socialism, syndicalism (the I.W.W.'s) and anarchism. When I read Tolstoi, I was an anarchist . . . [This] appealed to me. But not the American anarchism that I had come in touch with."[15] Years of equivocation would end with Day's conversion to Catholicism. After converting, and settling in on a love-centered ethics, she came to find Tolstoy's claim undeniable: Christian love is incompatible with coercion, violence, and centralized political decision-making processes.

Day's religious ethics provides perhaps the clearest twentieth-century statement of Christian anarchism in the American context, which is striking in that Roman Catholicism has been one of the main objects of anarchist criticism during the past century. Part of the lasting significance of Day's activist career is that she demonstrated the way in which traditional Catholic piety could be channeled in radical political directions. After converting to Catholicism in the late 1920s, Day would self-consciously submit to ecclesiastical authority, however, she appealed to Catholic dogma, namely, the distinction between "truths of the faith" and the idea of the "autonomy of the temporal order" in order to establish her license to assert her view that anarchism is an (if not "the") appropriate form of social organization for a Catholic Christian.[16]

Chapter 2 is comprised of two major parts. In the first part, I will primarily explicate Day's religious commitments as they relate to her conception of God, the person, community, and love, mostly by indicating the particularly religious—and unifying—function that Day attributes to love. More specifically, in the first section of Chapter 2, I consider Day's religious odyssey, focusing on important aspects of her move toward joining the Roman Catholic Church. In the second section, I give attention to Day's articulation of her religious ethics in the light of her interpretation of Catholicism.

After considering Day's conversion to Roman Catholicism, I analyze the details of Day's political philosophy, including her criticisms of the modern sociopolitical order and her positive sociopolitical prescription. Further, I highlight aspects of her thought and activism that connect her directly to the nonviolent activist tradition, putting on display the way in which Day combines crucial aspects of Thoreau's and Tolstoy's normative visions. In particular, Day embraces a type of realized eschatology that Tolstoy emphases in *The Kingdom of God Is Within*. And similar to both Tolstoy and Thoreau, Day embraces voluntary poverty and suggests the liberatory character of asceticism. For Day, asceticism—the self-regulation of desire in the light of authentic needs—when politically charged carries all of the way to the level of the state. Asceticism forces the moral agent to subsist conscientiously, thus liberating the agent to imagine alternative modes of being, including social and political practices at the institutional level. In this way, Day's political vision is rooted in the kind of imaginative ethos that is often dismissed as unrealistic or utopian. It is through concrete action that the activist undermines the purchase of this charge, and so for Day, imagining an alternative social reality and the viability of the vision hinges on what we might term "revelatory praxis." Such praxis sets out to *reveal* what is in fact necessary.

Along with Tolstoy and Thoreau, Day contends war, presidents, and the territorial (welfare-police) state are false necessities. Convinced that centralization is unnecessary and undesirable, Day embraced strong anarchism and insisted that morally responsible persons must refrain from supporting the territorial state and must enact alternative social practices that demonstrate that the territorial state is unnecessary. This enactment of an alternative is a precondition to the realization of a postterritorial state social order.

It will be clear by the end of my analysis that Day's political vision was a religious vision: she asserted that social transformation is something that has to do simultaneously with God and other persons and she claimed that cultivating and sustaining the qualities of character necessary for a perpetual revolution requires the vehicle of the Roman Catholic Church with its liturgy and sacraments. Taken together, the sections that comprise Chapter 2 show that, on Day's view, God is encountered through acts of love, love precludes violence, and only in community and in interpersonal relationships can persons realize their higher selves. As such, Day identifies decentralized associations and cooperatives—houses of hospitality and farm communes—as the appropriate institutional arrangements by which to usher in the new sociopolitical order, the beloved community.

In Chapter 3, "The Dilemma of the Black Radical: Bayard Rustin's Ambivalent Anarchism," I turn to the social and political philosophy of African American Quaker public intellectual and social activist Bayard Rustin. Rustin is not ordinarily described as an anarchist and he did not embrace the anarchist label. While at first glance, Rustin might not seem to fit the anarchist mold, I wish to show that his substantive commitments can be interpreted so that it is clear that they have anarchist implications. In this way Rustin might be regarded as an implicit anarchist, and I am confident that even skeptical readers will find that closely analyzing Rustin's substantive commitments reveals that Rustin presents an ambiguous case. This ambiguity is in fact what makes reflecting on Rustin instructive, with the ambiguity providing an occasion to clarify what constitutes anarchism as an ethic and political philosophy. And at the same time, the anarchist lens itself puts into focus critical aspects of Rustin's political philosophy. With Rustin in the frame and the character of anarchism clarified, through my analysis of Rustin, I hope to make clearer how pervasive the anarchist spirit has been among radicals on the American scene. At the very least, it shall become clearer how compatible anarchism can be with certain practical commitments and how incompatible it is with others.

Rustin participated in nearly every major progressive social movement in post-World War I America, which poses significant challenges for a student of his life and work. Rustin's biographers such as Jervis Anderson, John D'Emilio, and Daniel Levine all more or less respond to this issue by dividing Rustin's life based on the organization that he was working for or the issues that he was devoted to at a given point in time. The first stage was his communist phase, where he worked as a Young Communist League organizer. The second period was his work with Fellowship for Reconciliation (FOR) and then War Resisters League (WRL), where he melded radical pacifism with civil rights activism. Then during the 1960s he renounced his absolute pacifism, left WRL, and resigned as an editor of the leftist journal *Liberation*. At that stage he became intricately involved in the operations of the Southern Christian Leadership Conference (SCLC), an organization that Rustin helped create, along with Ella Baker, Stanley Levinson, Fred Shuttlesworth, Martin King. When Rustin's SCLC involvement waned, after the passage of the Civil Rights Act, he then set up shop at the A. Phillip Randolph Institute, funded in part by the American Federation of Labor. Finally, from the beginning of the 1970s, he became the chair of the board at Freedom House, concentrating on cultivating grassroots social movements in authoritarian societies around the globe.

I treat Rustin's life in two overlapping phases beginning with the phase during which he combined a Quaker-inspired radical pacifist position with an idea of perpetual political disobedience in the face of social injustice. Building on my consideration of pacifism in Chapter 2, in Chapter 3, I will show how Rustin's Quaker-inspired radical pacifism implies a version of anarchism. In particular, I argue that radical pacifism, if consistently expressed, has strong anarchism as its consequence. Since many African American Christians embraced radical pacifism during the mid-twentieth century, my consideration of Rustin's career as a radical pacifist suggests where we might turn in order to find African American anarchists or African Americans with political commitments that are consistent with strong anarchism. Yet, there is a rub here too; for, meditating on Rustin's experience will highlight the tests confronting African Americans who would embrace such an ethic.

In the latter half of Chapter 3, I explore Rustin's dramatic turn away from radical pacifism. Rustin's mid-1960s pivot finds him arguing explicitly for the necessity of a strong centralized state as a means to eradicate poverty and eliminate racial oppression, separating him from Dorothy Day in ways that are important to understand. Although both Day and Rustin embraced a Christian theological ethic that entailed a commitment to pacifism, their differing views about the role of the territorial state led them in remarkably different directions. With Rustin it becomes evident how difficult it is for one committed to racial justice and economic justice (eradication of poverty) to maintain a radical pacifist or strong anarchist position and prescribe decentralization. For, racial and economic justice in the American context has nearly always been pursued by means of the national government and an absolute rejection of political violence would seem to rule out relying on state action. Rustin appreciated this. But even as he renounced his radical pacifism, he maintained a commitment to perpetual political disobedience.

Rustin's commitments, after he relinquishes his radical pacifism, raise a thicket of profoundly important political philosophical questions and point to the paradox of black radicalism. In the later phase of his career, Rustin adopts views that would appear to rule out his being referred to as an anarchist. However, in Chapter 3, I attempt to refine my conception of anarchism and reflect on whether a rigorous commitment to political disobedience can be regarded as *entailing* a commitment to weak anarchism. My analysis reveals that a commitment to a strong centralized state does not necessarily mean that one has to posit that individuals have *moral* duties to obey political commands or the law in virtue of its being the law.

The reflection in Chapter 3 specifically sets the stage for exploring the affinities between anarchists and the political philosophies of persons belonging to the black radical tradition. As Michael Dawson and others have pointed out, black radicals typically endorse two important theses. First, they argue for a state-centered view of social change. Second, they contend that extrajudicial agitation is necessary for the realization of social justice and the liberation of the oppressed. My contention is that a significant number of black radicals place a premium on the second of these theses, which brings them close to weak anarchism. Indeed, one of the virtues of weak anarchism as a classificatory term is that it provides an auspicious way to capture the praxis of a large number of radical social activists and raises an important question about the attitude toward authority—particularly political authority—that it is appropriate or pragmatically advisable for social justice actors to embrace in the contemporary sphere.

I should note that, more than in Chapters 1 and 2, my treatment of Rustin will be especially interpretive. I rely on artificial constructs, to some extent, to make the distinctions between phases, but by no means are the lines arbitrarily drawn. Rather the analytic units that are employed simplify the subject matter—the objects of study—providing for maximal clarity or clarification. Rustin enunciates a political philosophy with subtly different implications at various points during his activist career and, as I analyze Rustin's social and political philosophy, I am particularly concerned with the *implications* of the views that I attribute to Rustin during the respective stages that I take up. Further, I am interested in the positions that Rustin held in the respective periods more so than in his consistency over the course of his life, and so I will discuss inconsistency and shifts comparatively insofar as it bears upon a perceived principled contradiction or pragmatic assessment of the impracticality of a given principled stance.

My aim is to understand the implications of his explicitly held ethical commitments and to see how certain substantive ethical commitments relate to anarchist philosophy and praxis. To put this differently, I attempt to show how in practice and at the theoretical level certain principles—radical pacifism or a strict commitment to substantive social justice—can become the content of or basis for an anarchist ethic. Proceeding in the manner proposed will put us in a position to assess and understand how anarchist ideas, ideals, and attitudes relate to Gandhian theories of social change and the sociopolitical commitments of members of the black radical tradition, opening the door for a reconsideration of how we conceptualize anarchist practice, past and present social movements, and imagine possible radical coalitions in the present-future.

So in the main chapters I will make explicit the moral dimension of anarchism and will consider the way in which certain religious-ethical commitments connect with or constitute grounds for an anarchist philosophy or anarchist ethic. Thoreau, Day, and Rustin, on the basis of their respective concerns for racial and social justice, each emphasize moral autonomy, noncomplicity, and responsibility in a way that entails the rejection of the claims to authority characteristic of modern territorial states. These three moral exemplars, I hope to demonstrate, belong to or have at least greatly influenced the nonviolent anarchist tradition, a tradition that presents a formidable theory of immediate action or revolutionary practice. In the "Conclusion," I will consider the implications, for ethicists, historians of social movements, and activists, of making explicit the moral and religious sources of anarchism or, to put it in different terms, the anarchist dimension of certain moral and religious commitments. By referring to Thoreau, Day, and Rustin as anarchists, it should be evident how radical their respective ethical commitments were; but at the same time, by showing how each of the three, at various moments in their activist careers, can be properly understood as anarchists, I mean to show anarchism in a fresh light. In what follows, at once I aspire to render the familiar strange and make the strange familiar, with an eye toward haunting, inspiring, awakening, and prodding—perhaps.

# 1

# The conscience on fire:
# Thoreau's anarchist ethic

*My thoughts are murder to the State, and involuntarily
go plotting against her.*

HENRY DAVID THOREAU in "Slavery in Massachusetts"

*The good man, the man who infects hardly anyone, is the man
who has the fewest lapses of attention.*

ALBERT CAMUS, *The Plague*

*You will understand that to remain a servant of the written law
is to place yourself every day in opposition to the law of
conscience, and to make a bargain on the wrong side; and
since this struggle cannot go on forever, you will either
silence your conscience and become a scoundrel, or you will
break with tradition, and you will work with us for the
utter destruction of all this injustice, economic, social, and
political. But then you will be a revolutionist.*

PETER KROPOTKIN

## I

Many stories have been told about Henry David Thoreau. His 44-year life has
proved rich material for ideological contestations that stretch from at least
his death in 1862 up to the present. What Thoreau's detractors and devotees

agree on is that he was an iconoclast bent on breaking with conventions prevailing in Massachusetts social circles. What divides them is how they assess this break—the reasons, the extent, and the effects. For persons sure that American democracy is the last best hope for humanity, either Thoreau is not a democratic thinker and must be discarded, or his thought and action must be translated into an idiom that vindicates his democratic credentials. Hannah Arendt belongs to the former class while Nancy Rosenblum and George Kateb can be cast as principal players in the latter role. For persons certain that religious, supernatural, theological, or metaphysical ideas or orientations represent barriers to social progress, Thoreau must either be cast as a thoroughgoing naturalist or cast aside.

My aim here is to portray Thoreau's commitments in a way that calls into question prevailing stories about him. Taking my cue from political theorists and social critics, such as Isaiah Berlin, whose work stress the centrality of anthropological questions in modern political and social thought, my sense is that we will best apprehend Thoreau's political philosophical commitments if we familiarize ourselves with his ideas about the human person, the moral order, and the divine.

Let me begin this story, then, by trying to convince you that we must take seriously Thoreau's religion, which means turning to Thoreau's nineteenth-century milieu. His idiosyncrasies and iconoclasm notwithstanding, Thoreau had fellow religious travelers and his unconventional flourishes are best understood in relation to them. Born in 1817, Thoreau came of age in the 1830s, arriving for undergraduate study at Harvard College just as Transcendentalism and abolitionism were shaking up New England's educational, religious, political, and cultural life.

Transcendentalism emerged in the midst of religious revivalism, heated theological controversy, cultural contestations about the meaning of America, and political conflict that always teetered on the edge of violence. Such times are made for passionate ethical striving. Appropriately, as the nineteenth century progressed, "more and more, [American] religious thought was devoted to questions of ethics."[1] And as ethics or ethical questions pervaded religious discourse, quite naturally, theological questions about the nature of the human person—theological anthropological questions—assumed growing significance. According to Lewis Perry, "The conclusion seemed irresistible [among certain theologians and clerics] in the new republic: if God was lawgiver, then he must have implanted both knowledge of the law and the capacity to fulfill it in the constitution of man."[2]

The ethical turn in early to mid-nineteenth-century American religious thought had far-reaching effects on New England's religious practice and social life in general. In fact, the conclusion that God endowed human persons with the knowledge of and capacity to fulfill the moral law can be understood as both a cause and effect of antislavery and abolitionist activism. Moral controversy about race-based chattel slavery instigated religious debate about the nature of God, the moral order, political order, and human identity and nature. And for persons—from David Walker to William Lloyd Garrison to John Brown—convinced that black Africans were creatures of God and that slavery constituted an affront against God and God's law, religious fervor manifested as prophetic social criticism and activism. New England enthusiasts such as James and Lucretia Mott, Elizabeth Peabody, Margaret Fuller, Orestes Brownson, Wendell Phillips, Theodore Parker, and Bronson Alcott would found congregations, schools, newspapers, journals, reform organizations, and communes during our period, and so greatly effect American religious and activist life during antebellum and beyond.

All of this is important for our consideration because, while American Transcendentalism has been remembered mostly for its lasting contributions to (secular) American literature, the movement actually began in the 1830s among ministers and religionists dissatisfied with the extent of reform enacted by Unitarian Congregationalists, so that in many respects Transcendentalism started off as a Christian-dissident uprising focused on theology and theological anthropological disputes. Accordingly, several early participants in the "Transcendentalist Club" meetings—Frederick Henry Hedge, Ralph Emerson, George Ripley, and William Henry Channing—were first and foremost religious reformers, extending liberal and Unitarian strands of Congregationalism in radical directions.

American Transcendentalists were notoriously independent individualists, which militated against Transcendentalism's sustenance, over time, as a cohesive movement. But what united the disparate figures now routinely referred to as Transcendentalists were the theological anthropological assumptions that they eventually embraced. In short, Transcendentalists, Thoreau included, broke with Calvinist theology and theological anthropology. Inspired by Quakerism, the European Enlightenment, and German and English Romantics, the Transcendentalists had no place for the Calvinist's pessimistic view of postlapsarian human nature and the concomitant emphasis on the permeation of sin and "total depravity of man."[3] Significantly, American Transcendentalists replaced the Calvinist emphasis on sin-sick selves with a view of the "divine in all."[4] Lawrence Buell, correctly in my view, goes so far as to aver that "the central message of Transcendentalism itself [was] the idea of divine immanence."[5]

The trend toward radicalism among Transcendentalists gained momentum during Thoreau's final years at Harvard. He graduated in 1837, one year after and one year before Ralph Waldo Emerson published his groundbreaking masterpiece *Nature* and delivered his subversive "Divinity School Address" at Harvard, two statements spelling out the Transcendentalist theological and philosophical tenor: the divine rests both within nature and each individual, and "intuition" as opposed to revelation represents how humans arrive at truth. This basic proposition rests at the heart of Thoreau's religious imagination and any effort to understand his religiosity or his political philosophy must be attuned to Thoreau's meditations on the nature of the self and its relation to the divine—that is, his theological anthropology. Thoreau's wordplay, affinity for paradox and irony, aversion to systematicity, and reputation as a naturalist make attunement difficult.

Still, if we tend to Thoreau's theological statements with care, it will be hard to miss his profound religious sensibility, a sensibility rooted in a conception of a divine being. His complex religious views extend from his unorthodox conception of God; he explicitly expresses a belief in God, even if there is often ambiguity when he does so. This is no clearer than in a letter written to Harrison Gray Otis Blake, his spiritual companion, where Thoreau proclaims: "God Reigns! I say God. I am not sure that is the name. You know who I mean."[6]

As is often the case, this instance of ambiguity, the fruit of a fallibilistic impulse, is revealing, as subtle hints of Thoreau's mysticism come to the fore. The mystic, of course, is both overwhelmed by exposure to the deity and burdened by an inability to wholly grasp the nature of the deity. The "being" whose reign is known, yet whose name and nature is not, is the infinitely complex being that is typically referred to as God. The mystic knows better than to say whether the name that is typically bestowed on the being is the name that ought to be bestowed. Thoreau's terse statement to Blake is not necessarily an enunciation of a mystic's religious knowledge, but it does betray the inclinations of a mystic.

Thoreau's faith in the existence of God, and belief in the human person's capacity to know and experience this God, is especially on display in *A Week*, published in 1849, where Thoreau converts into prose his sensual encounter with the Divine, or the divine self, what Thoreau will refer to as "that everlasting Something":

> I see, smell, taste, hear, feel, that everlasting Something to which we are allied, at once our maker, our abode, our destiny, our very Selves; the one historic truth, the most remarkable fact which can become the distinct and uninvited subject of our thought, the actual glory of the universe; the only fact which a human being cannot avoid recognizing, or in some way forget or dispense with.[7]

And in *Walden*, published in 1854, Thoreau conveys a similar sentiment:

> I only know myself as a human entity; the scene, so to speak, of thoughts and affections; and am sensible of a certain doubleness by which I can stand as remote from myself as from another. However intense my experience, I am conscious of the presence and criticism of a part of me, which, as it were, is not a part of me, but spectator, sharing no experience, but taking note of it; and that is no more I than it is you.[8]

These pithy statements, essential to understanding Thoreau's thought, constitute a window not only into Thoreauvian theology but also Thoreau's epistemology and ontology, that is, his understanding of how and what persons can know about the character of reality (God) and the constitution of the self. Thoreau, in mystical form, is moved by faith and inspired by experience: in addition to being humbly confident that God reigns, he is conscious of the fact that God reigns with or even within the self; for, Thoreau knows that we are allied to "that everlasting Something" which is "our very Selves."[9] While not predominant in Thoreau's New England or America, a variant of this theological view constituted a distinctive feature of American Transcendentalist (transcendentalist) thought and caused much controversy in mid-nineteenth-century New England religious circles.[10]

The importance of this theological (anthropological) view, especially for the purposes of my analysis, lies in the implications that it had for questions of legitimate authority, particularly in relation to ecclesiology, church polity, politics, and ethics. Not only did the idea of "divine in all" or "divine immanence" extend the Protestant Reformation idea of a "priesthood of believers," undermining respect for traditional priestly authority, which I will say more about shortly, it also set the stage for an evasion of several ethical, particularly metaethical, dilemmas confronted by theologians and philosophers during the nineteenth century. By deifying the self, that is, locating God within the self, Transcendentalists were able to sidestep moral skepticism and avoid being too disturbed by cultural relativism.

Significantly, conceptions of God seem to presuppose the idea of worship. In the purest sense worship is the complete devotion to an object. In the case of religious worship, a deity or deities are typically the objects of worship. Religious theists take their respective gods to demand a host of acts, including sacrificial offerings, prayers, salutations, and so on. To be devoted completely to a given God or gods requires the performance of the appropriate act or range of acts. Akin to many religiously inspired social activists, Thoreau's religiosity does not primarily entail the performance of the kind of acts listed above. Instead, Thoreau is devoted to a God that demands moral self-perfection and adherence to moral laws that are fundamentally about the proper way to treat animate and inanimate beings. His religiosity, then, is profoundly ethical.

Thoreau may be unsure about the reigning deity's name, but he is resolute about the deity's role. Thoreau's God is the *ultimate* moral judge. As well, Thoreau, after stoics and deists, believes God to have created a world wherein nature, including human persons, is suffuse with moral meaning. The epistemological debates and attendant uncertainties that the Enlightenment and cross-cultural encounters had instigated in European thought did not undermine Thoreau's certitude with respect to moral truth. In fact, similar to later religious pluralists, Thoreau found themes unifying the diverse religious and social practices across the world, so that the areas of overlapping interest or agreement among diverse religions served to reinforce his moral stance. For Thoreau, reflecting on the character of human personality, society, and the natural environment discloses moral truth. So he rhetorically asks, "May we not see God? Are we to be put off and amused in this life, as it were with a mere allegory? Is not Nature, rightly read, that of which she is commonly taken to be the symbol merely?"[11] Thoreau insists that moral truth is God's truth and each person has the capacity—call it reason or conscience if you would like—to discern it.[12] Conscience is God's gift to humanity and the human person's guide on the path upward—higher living in accord with the higher law.

Thoreau's belief in God, objective moral truth, and human capacity to know come together in an evocative passage in *A Week*:

> I must conclude that Conscience, if that be the name of it, was not given us for no purpose, or for hindrance. However flattering order and expediency may look, it is but the repose of a lethargy, and we will choose rather to be awake, though it be stormy, and maintain ourselves on this earth and in this life, as we may, without signing our death-warrant. Let us see if we cannot stay here, where He has put us, on his own conditions. Does not his law reach as far as his light? The expedients of the nations clash with one another, only the absolutely right is expedient for all.[13]

Thoreau asserts that God is lawgiver, maintains that God's law determines absolute rightness, and contends that human persons, through "Conscience," can know God's law. Thoreau thinks that human beings are called to *become* moral and he fervently believes in the capacity of individuals to realize moral truths; knowing that we (human beings) *are* divine moral beings points toward what we should *do*. Yet he adds an important contention: recognition of God's law and, subsequently, the will to abide by it hinge on the prior choice to "be awake, though it be stormy."

Surrounded by neighbors who, in practice, have not chosen wakefulness, who have not determined to stay where God has put them, on God's conditions, at every turn Thoreau is confronted with actual behavior and social practices that appear to contradict his epistemological and ontological claims. Thoreau insists that "men do not fail commonly for want of knowledge." However, as Thoreau intimates in *A Week*, they do "want of prudence to give wisdom preference." Why is this? According to Thoreau, we struggle to give wisdom preference because we often establish "durable and harmonious [routines that] . . . all parts of [our] nature consent to."[14] So, on Thoreau's view, persons' failure to choose wakefulness is largely the effect of their having fallen into certain routines. The most detrimental routines and habits are often those enforced or imposed by social institutions, customs, and norms. Over time, such routines obfuscate important moral truths, particularly truths about the self, and too often such routines and habits deny in practice the value of the human person and the richness of individuality, encouraging the blind conformity and moral complacency that is constitutive of slumber.

It is to this problem of slumber that Thoreau answers in his vocation. Similar to other American Transcendentalists, from Elizabeth Peabody to Theodore Parker to Amos Bronson Alcott, Thoreau engages in what Jeffrey Steele names "rhetorics [sic] of regeneration," which amounts to a call for a "recovery of the self, as if from illness."[15] "Rhetorics of regeneration" or calls for conversion almost by definition sustain themselves on appeals to the unrealized, or what Ralph Waldo Emerson wonderfully refers to as the "unattained attainable self." For Thoreau, then, the posited self possesses powers wanting recovery. Thoreau's regeneration rhetoric serves as a moral conversion narrative that attests to what is in fact possible and aims to inspire self-improvement, self-reform, or self-culture, and so represents a remedy for the slumbering.

*Walden*, a text devoted to delving into this issue of slumber, aptly begins with Thoreau's well-known declaration: "I do not propose to write an ode to dejection, but to brag as lustily as chanticleer in the morning, standing on his roost, if only to wake my neighbors up."[16] Convinced that "moral reform is the effort to throw off sleep," Thoreau embarks on a project of moral reform that consists in waking neighbors up.[17] Indeed, while Thoreau collates myriad themes in *Walden*, perhaps none rises to the level of importance of the awakening motif that is reiterated throughout. *Walden* oscillates here and there between lamentation and hopefulness, as is appropriate for prophetic prose. Implicit is a complaint about the present predicated on knowledge of a possible alternative world; the text's opening premise is that there is unrealized promise. *Walden*'s narrator chronicles unfulfilled potential and thus testifies to the possibility of regeneration and conversion. It is for good reason that Thoreau's stay at Walden's Pond has been variously described as a spiritual retreat, a pilgrimage, and a quest for spiritual renewal and awakening.

Critical reflection on living well inspired his sojourn adjacent to that Concord pond. And critically reflecting on his life in the woods provided Thoreau with the material (experience) necessary to engage in rhetorics of regeneration. His task was to demonstrate in practice the veracity of his bold claims about the self, to vindicate his own faith in humanity. Persons are called to acknowledge their higher selves and to act in ways that accord with such selves. Taking for granted that there are a "mass of men," particularly in New England, who desire transformation yet wrongly doubt its possibility, Thoreau speaks to those persons who wish for a more meaningful existence, "to the mass of men who are discontented, and idly complaining of the hardness of their lot or of the times, when they might improve them."[18] Thoreau, of course, insists that awakening is possible and claims to know of "no more encouraging fact than the unquestionable ability of man to elevate his life by a conscious endeavor."[19]

Each reader is invited to follow Thoreau's lead, to explore his or her self in relation to social institutions and practices, the natural environment, and his or her own web of beliefs about the self, world, and deity. Thoreau endeavors to identify beliefs and practices or ways of being that edify and enhance and those that degrade and diminish moral life. Not unlike other nineteenth-century reformers and social critics, Thoreau identifies tradition—religious, economic, and political—and habits of consumption as primary barriers to moral reform. Tradition, in Thoreauvian parlance, stands for those practices that misidentify the limit of human potentiality and misconstrue the character of moral truth or rightness, thus engendering or imposing conformity and obedience to ineffective or immoral standards and practices. And when defending social practices and institutions (routines), persons, particularly apologists, nearly always presuppose certain limitations and by extension assert particular necessities, so as to engender and impose conformity and obedience.

Persons often present and accept mere conjecture about limitations as actual knowledge of limits. Thoreau illustrates the importance of this facet of social life through a parable that he derives from the conjecture on the subject of the qualities and properties of Walden's Pond. How persons relate to ponds, especially in terms of knowledge, is representative or symbolic of how they relate to the world—social or natural—generally speaking: "The pond rises and falls, but whether regularly or not, and within what period, nobody knows, though, as usual, many pretend to know."[20] Such conjecture is problematic insofar as it tends to distort (our conception of) reality and undermine our ability to know. Reflecting on the "stories" exchanged about Walden's Pond, Thoreau gets at how vital it is to traverse boundaries through experimentation and exploration, acts which presuppose ignorance: "There have been many stories told about the bottom, or rather no bottom, of this pond, which certainly had no foundation for themselves. It is remarkable how long men will believe in the bottomlessness of a pond without taking the trouble to sound it. I have visited two such Bottomless Ponds in one walk in this neighborhood."[21]

This connects to the problem of slumber in that the slumbering conform and obey blindly, and eventually lose sight of the role that choice plays in determining their character and the character of their experience; in this way, persons experience alienation[22] and relinquish subjectivity and individuality, which is tantamount to denying the divinity that resides within each person. Conceptions and ideals about the self attract so much of Thoreau's attention because, on his view, "What a man thinks of himself, that it is which determines, or rather indicates, his fate."[23] To slumber is to accept a false limit, to make a dead law one's own law; because we slumber—blindly conform and obey—"man's capacities have never been measured;

nor are we to judge what he can do by any precedents, so little has been tried."[24] In turn, evil, unjust, and ineffective practices such as those which were pervasive in nineteenth-century North Atlantic societies—with the continuation of colonialism, imperial conquest, slave economies, patriarchal oppression, and the emergence of modern industry—are often defended or rationalized by appeals to necessity and perpetuated on the basis of the cooperation of the slumbering, those who do not go through the trouble of discovering the truth.

As we might expect, Thoreau demands proof that our routines, habits, traditions are necessary for a meaningful human life and he insists that individuals, as divine beings, are moral subjects who must exercise moral agency, thus making moral decisions about how to live and which acts to perform or not perform in certain situations. In short, Thoreau advocates reclamation of moral responsibility. The opening pages of *Walden* register this advocacy:

> When we consider what, to use the words of the catechism, is the chief end of man, and what are the true necessaries and means of life, it appears as if men had deliberately chosen the common mode of living because they preferred it to any other. Yet they honestly think there is no choice left. But alert and healthy natures remember that the sun rose clear . . . No way of thinking or doing, however, ancient, can be trusted without proof.[25]

Thoreau sojourns at Walden's Pond in order to "learn what are the gross necessaries of life and what methods have been taken to obtain them" and so authenticate his social criticism by providing proof that certain habits, practices, and institutions that are often presented as natural or necessary are in fact dispensable.[26] He accomplishes this by illustrating the way in which our habits, practices, and institutions create a false sense of what is necessary. Making use of his life on the frontier, a life of simplicity, Thoreau aspires to get an objective view of the social life of most New Englanders, townspersons and farmers alike, by comparing it to his simple living at Walden's Pond.

The first part of *Walden* is fittingly entitled "Economy." By beginning thus, Thoreau acknowledges the importance of economic matters to human striving, and yet at the same time calls into question the economic theories and practices prevalent in America during the 1840s and 1850s. The decision to discuss the basic "necessaries" (necessities) of life under the title "economy" is meant to highlight the fact that (1) basic necessities are, as a factual matter, particular means to certain ends and (2) economic interests are rooted (or at least originate) in needs. After contemplating what is essential to bodily well-being and considering the purposes served by primary goods, Thoreau concludes that, at bottom, primary goods are required so that persons can "maintain their vital heat" and he homes in on three primary goods—food, clothing, and shelter.

These three goods are the means necessary for sustenance and societies are often organized around procuring them. And this is as it should be. Yet almost invariably, "even in democratic New England towns," persons allow these means to become ends and thus devote more time (life) to their pursuit than is actually necessary. In New England, says Thoreau, "men have become tools of their tools"[27] and "we do not ride on the railroad; it rides upon us."[28] Institutional practices turn out or bring into being persons with viscous appetites and thus unhealthy consumptive habits; and persons with such appetites and habits themselves generate inefficient and unjust modes of action and institutional practices. Most problematic, though, is the fact that all of this engenders unreflective behavior that in turn facilitates the process by which human persons become tools, so that human subjects are transformed into objects.

Thoreau's emphasis on the role that consumptive habits play in this process is a distinctive feature of his social analysis. Consumption matters for Thoreau in part because matters of consumption (1) are so intertwined in the final analysis with how we relate to other human beings and to the natural environment and (2) determine the kinds of institutions that we will likely deem necessary. Our sensual desires, when unchecked, undoubtedly have dire social implications. The greedy often claim to need slaves. The same is true of imperial and colonial masters with respect to colonial subjects. Thoreau's insight about the relation of consumptive habits and greed to economic exploitation and political oppression is unoriginal yet key to understanding his thought. When he claims that "the luxury of one class is counterbalanced by the indigence of another," observes that "on the one side is the palace, on the other are the almshouse and 'silent poor'," and cites the wars fought in order to secure a low price for sugar, to sweeten tea, he is diagnosing a problematic—the modern predicament—that his normative social vision is framed to eradicate.[29]

Sugar no longer significantly shapes the foreign policies of territorial states. But goods such as oil have replaced it. And so unbounded appetite or desire, call it gluttony, nonetheless invades the realm of the political and ordinarily wreaks violence. As Thoreau says toward the end of *Walden*, undoubtedly thinking about imperialist America and European colonial powers such as Britain and France: "The gross feeder is a man in the larva state; and there are whole nations in that condition, nations without fancy or imagination, whose vast abdomens betray them."[30]

It is in such a milieu—of rampant materialism, economic exploitation, and political oppression—that Thoreau commends asceticism, a central aspect of his ethics, and a fundamental component of his conception of philosophy. Thoreau, in *Walden*, tells the reader that the philosopher practices "better methods" of practical living than others in that the philosopher accords goods their appropriate place and loves "wisdom so as to live according to its dictates, a life of simplicity, independence, magnanimity, and trust."[31] The philosopher possesses the prudence to give wisdom preference. Philosophers are awake and wise. And wisdom dictates a simple life—the life of an ascetic. For Thoreau, then, the philosopher is by definition an ascetic. Three terse lines illuminate the character of Thoreauvian asceticism and the reason(s) that Thoreau regards asceticism as imperative. To begin, according to Thoreau, "None can be an impartial or wise observer of human life but from the vantage ground of what *we* should call voluntary poverty."[32] Further, voluntary poverty is viable only when one minimizes one's consumption and one's participation in economic trade or exchange. In his standard ironic tone, Thoreau announces his resistance to and rejection of conventional (entrepreneurial) wisdom: "Instead of studying how to make it worth men's while to buy my baskets, I studied rather how to avoid the necessity of selling them."[33] And finally, Thoreau crafts a fresh proverb in order to underscore his larger point about the philosopher's methods of living: "A man is rich in proportion to the number of things which he can afford to let alone."[34]

These are not just catchy phrases. Again, asceticism rests near the heart of Thoreau's ethics and Thoreau prescribes asceticism or simple living for a mélange of profoundly important reasons. It provides clarity of thought and the freedom of action that comes with having little vested interest in extant unjust conditions, which makes it possible to avoid complicity with injustice.[35] Asceticism, then, is a technique for attaining clear-sightedness or impartiality. It thereby furnishes a context in which an authentic self and authentic need can be disclosed, setting the stage for the maximization of moral and material independence. In other words, asceticism is therapy for slumbering souls, numb to the world, a way to erase the distance between oneself and God and the divine within one's self. So Thoreau declares,

> Chastity is the flowering of man; and what are called Genius, Heroism, Holiness, and the like, are but various fruits which succeed it. Man flows at once to God when the channel of purity is open. By turns our purity inspires and our impurity casts us down. He is blessed who is assured that the animal in him is dying out day by day, and the divine being established.[36]

Thoreau wants his readers, especially those leading "lives of quiet desperation," to appreciate that an ascetic life is possible in practice and to see that it makes achievable the awakening that is (or should be) desired and is needed. He takes for granted our divine nature and then attempts to convince us that divine beings ought to have chosen better methods of living than most of us have; Thoreau-the-philosopher (tentatively) illuminates what it is to be human and provides instructions as to how to become fully what one is. Set aside whether or not it is practically possible for Thoreau's readers, having reflected on his prodding, to embark upon the kind of sojourn that is the object of reflection in *Walden*. To a degree, Thoreau's primary aim is to, through Socratic questioning and (sometimes ironic) rumination, spur self-examination and reconsideration of the given, including the character of the self. Thoreau's faith is that such examination will lead to better choices or reformed ways of individual and collective being.

This last point is vital since so many political realists, postmodern theorists, and anti-Kantian thinkers, in recent years, tend to conflate talk about noncomplicity with naive quests for (self-centered) purity; reduce celebrations of the individual or individuality to asocial solipsism; and to dismiss any talk about ascetic withdrawal as (self-centered) escapism.[37] Thoreau has been charged with the above vices periodically for decades and one virtue of the story that I am telling about him is that it concentrates on aspects of his thought that contest these charges and invites a reconsideration of the tendency among so many contemporary critical thinkers to disparage individuality, autonomy, inwardness, deontological ethics, and other values that are often associated with but are not the exclusive province of liberal or Kantian thought. To be clear, my goal here is not to defend Immanuel Kant or political liberals such as John Rawls. Yet I do mean to show that while Thoreau is a proponent of individuality, inwardness, introspection, and perhaps even conscientious self-isolation, he does not regard a turn inward and away as a means by which to avoid dealing with the corrupt and unjust character of a given society's institutional practices and arrangements. Rather, as John L. Thomas notes, the Transcendentalists, Thoreau included, "turned inward to examine the divine self and find there the material with which to rebuild society."[38] For Transcendentalist reformers, the turn inward and away facilitates the cultivation of habits, attitudes, and ethoi that themselves reform or revolutionize the social world. In this way, the inward turn and movement away is always already socially and politically charged.

Thoreau stands out among Transcendentalists for the sustained way in which he fastidiously accounts for how slumbering occurs and how awakening might be realized. As we take the next turn in this story about Thoreau's life and thought, the concern will be with how the moral conversion or awakening that Thoreau aspires to instigate implicates the political and connects directly to the modern territorial state. In the coming sections I show that awakening is connected to the territorial state in that, from Thoreau's vantage, few institutions play as negative a role in the moral degradation and oppression of individuals as does the modern territorial state. The territorial state is problematic because of (1) the way in which it oppresses large segments of the human population and (2) the way in which cooperation with and agency on behalf of the state stymies moral sensibility. The territorial state, Thoreau suggests, is unnecessary, at least for the morally conscientious, so that awakening implies or entails political resistance.[39] This basic descriptive account and understanding of the territorial state prevails throughout Thoreau's writings and activist career. And we should keep this fact about Thoreau's conception of the state in mind when reading and reflecting on *A Week* and *Walden*, as doing so allows us to appreciate the political implications of the claims presented in these texts. If I have so far presented them as religious texts about the divine status of the human person, this is because on some levels they are and because the task up to this point has been to present Thoreau's too often neglected religiosity. We are now ready to take note of Thoreau's prophetic voice as it reverberates in the political domain, proving true Isaiah Berlin's insight that "our political notions are part of our conception of what it is to be human," and showing how Thoreau's principal texts, especially *Walden*, double as religious and political tracts, with the political shadowing the religious and vice versa.[40]

# II

Few dates could be more politically significant than the date on which Thoreau chose to relocate to those now famous Concord woods. Thoreau moved to Walden's Pond on July 4, 1845.[41] And his decision to withdraw to the woods on such a politically significant date should inform the meaning that we attribute to his withdrawal and guide how we interpret the masterpiece that he crafted while sojourning in the woods. We can understand him to have been declaring his independence from the United States of America on the very anniversary of Americans' declaration of independence from King George's Britain. In the midst of the entrenchment of Jacksonian democracy, the rise of James Polk and imperialist expansion, and the consolidation of the Southern slaveholder's aristocracy, Thoreau set out to demonstrate in practice which purported necessities are true and which are false.

Recognizing that Thoreau includes the territorial state among false necessities and contends that awakening precludes cooperation with it is vital to comprehending Thoreau's political philosophy, which is why it has been essential to delineate Thoreau's theology and theological anthropology and to consider the role of the ideas of slumber, awakening, and false necessity in Thoreau's thought. To make the fact that Thoreau regarded the territorial state as a false necessity clearer, we will have to reflect on his explicit references to and criticisms of the territorial state, law, authority, and political action as they appear in *A Week*, *Walden*, "Resistance to Civil Government," and "Slavery in Massachusetts." Analyzing these works in concert promises to enrich and develop our understanding of Thoreau's political morality and lay bare the anarchist dimension of Thoreauvian ethics.

The character of Thoreau's writing process shaped his oeuvre in ways pertinent to my analysis. He wrote incessantly and was committed to the view that writing is rewriting. Further, he was always working on more than one piece at a time. In accord with this, Thoreau composed his great political essays at the same time that he was writing (or revising) *A Week* and *Walden*, which undoubtedly accounts for the extensive thematic overlap and continuity with respect to the substantive content in the respective pieces. What's more, because Thoreau shares the prophet's penchant for repetition and reiteration, the argumentative structures in most of his writings bear remarkable resemblance to one another. No less than in *A Week* and *Walden*, in his more explicitly political essays and reform papers, Thoreau calls his audience's attention to (1) the divine nature of persons, (2) the need for awakening, and (3) the injustice of the state. Thoreau consistently takes the problem of slumber as his starting place. And subsequently, in his own way, after his own fashion, he prophesies deliverance. With respect to the political, Thoreau's message is always: The modern state is unjust; it is a false necessity or an inexpedient institution; acting on its behalf makes one an agent of injustice, stultifying one's moral sense; awakening entails noncomplicity with unjust practices, renunciation of false necessities, heightened moral sensitivity, and thus the elimination of the territorial state.

Thoreau's criticism of the political realm largely constitutes an attempt to demystify and demythologize standing political institutions and practices. In particular, he subverts predominant myths about the law and state officials by offering descriptions of the function of the former and the latter that counter conventional accounts. Rulers, says Thoreau, have claimed that in order to be morally good, one must comply with the law, that is, one must be law abiding. Such rulers have insisted that obedience to positive laws of the state is a precondition to realization of individual moral virtuousness and also the common good. But in actual fact, says Thoreau, blindly complying with the laws or commands issued by political authorities merely impedes the realization of just conditions; it perpetuates injustice. And to respect the law and to comply with or to labor on behalf of the state is to surrender one's moral autonomy, induce slumber, and become an agent of injustice.

Thoreau makes this point in several evocative passages that are worth quoting at length. His charge in "Resistance to Civil Government" is especially direct:

> It is not desirable to cultivate a respect for the law, so much as for the right. The only obligation which I have a right to assume is to do at any time what I think right. Law never made men a whit more just; and, by means of their respect for it even the well-disposed are daily made agents of injustice. A common and natural result of an undue respect for law is, that you may see a file of soldiers, colonel, captain, privates, powder-monkeys and all, marching in admirable order over hill and dale to the wars, against their wills, aye, against their common sense and consciences, which makes it very steep marching indeed, and produces a palpitation of the heart. They have no doubt that it is a damnable business

in which they are concerned.... Now, what are they? Men at all? or small moveable forts and magazines at the service of some unscrupulous man in power?[42]

The mass of men serve the State thus, not as men mainly, but as machines, with their bodies. They are the standing army, and the militia, jailers, constables, *posse comitatus*, and company. In most cases there is no free exercise whatever of the judgment or of the moral sense; but they put themselves on the level with wood and earth and stones, and wooden men can perhaps be manufactured that will serve the purpose as well. Such command no more respect than men of straw, or a lump of dirt.[43]

This passage can be interpreted in the light of Thoreau's consideration of the detriments of slumber and the impediments to awakening in *Walden*. The territorial state, instead of elevating human social life, initiates a process of alienation; for, by way of "respect for" the law and obedience to the territorial state human persons are transformed into machines who act against conscience rather than with it. With the significance of the mutually reinforcing interplay between belief and action in mind, Thoreau plainly states his view of the fact that the territorial state (particularly the American government) is a false necessity. To that end, toward the beginning of "Resistance to Civil Government," Thoreau writes:

[The American] government never itself furthered any enterprise, but by the alacrity with which it got out of its way. It does not keep the country free. It does not settle the West. It does not educate. The character inherent in the American people has done all that has been accomplished; and it would have done somewhat more, if government had not sometimes got in its way.[44]

Thoreau presents the same idea in *A Week*, in a suggestive passage that flows seamlessly from Thoreau's celebration of "Conscience," which was presented in the earlier section. Read together, the two passages further elucidate the way in which Thoreau's theological and ontological assumptions undergird his political philosophy. In the long but elucidative passage, Thoreau intimates,

To one who habitually endeavors to contemplate the true state of things, the political state can hardly be said to have any existence whatever.... In my short experience of human life, the outward obstacles, if there were any such, have not been living men, but the institutions of the dead ... [And] it is not to be forgotten, that while the law holds fast the thief and murderer, it lets itself go loose. When I have not paid the tax which the State demanded for that protection which I did not want, itself has robbed me; when I have asserted the liberty it presumed to declare, itself has imprisoned me . . . I do not wish, it happens, to be associated with Massachusetts, either in holding slaves or in conquering Mexico. I am a little better than herself in these respects . . . I love man-kind, but I hate the institutions of the dead un-kind.[45]

Thoreau complains that in an effort to "execute . . . the wills of the dead," persons are willing to serve as tools. Political officers or officials are most susceptible to the moral detriments of this tendency. While acting as a neighbor, a person will tolerate or even support persons who assert "the value of individual liberty over the merely political commonweal." But the state necessarily denies this value and persons who serve the state abandon moral virtue in the name of political obedience: "[The state's] officer, as a living man, may have human virtues and a thought in his brain, but as the tool of an institution, a jailer or constable it may be, he is not a whit superior to his prison key or his staff." In Thoreau's view, this phenomenon constitutes a tragedy in that because men are willing to do "outrage to their proper [divine] natures" and "lend themselves to perform the office of inferior and brutal ones," slavery and war are introduced into social life.[46]

A similar assertion about the modern state and its agents emerges in *Walden*. In particular, in a section entitled "The Village," Thoreau recounts his arrest for tax refusal and denies the authority of Massachusetts (i.e. the State), referring to it as a "dirty institution" rather than an "institution of the dead," but the point is the same. Thoreau regards the state as an unjust and inexpedient institution—a false necessity—that molests, jails, and robs the just while slaveholding and wars of conquest go on in its name or with its power:

> I was seized and put into jail, because, as I have elsewhere related, I did not pay a tax to, or recognize the authority of, the state which buys and sells men, women, and children, like cattle at the door of its senate-house. I had gone down to the woods for other purposes. But, wherever a man goes, men will pursue and paw him with their dirty institutions, and, if they can, constrain him to belong to their desperate odd-fellow society. It is true, I might have resisted forcibly with more or less effect, might have run "amok" against society; but I preferred that society should run "amok" against me, it being the desperate party . . . I was never molested by any person but those who represented the state.[47]

Finally, a few years later, in the essay "Slavery in Massachusetts," the famed 1854 piece that Thoreau composed as a protest against the Fugitive Slave Act of 1850 and the trial of runaway slave Anthony Burns, Thoreau once more calls into question the necessity of the territorial state. In particular, he again denies that it, in this case the state of Massachusetts, provides protection and asserts that it fails to effectuate just conditions, two goods often attributed to state action and pointed to in order to argue for its necessity. Dressing trenchant criticism in his characteristic sarcasm, Thoreau doubts that he needs a governor: "I think that I could manage to get along without one. If he is not of the least use to prevent my being kidnapped, pray of what important use is he likely to be to me? When freedom is most endangered, he dwells in the deepest obscurity."[48] Still speaking about the governor (of Massachusetts), Thoreau adds: "What I am concerned to know is, that that man's influence and authority were on the side of the slaveholder, and not the slave—of the guilty, and not of the innocent—of injustice, and not of justice."[49] But not only do territorial states lend their weight to unjust causes, they also imprison many of the only persons actually committed to securing the values that state officials claim as the ends for which the state exists to procure. According to Thoreau, "While the Governor, and the Mayor, and countless officers of the Commonwealth, are at large, the champions of liberty are imprisoned."[50]

The above passages present a basic outline of Thoreau's account of the territorial state and are best understood in relation to Thoreau's emphasis in *Walden* on identifying false necessities and eliminating impediments to a flourishing moral life. As I have already suggested, on Thoreau's view the territorial state—with its governors, judges, and laws—does not in practice serve a positive function. Myth would have us believe that state officials protect freedom and secure justice. Thoreau, of course, contends that the state, in actuality, perpetuates injustice and facilitates alienation.

Especially troubling for Thoreau is the effect that the practices of the territorial state and obedience to it have on our self-conceptions and moral senses—our perceptions or conceptions of human nature and moral truth or rightness. The myths that circulate about the state (political ideology), and the conformity that it engenders, have grave consequences for moral and social life. As Thoreau puts it: "Under the name of order and civil government, we are all made at least to pay homage to and support our own meanness. At the first blush of sin, comes its indifference and from immoral it becomes, as it were, unmoral, and not quite unnecessary to that life which we have made."[51] Under the weight of myth and conformity, then, we become conditioned to condoning what prior to conditioning we would have deemed or demeaned as immoral; we come to regard artificial things as natural, unnecessary institutions as necessary, suffering and cruelty as unavoidable; we degrade ourselves and others, denying our value or dignity; we condone racial apartheid and imperialist wars; we accept (or believe) the territorial state as necessary when it in fact is not; in turn, we do things that we ought not to do.

Thoreau responds to this sociopolitical problematic with a multifold prescription that includes practices that have already been alluded to. These practices can be divided into three categories that deserve enumeration: (1) self-reflection or self-examination, (2) truth-telling or social criticism, and (3) principled action (and principled action includes asceticism, experimentation, and disobedience). These three interrelated practices (or practice areas) constitute the remedy, the elemental part of Thoreau's moral or social reform program, and can be properly regarded as Thoreauvian religious ethical (religio-ethical) duties, as they all relate back to Thoreau's theology and concomitant theological anthropology (i.e. theologically informed conception of the human person). As I indicated in my earlier consideration of *A Week* and *Walden*, Thoreau believes that accurately describing the character of the self and the effects of our institutional practices are preconditions to the reclamation of moral responsibility and the adoption of alternative practices.

For Thoreau, self-examination, truth-telling (social criticism), and principled action are indispensable to the effort to overcome the complacency and unjust conditions borne of myth and custom. Ultimately, only by self-examination, a recovery of the divinity within and our moral sense—and hence reclamation of moral responsibility—can we be liberated. The expectation, of course, is that self-examination and truth-telling will culminate in principled action, and reflection on this principled action will in turn become the basis for additional truth-telling. These interrelated practices are crucial for the clarity that they bring. They cast light. The light reveals (or even presents) a line of demarcation: are you on the side of justice or injustice?

Examining oneself, contemplating one's purpose and nature, brings into view the character of one's duties, directing one's attention to the moral principles or rules that determine what constitutes just or unjust action. In Thoreau's case, these principles or rules, rooted in his religious impulse, provide the basis for social criticism and determine what constitutes *principled action*. So, for Thoreau, principled action consists of action based on moral rules or principles—doing one's moral duty. The most significant moral duty for our present purposes is the duty to be just or to avoid being an agent of injustice. Importantly, Thoreau's conception of justice is inseparable from his doctrine of noncomplicity. A straightforward articulation of the doctrine of noncomplicity comes in "Resistance to Civil Government":

> It is not a man's duty, as a matter of course, to devote himself to the eradication of any, even the most enormous wrong; he may still properly have other concerns to engage him; but it is his duty, at least, to wash his hands of it, and, if he gives it no thought longer, not to give it practically his support. If I devote myself to other pursuits and contemplations, I must first see, at least, that I do not pursue them sitting on another man's shoulders. I must get off him first, that he may pursue his contemplations too.[52]

Whether or not this doctrine is onerous, of course, depends on the relative moral sensitivity or rigorousness of the deliberating moral agent. Although one might invoke a doctrine such as this one in order to exonerate, Thoreau, an ever so rigorous moralizer, invokes it in order to indict. And Thoreau's interest in combating slumber and moral indifference should inform how we interpret, in political philosophical terms, his version of the Golden Rule or ethic of reciprocity and the political disobedience that it motivated.

# III

The anarchist implications of Thoreau's doctrine of noncomplicity and tax refusal might elude us if we fail to recognize that Thoreau, not unlike other social activists of his day, embracing voluntarism, regarded the state as one among many voluntary associations. The voluntarist impulse undoubtedly emerged as a salient factor in European social and political affairs in the aftermath of the Protestant Reformation. And Europeans' colonization of land in the Americas, especially North America, only intensified this trend, given the disruption of traditional social hierarchies, customs, and practices that migration produced. For our purposes, it is enough to understand the relevance that voluntarism came to have in what is often referred to as the "come-outerism movement," a movement comprised of abolitionists during the early to mid-nineteenth century.[53]

In that movement, religious reformers, including William Lloyd Garrison, called for persons to "come out" of union with sin and certain Christian denominations and churches—denominations and churches that come-outers took to be committed to an adulterated or corrupt form of Christianity as a result of their support and endorsement of white supremacy and slavery. By the late 1830s activists had turned to calling for individuals to come out of union with government. For example, in 1839, Adin Ballou and several other Christian pacifists, who would later found the Hopedale community, in the publication *Standard of Practical Christianity*, renounced allegiance to "all the governments of the world." At about the same time, Garrison, Bronson Alcott, and George Ripley issued similar separate statements.[54]

To be sure, there are important differences among these figures. Thoreau, for example, while an advocate of "noncooperation" with forces of evil or injustice (noncomplicity), did not base his commitments on the biblical injunction against violence as did "nonresistants" such as Ballou and Garrison. And Garrison and Ballou disagreed with one another about whether or not chattel slavery constituted the principal injustice propagated by the American state or merely one injustice among many. But these differences, while important, should not detract from what the above figures held in common. First, they each responded to state sanctioned racial oppression by commending individual moral responsibility and moral autonomy. In addition, they rigorously applied their ideals of justice and all found the American state wanting. Consequently, they asserted that individual persons, in virtue of their status as moral agents, created by God, had a moral duty to withdraw support from the modern territorial state. They discussed this duty in terms of "disunion," "nonresistance," "noncomplicity," and "noncooperation." In this way, they belong to a line of American revolutionaries who, as Staughton Lynd points out, "agree that a political philosophy based on [moral] freedom leads to the reconstruction of society as a voluntary association of individuals" and conceived of government as one "among many voluntary associations."[55]

Thoreau's subscription to voluntarism was already evident in 1840, the year that he was confronted by the state of Massachusetts for his refusal to pay the church tax, a tax the payment of which was then required by law. In response, he wrote to the Concord town clerk, informing him that "I, Henry Thoreau, do not wish to be regarded as a member of any incorporated society which I have not joined." Akin to other religious reformers and activists in nineteenth-century New England, it would not be long before Thoreau extended his voluntarism so that it included resistance to both the church and the state. By 1842, Thoreau, of course, refused to pay a Massachusetts poll tax in resistance to a government that he believed to be fundamentally unjust in its practices toward Native Americans, Mexicans, and enslaved African Americans. Many who would be unable to identify Thoreau as the author of *Walden* know him for his tax refusal during the 1840s. That political disobedience became the experience that Thoreau immortalized in his classic occasional piece "Resistance to Civil Government."

Theorists and social critics have often devoted themselves to describing revolutionary action or interpreting revolutions. A list of such theorists includes Kant, Thomas Paine, Edmund Burke, Alexis de Tocqueville, Frederick Douglass, Karl Marx, and Hannah Arendt. Thoreau, perhaps appropriately given his status as a prophet of the American Renaissance, interprets his own action. Thoreau resists the territorial state because "it is not desirable to cultivate a respect for the law, so much as for the right." And, again, he maintains that "the only obligation which I have a right to assume, is to do at any time what I think right."[56] Consistent with this view, in "Resistance to Civil Government," Thoreau relates,

> It is for no particular item in the tax-bill that I refuse to pay [the poll tax]. I simply wish to refuse allegiance to the State, to withdraw and stand aloof from it effectually. I do not wish to trace the course of my dollar . . . but I am concerned to trace the effects of my allegiance. In fact, I quietly declare war with the State, after my fashion.[57]

The implications of Thoreau's doctrine of noncomplicity and his descriptive account of the territorial state should be clear. Thoreau's commitment to the doctrine of noncomplicity and his belief in the revolutionary effect of action based on principle motivated his resistance to civil government, including his tax refusal. By extension, we can say that the doctrine of noncomplicity underwrites Thoreau's political disobedience and his rejection of the legitimacy of the modern territorial state. Indeed, more to the point, in view of his religious-ethical commitments generally speaking, Thoreau advocates abolishing the territorial state. His most explicit statements to this effect probably come in "Resistance to Civil Government." There Thoreau declares:

> I heartily accept the motto—"That government is best which governs least"; and I should like to see it acted up to more rapidly and systematically. Carried out, it finally amounts to this, which also I believe—"That government is best which governs not at all"; and when men are prepared for it, that will be the kind of government which they will have. Government is at best but an expedient; but most governments are usually, and all governments are sometimes, inexpedient. The objections which have been brought against a standing army, and they are many and weighty, and deserve to prevail, may also at last be brought against a standing government.[58]

And he concludes, "When the friction comes to have its machine, and oppression and robbery are organized, I say, let us not have such a machine any longer."[59]

All of this beckons toward anarchism. Yet just after asserting that arguments against standing armies and standing governments deserve to prevail, Thoreau backs away, seemingly reversing course. Shifting his tone, he writes: "[To] speak practically and as a citizen, unlike those who call themselves no-government men, I ask for not at once no government, but at once a better government. Let every man make known what kind of government would command his respect, and that will be one step toward obtaining it."[60]

Thoreau is often understood to be rejecting anarchism in this passage, where he differentiates himself from no-government men (such as William Lloyd Garrison), and suggests that he wants "at once a better government." But I would like to suggest a different interpretation. A close reading of the text, in its context, reveals that here, where Thoreau seems to be refuting an anarchist thesis, he is in fact articulating the content for an anarchist conception of government. This might seem a strange assertion. In some ways it is. Yet it will appear more plausible if we do at least two things. First, we must keep in mind that anarchism does not entail a rejection of government or political organization; rather, anarchism only entails a rejection of certain forms of government or means of governing.[61] In addition to this, we need to pay careful attention to the kind of government that Thoreau suggests would command his respect.

To solve this puzzle we need only to contemplate the closing paragraphs of the essay, "Resistance to Civil Government." There Thoreau, who had earlier in the essay denounced the American constitution as evil, concedes that one can evaluate institutions from multiple perspectives, including a "lower point of view." In consequence, he acknowledges that it is possible to reach relative moral judgments with respect to certain institutions. However, Thoreau denies that one should rest content with the lower point of view and reiterates his judgment, of the Massachusetts and American states, from a higher plane. He writes,

> Seen from a lower point of view, the Constitution, with all its faults, is very good; the law and the courts are very respectable; even this State [Massachusetts] and this American government are, in many respects, very admirable and rare things, to be thankful for, such as a great many have described them; but seen from a point of view a little higher, they are what I have described them; seen from a higher still, and the highest, who shall say what they are, or that they are worth looking at or thinking of at all?[62]

With faith that social progress is facilitated by achieving the clarity that comes with the higher point of view, Thoreau reaffirms his commitment to higher-level criticism, and articulates the criteria by which he will judge political institutions. That is, he "makes known what kind of government would command his respect," which is a step toward attaining it:

> The authority of government, even such as I am willing to submit to . . . is still an impure one: to be strictly just, it must have the sanction and consent of the governed. It can have no right over my person and property but what I concede it.

He goes on,

> The progress from an absolute to a limited monarchy, from a limited monarchy to a democracy, is a progress toward a true respect for the individual. Is a democracy, such as we know it, the last improvement possible in government? Is it not possible to take a step further towards recognizing and organizing the rights of man? There will never be a really free and enlightened State, until the State comes to recognize the individual as a higher and independent power, from which all power and authority are derived, and treats him accordingly.[63]

Notice that, in the above, Thoreau is not simply criticizing the American state on account of its defense of slavery, its imperialist militarism, or its domestic repression. Instead, the enunciation of his normative ideal amounts to an implicit rejection of representational democracy as a form of government. While Thoreau regards the constitutional democracy operative in nineteenth-century America as superior to the political forms that preceded it in European countries, he refuses to regard democracy as mid-nineteenth-century Americans knew it as the best possible *form* of government. The American Revolution did not spell the end of history.

This all points to the fact that a given political philosophical orientation is as much an attitude regarding history (and its present) as it is anything else. The historical gaze gives life to political philosophy and what we look at determines what we see. So in the debate about preferable forms of government, at least with respect to contemporary normative social-political thought, the better part of the weight rests on our evaluations of actual social practices. It is hence of great consequence that Thoreau insists on judging from a "higher view" and calls attention to the dark side of America, constitutional democracy, and modern territorial states.

With respect to America, self-identifying anarchists have focused on the faces at the bottom of the well, the dispossessed, and the excluded. Adopting a critical lens, anarchists insist that any celebration of the American Revolution be accompanied by remembrance of Native Americans, African slaves, lower class Europeans, women. They insist that celebration of the US Constitution be accompanied by an acknowledgment of the considerations that influenced the structure of the constitution; they note the effect that interest in compromise, oppression, conquest—the wars with Native Americans, the Mexicans, the Spaniards, slave aristocracy—had on the configuration of American political institutions. The United States' representational democratic federalism, say anarchists, is as much the by-product of greed and cruelty as anything else. To substantiate this claim, anarchists point to the constitutional debates; analysis of the debates at the constitutional conventions is instructive for what it reveals about the rationale that informed the ultimate structure of the constitution; the quest for an empire and a commitment to maintaining a slave economy are betrayed by the differences between the Articles of Confederation and Perpetuation and the American Constitution. It is reasonable to conclude, on the basis of this history, that the US Constitution was written as a proslavery and proimperialist document. Anarchists refer to the above and more in order to counter claims about the goods that a given territorial state delivers. From the anarchist vantage, it is not clear that the American state is not being used as a tool by the few, to paraphrase Thoreau.

Thoreau's higher view, if I am correct, poses a direct challenge to theorists, including liberal and republican democrats, who maintain the value of representational democratic territorial states on empirical and functional (or instrumental) grounds. Such theorists, of course, assert that the territorial state with its legal regime is valuable for the goods that it provides for human persons. In particular, these theorists contend that a powerful centralized authority such as the state generates norms and enforces them; it creates and protects indispensable individual human rights and freedoms, which is said to prevent or at least minimize injustice and domination. But, as we have seen, the claim that the territorial state is necessary for the realization and protection of rights and freedom is just the sort of claim that Thoreau rejects.

Thoreau suggests that the state, with its legal regime, is a dead institution that does not in practice serve the function that many theorists assert, so that it can be regarded as a false necessity. It quarrels with and attempts to subjugate foreigners. It taxes and conscripts persons in order to carry out its unjust designs, attempting to make all persons complicit in its unjust practices—it desperately runs amok against those who refuse to support its unjust practices, practices which themselves serve to perpetuate superfluous consumption. Thoreau regards the modern territorial state as a product of superfluous consumption and the practical means (exploitation, oppression, and repression) for the sustenance of such consumption, especially among elites, and contends that serving as an officer of the state is to serve as a "tool of an institution," which entails acting in ways that are inappropriate (or "not proper") for a (divine) human being. And since one cannot belong to a political order that engages in systematic domination and oppression—an order that enslaves some, represses some, and invades some—without being diminished from a moral vantage, Thoreau denied that he had benefited from the nineteenth-century American-Massachusetts political order, denied its moral legitimacy, and refused to be associated with or pledge allegiance to it. Thoreau is unequivocal in his negative assessment of the function of modern territorial states, even constitutional democracies. The American constitutional democracy, as inexpedient and as unjust as it was, convinced Thoreau that such a form of government was inadequate (for divine beings); one could not be associated with the territorial state and at the same time be faithful to God and the higher law.

Significantly, Thoreau derives general positive normative principles from his reflection on the particular defects of the American and Massachusetts governments. We might say that the democratic experiments in the Americas revealed or exposed short-comings of constitutional representational democracy and majoritarian or electoral decision-making procedure that molded Thoreau's idea about the shape that a better form of government would have to take. And, so he asks, "Is it not possible to take a step further towards recognizing and organizing the rights of man?"

Thoreau's answer to the above question is clear: it is desirable and possible to replace the representational democratic government with some other form and a morally preferable form of government would be a government that individual persons voluntarily consent to in advance of executive action by that government. He thus maintains that political authority, to be legitimate or "strictly just," must be derived from the explicit consent of every individual person who is to be subject to the authority in question. All power and authority in a morally acceptable political order would be derived from the "individual as a higher and independent power."

The government, or form of government, that would command Thoreau's respect would be a government that respected persons' moral autonomy such that they were neither oppressed by the government in question nor forced to play a role in oppressing others.[64] In describing his ideal form of government, Thoreau delineates a form of government that is probably best described in terms of anarchism, as the idea that only mutual consent can generate legitimate political authority and so putative political obligations is constitutive of anarchist thought.

As I noted in the "Introduction," a basic component of anarchism is the assumption that persons are voluntary participants in certain domains of social and political life; persons can become subjects owing certain duties to other persons or institutions only by voluntarily submitting to them. Especially relevant for our purposes is the issue of *political* authority. According to anarchists, political decisions *imposed* from above by others do not give rise to *moral* obligations. Any authority that attempts to impose such decisions on persons is regarded as both unjust and illegitimate.[65] For anarchists, a political entity is legitimate—perhaps we could say legitimate in the fullest sense—only insofar as the entity in question operates based on the explicit consent of persons said to be subject to that entity's authority. Anarchists, then, reject the legitimacy of the territorial state owing to a theory about the function of the state as a facilitator of economic exploitation and domination generally speaking, both as a domestic and international matter, and because of the way in which territorial states reach decisions about law and policy. It should be clear that Thoreau's religious-political ethic involves a commitment to noncomplicity that includes a duty to dissociate from political regimes that are systemically unjust either in the laws and policies they enact, the decision-making processes that they adopt, or the way in which their laws and policies are implemented or enforced. In the end, Thoreau rejected constitutional democracy because he concluded that moral life in constitutional democratic orders is wanting and because he had a vision of what could and would be if only persons were to heed their callings, that is, answer to the divinity within.[66] We see now how Thoreau's metaphysics of the self inform his ethics and his political philosophy. Thoreau understands God and religion in ethical terms; he deifies the self; he posits the existence of an objective moral order; and he maintains that human persons have (unmediated) access to moral truth. These moves paved the way for Thoreau's rejection of nonvoluntarist conceptions of political authority. Some reject this vision as utopian, naïve, or unrealistic. And such rejections may be well founded. But this does not undermine the fact that this is Thoreau's vision. On my view, Thoreau's religious-ethical commitment to noncomplicity motivates an anarchist ethic. We can say, then, that an anarchist government, similar to the one predicted by Proudhon—a government with no master—is the kind of government that would command Thoreau's respect.

To appreciate why I say this, we should think about how anarchists differ from political liberals in terms of how they assess whether a given political entity is legitimate. Political liberals ordinarily concentrate on the degree to which the state's procedures adhere to a certain form. This is a preoccupation that political liberals share with anarchists. What separates them is the form that they identify as qualifying as legitimate. In practice, liberal democratic theorists are essentially persons who identify representational democracy as the best form of government and argue that this form, because it is the best form, is legitimate. Anarchists, then, are persons who identify anarchy (or perhaps direct consensus democracy) as the best form of government. Again, I realize that this way of putting it will likely strike most persons as nonsensical. But one of the things that I hope to accomplish in this work is to make clear the degree to which what we contemporaries call anarchism is first a rejection of the legitimacy and thus the authority of modern territorial states, including representative democratic ones, and second a proposal about what form government would have to take in order to be deemed legitimate and so authoritative. My claim about how we should understand anarchism is rooted in my understanding of the importance of the fact the positive political philosophical use of the term anarchism emerged in the mid-nineteenth century with the emergence of the modern territorial state, with Proudhon being the first self-declared anarchist. Anarchists (i.e. modern or contemporary anarchism) have rejected the legitimacy of the modern territorial state and offered concrete alternatives to it.

# IV

But even if we concede that Thoreau is an anarchist, there is still the question as to whether he should be classified as a weak anarchist or as a strong anarchist. In the "Introduction," I suggested that the question as to whether one has a duty to comply with the territorial state can be distinguished from the question about whether or not one has a duty to defy, withdraw from, or seek to eliminate the state. To reiterate, some anarchists, *strong* anarchists, contend that there is a duty to withdraw support from existing territorial states while others, namely *weak* anarchists, do not. Both strong and weak anarchists maintain that there is no general moral duty to obey the law in virtue of its being the law; rather one has a moral duty to consider the substance or content of a given law, or the consequences of compliance, so that one takes into consideration nonlegal moral norms and other practical considerations before determining whether to comply with a given legal or political command. One may have reasons to obey the law, but they are not reasons that have to do with the law's status as law. What distinguishes *weak* anarchists from *strong* anarchists, then, is that the former do not hold that one has a duty to oppose, to withdraw from, or to seek to eliminate the territorial state.

According to weak anarchists, such as A. John Simmons, some territorial states may on reflection be said to provide social goods that one has a natural duty to support, and so one may support the territorial state as a way of securing those goods. But even in such a case, says Simmons, there is no general moral duty to obey the laws and commands of the state in virtue of their being the laws and commands of the state; one must only obey a political entity if the entity in question exists and operates on the basis of the actual, explicit consent of the governed; in other words, only the fact of individual consent can legitimize political authority; and where there is no legitimate political authority, there are no political obligations per se, which is a stance that probably separates weak anarchists from political liberals and democratic republicans.

Insofar as we concede that anarchists do not reject all forms of political organization, my sense is that Thoreau is best described as a proponent of *strong* anarchism, as he clearly contends that there is a moral duty to withdraw support from the territorial state and maintains that a benefit of doing so is that it will spell the territorial state's demise. However, there is resistance to classifying Thoreau in this way. David Miller, for instance, in his superb text on anarchism, suggests that Thoreau rejects the authority of the modern state yet does not advocate for its elimination. Miller relates that weak anarchism

> entails the view that the state has no right to tell me or anyone else how to behave. One can believe this and respond in a wholly passive way, evading inconvenient or immoral state dictates whenever possible and complying with them when forced to do so, but taking no positive action to get rid of the state and having no constructive view about what might take its place. Men like Thoreau would fit roughly into this category.[67]

Miller goes on to point out, correctly, that weak anarchism does not necessarily provide "any recipe for destroying the state or other coercive institutions."[68]

Although Miller's portrayal of weak anarchism more or less mirrors my own, I think that Miller overlooks aspects of Thoreau's sociopolitical vision that, when acknowledged, make it difficult to classify him as a weak anarchist as opposed to a strong anarchist.[69] It is true that Thoreau did not present a systematic constructive view about what might replace the territorial state. Yet he did in fact specify criteria by which to determine the legitimacy of a given form of government. Further, it is not entirely accurate to suggest, as Miller does, that Thoreau took no positive action to get rid of the territorial state. To appreciate this latter point, we only need to understand the revolutionary character of Thoreau's doctrine of noncomplicity, his appeal to conscience, and his related tax refusal, facets of Thoreauvian ethics that have been important for modern social movement activists, particularly proponents of nonviolent direct action and nonviolent revolution such as Lev Tolstoy, Mohandas Gandhi, Dorothy Day, Bayard Rustin, and Howard Zinn.

Thoreau's significance for such revolutionaries notwithstanding, the revolutionary and thus stridently political character of his activism have often been unacknowledged. This stems largely from the fact that many interpreters of Thoreau's thought divorce his appeal to conscience from his theological anthropology, his understanding of the state, and his theory of social change, and then charge him with being overly concerned with himself, unconcerned with social suffering and injustice, and passive in the face of injustice. I have already suggested that it is wrong to attribute the vice of individualism or self-centeredness to persons who assert the primacy of moral autonomy. But if one does not appreciate the degree to which Thoreau's social activism and theory of social change are rooted in and connected to a particular conception of conscience, then it is easy to portray him as self-centered and indifferent in the face of injustice.

Hannah Arendt does just this in an essay on political obligation in which she criticizes Thoreau's social engagement. In particular, Arendt frames her criticism of "Thoreau" as a criticism of "conscience" proper. Adopting a rather narrow conception of conscience, Arendt tells her readers that conscience is problematic because it is not "primarily interested in the world where the wrong is committed or in the consequences that the wrong will have for the future course of the world."[70] And this points to exactly what troubles Arendt when it comes to Thoreau. She finds him insufferably vested in "the rules of conscience." In Arendt's mind, Thoreau's concern with conscience amounts to a problematic preoccupation with the self, or specifically, moral purity. In her words, "the rules of conscience hinge on interest in the self."[71]

The self/world dichotomy that Arendt takes for granted undergirds her claim that Thoreau abandons the world for his own sake. Ironically, Arendt cites Thoreau's famed charge, "The people must cease to hold slaves, and to make war on Mexico, though it cost them their existence as a people," as evidence of Thoreau's lack of concern for the "world." And to drive home her point about Thoreau's problematic indifference to worldly concerns, Arendt contrasts Thoreau with Abraham Lincoln. Lincoln, Arendt tells us, offered himself as a sacrifice so as to save the American territorial state, whereas Thoreau prescribed sacrifice in the name of dissolving the Union. That Arendt should criticize Thoreau on account of his response to injustice is ironic, and not simply because one would think that Thoreau's concern for human persons is especially on display in his trenchant criticism of chattel slavery. It is also ironic in the light of Arendt's having devoted so much of her career as a theorist to arguing for a conception of "the political" that aligns with Thoreau's and anarchists' in interesting ways, a point that I will return to in the conclusion to this book.

For now, though, we simply need to understand why Arendt's description of Thoreau's sociopolitical action fails to capture its moral and political significance. As far as I am concerned, one can only characterize Thoreau as being unconcerned with the world if one assumes two things. First, one must assume that conscience is a private matter. And second, one must assume, as Arendt sometimes seems to, that if one is to show concern for the world, then one should (always) act in a way that improves a *given* political order. In other words, one must assume that a concern about conscience is merely about an inward-looking moral freedom rather than "outward" expression that motivates sociopolitical action aimed at the increase of freedom or justice in the "world."

It should be clear how Thoreau's appeal to conscience differs from the inward-looking, self-absorbed agent that Arendt describes. Thoreau's concern about injustice or wrongs in the world and his desire to undermine unjust practices is given expression through his appeals to conscience and his emphasis on the role that conscience plays in bringing about positive social change. So it is simply untrue that because, unlike Lincoln, Thoreau did not care to "destroy slavery in order to preserve the Union" but to "destroy the Union so as to destroy slavery," he (or his appeal to conscience) was not primarily interested in the world where wrongs are committed. Furthermore, it is untrue that, because Thoreau eschewed traditional formal political participation, he was unconcerned with the (social) world. By understanding how profoundly concerned Thoreau was with wrongs committed in the world, we can begin to understand how thoroughly alienated he was from the American territorial state.[72] Arendt's narrow conception of conscience precludes her from appreciating this, the character of Thoreau's political vision, and the significance of conscience (or action based on principle) for contemporary social justice activism.[73]

Because normative ethical prescriptions take on a special value when related to a specific context, it is quite pertinent that Thoreau lived at what might be referred to as the dawn of modernity, in a society with increasingly centralized institutions. He thus came of age in a world in which an injustice anywhere had begun to count as an injustice everywhere, making it quite difficult to wash one's hands of the many wrongs that marked the social world. This aspect of modern life has left many in the modern world feeling impotent in the face of injustice. Yet this same social reality has inspired radical activism too, leaving countless radicals convinced that liberation depends on the acts or action of individual persons.

Such activists have contended that it is in a context in which a centralized entity, such as the territorial state, attempts to universalize complicity with injustice that individual resistance based on principle—rebellion—can have its most dramatic effect. As Barbara Packer eloquently puts the matter, "Rebellion needs something rigid to overthrow."[74] Few things are more rigid than the territorial state's claim to legitimate authority, which includes the right to issue commands that persons have a duty to obey. Thoreau realized this. So he says, "One would think, that a deliberate and practical denial of its authority was the only offense never contemplated by government."[75] It is in the light of this that he would stress the revolutionary implications of moral rigorousness. In a set of lines teeming with urgency, Thoreau dramatizes the significance of principled action and gives voice to a sentiment that has moved radical activists around the world for more than a century: "Action from principle—the perception and the performance of right—changes things and relations; it is essentially revolutionary, and does not consist wholly with any thing which was. It not only divides states and churches, it divides families; aye, it divides the *individual*, separating the diabolical in him from the divine."[76]

Thoreau's conception of action from principle is best understood in relation to his doctrine of noncomplicity and his idea of conscience. Right moral action, for Thoreau, involves acting in a way that reflects one's moral autonomy or freedom; and to be morally virtuous or good entails avoiding complicity in the various forms of social injustice that are propagated daily. And because, as we have seen, for Thoreau, the territorial state was a leading purveyor of social injustice, a person could only be truly free, as a moral matter, when refusing to contribute to the state. In the realm of the political, blind obedience and conformity are the cause of death, destruction, and dehumanization. The oppressed can only attain material freedom—that is, liberation—if persons who contribute to the territorial state cease to do so, which is why Thoreau withdrew his allegiance from the state and refused to pay state taxes. It is in this way that action from principle is essentially revolutionary, changing things and relations.

Notice that the revolutionary character of action from principle parallels the purifying nature of asceticism (or chastity). To a degree, asceticism, as Thoreau relates its meaning, is an example of action from principle. Asceticism can be understood as conscientious consumption in a materialistic capitalist society; it is revolutionary in character because it brings one closer to the divine, changes one's practices, and thus has a transformative impact on the wider social structure. If in the face of capitalistic economic practices, action from principle entails the life of an ascetic, political disobedience is the form that action from principle takes in the face of territorial state politics. Conscience (and the doctrine of noncomplicity) dictated Thoreau's resistance to the state and led him to oppose, to withdraw from, and to seek the elimination of the territorial state. It is for this bundle of reasons that Thoreau's tax refusal, which he based on an appeal to conscience and rooted in the doctrine of noncomplicity, was at bottom revolutionary.

Thoreau maintained that, because the sustenance of the territorial state depends on compliance with it, withdrawing support from it constitutes the most effective means by which to undermine its operation. Consistent with this, in "Resistance to Civil Government," he prophesies: "I know this well, that if one thousand, if one hundred, if ten men whom I could name,—if ten *honest* men only,—aye, if *one* HONEST man, in this State of Massachusetts, *ceasing to hold slaves*, were actually to withdraw from this copartnership, and be locked up in the county jail therefore, it would be the abolition of slavery in America."[77] Thoreau continues his eloquent appeal,

> Cast your whole vote, not a strip of paper merely, but your whole influence. A minority is powerless while it conforms to the majority; it is not even a minority then; but it is irresistible when it clogs by its whole weight. If the alternative is to keep all just men in prison, or give up war and slavery, the State will not hesitate to choose. If a thousand men were not to pay their tax-bills this year, that would not be a violent and bloody measure, as it would be to pay them, and enable the State to commit violence and shed innocent blood. This is, in fact, the definition of a peaceable revolution, if any such is possible. If the tax-gatherer, or any other public officer, asks me, as one has done, "But what shall I do?" my answer is, "If you really wish to do any thing, resign your office." When the subject has refused allegiance, and the officer has resigned his office, then the revolution is accomplished.[78]

While his empathy is rarely discussed, the above makes clear that it is precisely because Thoreau is concerned about the so-called world, inclusive of his own self, that he rejects constitutionalism and the majority-principle, and prescribes political disobedience. Thoreau's spirited plea is inspired by compassion and indignation in the face of social suffering and social injustice; he recommends tax refusal because paying taxes "enables the State to commit violence and shed innocent blood." Thoreau's call for moral actors to withdraw support from the state is motivated by an interest in undermining an unjust practice and thus preventing social evils.

Reflecting on Thoreau's ethics in relation to anarchist philosophy elucidates why it is misleading to characterize Thoreau as some sort of egoist and points to an important aspect of anarchism. Anarchism is often referred to as a philosophy of freedom, but too few understand that many anarchists esteem, prescribe, and prioritize moral autonomy and voluntarism for *other-regarding* reasons. Most leading anarchists assert that persons should reject the territorial state's legitimacy and deny its authority because of the fact that the state takes advantage of deference and turns persons into tools that are employed in order to oppress and repress—harm and sometimes kill—other persons. And most religiously motivated anarchists give special emphasis to or make explicit these kinds of other-regarding moral or ethical reasons for embracing anarchism and conceptions of moral autonomy. Thoreau deserves to be counted among this latter group.

For Thoreau, a rejection of the majority-principle is the principal means by which to move toward a state of justice, which is to move toward a society in which the territorial state has been eliminated. As the text quoted above makes explicit, Thoreau desires to effectuate a revolution (because of the unjust nature of the status quo). And of utmost import, he imagines (the possibility of) a "peaceable revolution" being accomplished on the basis of individual persons acting in accord with the dictates of conscience against the state.[79]

In "Slavery in Massachusetts" Thoreau reiterates his rejection of the authority and legitimacy of the American political regime, and again calls attention to the importance of the cultivation of moral sensitivity, that is, conscience. Thoreau maintains that persons ought to obey and serve God and develop into "men of probity." Judges and lawyers leave much to be desired on Thoreau's view because they refuse to exercise judgment and thus deny critical truths about their nature as divine beings and this denial undermines the possibility of realizing just social conditions. He bluntly denounces lawyers and judges, contending that they are owed little respect because "They consider, not whether the Fugitive Slave Law is right, but whether it is what they call *constitutional.*" Such persons, silencing the voice of conscience, "persist in being the servants of the worst of men, and not the servants of humanity." Thoreau declares,

> The question is not whether you or your grandfather, seventy years ago, did not enter into an agreement to serve the devil, and that service is not accordingly now due; but whether you will not now, for once and at last, serve God,—in spite of your own past recreancy, or that of your ancestor,—by obeying that eternal and only just constitution, which He, and not any Jefferson or Adams, has written in your being.[80]

One might disagree with Thoreau's understanding of God, the self, society, and conscience. But it should be apparent that Thoreau's appeal to conscience was both rooted in a concern about injustice and aimed at inspiring social change. To neglect the fact that this is how conscience functions in Thoreau's and contemporary social justice activism is to miss one of the more remarkable characteristics of sociopolitical life in recent centuries; from at least the early part of the nineteenth century, conscience has operated as and been understood as a voice of political dissent, calling into question (immoral) consensus and blind conformity.[81] And political and religious radicals have been the modern bearers of conscience, with Thoreau standing out among these bearers.

Robert Richardson's captivating biography of Ralph Waldo Emerson is memorably entitled, *Emerson: The Mind on Fire*. This title captures what

Richardson regards as a central aspect of Emerson's strivings. Emerson lived a life of the mind. My concern here has been to bring to the surface the central elements of Henry David Thoreau's religious, ethical, and political strivings and to come to terms with the political implications of Thoreau's commitment to living a life of principle. The life of principle is the life of conscience. Thoreau's conscience was ablaze. This is evident throughout his writings. At every turn Thoreau confronts us with a challenge. He demands that we make explicit to whom or what we are allegiant. He asks us to announce our commitments. Thoreau asks, in so many words, Do you have conscience or not? Fitting for a revolutionary with a conscience on fire, Thoreau gave the world prophecy in prose form—prose composed to ignite.

Thoreau's call for persons to wake up is a call for regeneration that involves cultivating moral virtues that enable one to rely on one's own conscience and judgment. And the assumption is that the content of conscience is universal and, again, that acting on the basis of conscience will instigate social change. In John Thomas's words, Transcendentalists, including Thoreau, contend that,

> Every man may safely trust his conscience, properly informed, because it is the repository for divine truth. When men learn to trust their consciences and act on them, they naturally encourage others to do the same with the certainty that they will reach the same conclusions. Individual conscience thus creates a social conscience and a collective will to right action. Concerted right action means moral revolution.[82]

Thoreau's emphasis on exemplary moral action was rooted in his particular conception of moral reform and social change. He believed that political, religious, and social attitudes and actions are contagious. An individual act of defiance may appear nil in isolation, yet bold action inspires bold action. When communities of persons begin to confess the truth, and act in accord with it, others will begin to act in ways consistent with that truth as far as it is possible to do so.

In this way, Thoreau and Tolstoy are in agreement. Tolstoy wrote, in *The Kingdom of God Is Within*, "Only boldly profess the truth to which we are called, and we should find at once that hundreds, thousands, millions of men are in the same positions as we, that they see the truth as we do, and dread as we do to stand alone in recognizing it, and like us are only waiting for others to recognize it also."[83] Gandhi's attraction to Thoreau and Tolstoy had to do with this radical faith in the possibility of inspiring courageous action and swaying public opinion with nonviolent action—soul force.

Thoreau puts in sharp relief the connection among who we are, what we do, and the social circumstances in which we find ourselves (which is precisely the reason that Thoreau's life and thought has inspired so many radical activists). As theorists of social change and revolution note, cooperation is presupposed in nearly every oppressive situation; noncooperation with oppressive authorities is a must. It is thus imperative for persons in oppressive situations to realize the dynamic relationship between cooperation and the oppressive states of affairs. Thoreau calls on persons to do what they know is right, to dispense with hypocrisy, double standards, blind conformity, and indifference. And he trusts that if persons are reflective, then they will understand what right action entails, and thus find cause to defy certain social practices.

We could say, then, that for Thoreau revolution must begin with a refusal to evade responsibility. In that way revolution begins with asking the ethical question. Will I obey authorities that command me to kill unjustly? Will I torture? Am I to hand over a fugitive slave? Each person must determine for him or herself whether or not to consider torture as wrong or not; whether she will or will not join the firing squad; serve as warden of a prison which jails people for having broken laws that are widely regarded as unjust.

Thoreau posits the necessity of a coincidence of refusals and turns to prophecy and warning because he understood well that an isolated act of disobedience could not itself accomplish the revolution. It initiates the revolution; it solicits fellow revolutionaries; but it does not accomplish it. But, "Revolutions are never sudden," as Thoreau notes.[84] They begin with self-examination and the revolutionary call that is connected to action from principle.[85] Thoreau's writings and action were attempts to incite and provoke awakenings. Recall his announcement in *Walden*: "I do not propose to write an ode to dejection, but to brag as lustily as chanticleer in the morning, standing on his roost, if only to wake my neighbors up."[86] The prophet's call and action are replete with hope and faith. One who issues the call says: Awakening is possible. Thus, Thoreau, in appealing to conscience, hopes that his appeal awakens a public. An awakened plurality, refusing to support the territorial state, ushers in the death of the state. And because, for Thoreau, the modern territorial state is a false necessity engaged in unjust practices that oppress, degrade, and repress human persons, it is this death that would make social and political freedom possible—it would initiate the liberation of the slaves and an end to American imperialism.

In perhaps one of his most revealing comments, for our purposes, offering his take on the meaning of "America," Thoreau contends that by putting life in perspective and understanding what is truly necessary, a "true America" might emerge. The meaning of America has been contested territory from the beginning of European conquest and settlement of the New World. Economic and political crises, technological innovations, and natural disasters, when they occur, intensify contests over social and institutional norms and practices and thereby deepen debates over meaning. Such contests may proceed by words or swords, so to speak. The nineteenth century, the American state's first century, hosted a wave of crises and dramatic events that challenged contemporaries' understandings of America or the ideal of America. From the war of 1812 to the Compromise of 1820, the emergence of Monroe Doctrine, the Nullification Crisis, the Fugitive Slave Act, the case of Dred Scott, and the Native American Removal Act, the meaning of America was contested and in flux.

America, say some, is economic freedom. America, say others, is religious freedom. America is Eden. America is Empire. Some posit America as the realization of utopia; they equate the status quo with the Ideal. But others insist that we avoid confusing our norms with extant material social arrangements. For these latter figures, what needs to be defended is not the status quo, but a vision, such that the vision might seize here and there a person or collectivity, orienting action in a way that might pave a way for its realization. America could and should be this or that, say these characters. Thoreau, of course, belongs to this latter group—the visionaries.

When Thoreau lays down his understanding of the meaning of America, as we might expect, it is an understanding intricately intertwined with his religious and political notions. Thoreau proclaims in *Walden*,

> The only true America is that country where you are at liberty to pursue such a mode of life as may enable you to do without these [false necessities such as tea or coffee], and where the state does not endeavor to compel you to sustain slavery and war and other superfluous expenses which directly or indirectly results from the use of such things [as tea or coffee].[87]

Thoreau posits America as a place where action based on principle has become the norm and an anarchist government has become a true possibility. Holding on to the vision hinges on adopting the appropriate posture vis-à-vis standing institutions. Disobedience keeps complacency at bay and militates against a tendency to mistake the status quo for the ideal. In consequence of his ideal conceptions of the self and government, Thoreau refuses to recognize the authority of the territorial state. Rather than comply with the territorial state—institutions of the dead—we ought to endeavor to "stay where God has put us, on his own conditions." The territorial state should be dispensed with because its practices conflict with human nature and dignity—both of the oppressed and the oppressors—properly understood. Since doing away with the modern territorial state hinges on the awakening of persons, in his effort to wake his neighbors up, Thoreau sounds a political alarm: Persons who do wake up will realize that the territorial state is unnecessary and alter their methods of living, thus paving the way for and also constituting revolution—the realization of "the only true America."

It is this conviction, I believe, that moved Thoreau to celebrate the life and death of the militant abolitionist John Brown. In "A Plea for Captain John Brown," Thoreau praises John Brown because, unlike too many New

Englanders, "[Brown] did not set up even a political graven image between him and his God."[88] Brown was thus unwilling to defer to the authority of any government. According to Thoreau, "No man in America has ever stood up so persistently and effectively for the dignity of human nature, knowing himself for a man, and the equal of any and all governments. In that sense he [John Brown] was the most American of us all."[89] On my reading, Thoreau's paean to John Brown connects directly to Thoreau's enunciation of the form of government that would command his respect and his assertion about the means by which to realize that government (in his essay "Resistance to Civil Government"). To that end, we can say that according to Thoreau, the true America will be a place in which governments honor and respect the irreducible dignity of individual human persons. And it is true Americans who must bring into reality "the only true America." For Thoreau, the true Americans will "acknowledge no master in human form," which means of course that true Americans will regard no human persons as slaves. Moreover, they will realize that a preoccupation with electoral politics, constitutionalism, and obedience/conformity distracts us from cultivating the qualities of character that are critical to sustainable social change. They will understand, with John Brown, that "The fate of the country does not depend on how you vote at the polls—the worst man is as strong as the best at that game." They will appreciate that more important than "what kind of paper you drop into the ballot-box once a year [is] what kind of man you drop from your chamber into the street every morning."[90]

The above religious and political vision is reiterated throughout Thoreau's writings, including *A Week* and *Walden*. Although *A Week* and *Walden* are not always read in order to narrate Thoreau's political philosophy, doing so here has been instructive. In particular, connecting his understanding of awakening and asceticism to the problems of false necessities and conformism has highlighted precisely what Thoreau finds problematic about the modern state and made clear that a Thoreauvian ethic leaves little space for the modern territorial state, given its assertions of authority and role in perpetuating unjust social conditions.

The fact that Thoreau emphasized self-reformation has led many to charge him with passivity in the face of injustice (Arendt) and to conclude that he did not advocate for the abolition of the modern state (David Miller). To avoid this kind of misunderstanding, I have directed attention to two fundamental yet often neglected facets of Thoreau's ethics. First, I have stressed the fact that Thoreau believed that "a moral reform must take place first, then the necessity of [social reform] will be superseded, and we shall sail and plough by its force alone."[91] It is notable that Thoreau was sympathetic to communitarians who established utopian communities, but he doubted the viability of their enterprises because they, particularly Fourierists, struck Thoreau as excessively materialist. Thoreau's "A Paradise (to be) Regained," published in the *Democratic Review* in the early 1840s offered an alternative to Fourier's socialist doctrine and the transcendentalist communitarian vision of George Ripley and others. Communitarians and communists of the 1840s and 1850s were materialists, the most of extreme of whom were of the view that reformed material (social) conditions could lead to the transformation of human character and social relations generally. It is not as though Thoreau doubted the relationship between social arrangements and the character of individual persons. Few thoughtful human persons have ever doubted this. And while liberals are so often accused of neglecting the importance of "tradition," even liberals are cognizant of the significance of social order, which is why liberalism is so often associated with either a particular kind of economy or a specific type of governmental arrangement. What separates the materialists and idealists is the degree to which they emphasize the need for institutional change on the one hand and individual conversion or awakening on the other. In the end, Thoreau identifies neither with the idealists nor the materialists. Instead, he posits, perhaps paradoxically, consciousness as an effect of social process and the raising of consciousness as a precondition to reformed behavior. For Thoreau, self-reform is a precondition to or even tantamount to social reform. This connects to the second point that I have stressed. Thoreau insisted that it is desirable and possible to replace the modern institutions, including representational democracies, with higher forms.

When these aspects of Thoreau's ethics are brought into the frame, it is difficult to deny the revolutionary dimension of his thought. Given the aspects on display, I think that it is evident that Thoreau did in fact prescribe a recipe for destroying the territorial state: a conscience on fire is the recipe for the state's demise. In the light of all of this, if we accept that Thoreau is in fact an anarchist, as I have maintained, then we are on solid ground when claiming that Thoreau is classifiable as a *strong* anarchist.

# V

In this chapter, I have analyzed Thoreau's thought and activism in terms of a view of anarchism that differs from common conceptions; I have described a familiar American icon in strange terms. The strangeness notwithstanding, to my mind, the most crucial question in our interpretive analysis of Thoreau's ethics is whether the term anarchism fits him better than most other terms. Descriptive case studies in the field of "religion, ethics, and politics," drawing on American pragmatism, seek to provide clarity about how religious-ethical principles congeal so as to motivate sociopolitical action or vice versa. This analytical enterprise entails attaching particular descriptive terms to the subjects and objects of study. Such analysis, to be successful, requires employing maximally clear concepts or descriptive terms and consistently applying these concepts or terms to the phenomena in question. Social action that is interesting enough to warrant analysis ordinarily resists easy description or reduction to single terms, so that when we attach single (descriptive) nouns or adjectives to complicated subjects and objects, we are likely to miss something. I have undoubtedly missed some things in this chapter. Yet, on the whole, I am confident that I have accurately spelled out how anarchism is understood by most self-described anarchists and students of anarchism and I have consistently employed the concepts in question. Further, I have wholeheartedly striven to represent and explicate Henry David Thoreau's vision in a way that is faithful to the spirit of Thoreau's life/thought as I understand it.

In particular, I have invoked anarchism (an "ism") both in order (1) to direct attention to the substance of Thoreau's thought and the significance of his political disobedience and (2) to elucidate (if not explicitly then at least implicitly) the way in which other "isms" fail to adequately capture Thoreau's normative vision. Yet at the same time, paradoxically, in order to avoid letting any "ism" get in the way, I have tried to concentrate on the substance of Thoreau's commitments in relation to a noncontroversial description of the practices and aspects of territorial states, including representational democracy. Anarchism is certainly not a category or descriptive term without limitations, yet, again, the measure of its appropriateness is the degree to which it clarifies or captures Thoreau's commitments as well as or better than the alternatives. Accordingly, I have concluded that Thoreau can be plausibly described as an anarchist (only) after reflecting deeply on the meaning of anarchism in relation to other political philosophical and theoretical categories and meditating on the implications of Thoreau's religious-ethical vision.

Some, I suspect, might be reticent to classify Thoreau as an anarchist not because they disagree with how I have defined anarchism, but because they believe that Thoreau was somewhat ambivalent in his criticism of the modern state. This assertion about Thoreau's ambivalence is predicated on the claim that Thoreau presented direct or specific rather than general criticisms of the modern state. A person who embraces this view might contend that it is difficult or even impossible to say for certain whether anarchism is a term that fits, given the way in which Thoreau's criticisms of the American and Massachusetts states (seem to have) centered on slavery and the Mexican-American War. This way of thinking about Thoreau gives rise to a chain of counterfactual questions. What would have become of his thought had he lived through the end of America's Civil War or long enough to see the passage of the thirteenth and fourteenth amendments to the US Constitution? Would Thoreau's sharp criticisms of the state have become blunt with the passage of time and constitutional amendments? It is possible. Yet if I have clarified anything at all in this chapter, I hope that it is the degree to which Thoreau criticized the modern state on multiple related-yet-distinct bases. He undoubtedly disparaged the American and Massachusetts governments for their respective roles in perpetuating a slave-based economy. But Thoreau also took umbrage with American imperialism and colonialism, including the treatment of "Native Americans."

In consequence, even if we accept the suggestion that the American Civil War actually ended with the abolition of slavery rather than simply with an alteration of its form, then there is still the fact(s) of American imperialism and colonialism. In fact, developments that occurred during the period between Thoreau's death toward the beginning of the American Civil War and Dorothy Day's birth in 1897 mostly substantiated Thoreau's contentions about the evils of the American territorial state. Immediately after the Civil War, a coterie of generals who had honed their martial skills in Oregon Territory and California during the Gold Rush and the Mexican-American War that followed on its heels, and went on to attain a place in the pantheon of American military as heroes of the Civil War, turned their attention and their rifles toward Cherokees, Creeks, and other Amerindians scattered throughout the American South and Southwest. During the Indian wars and with the Indian Appropriations Act of 1871, the "natives" were "resettled" on reservations, making way for destiny, Manifest Destiny. This all coincided with elaboration and entrenchment of the Monroe Doctrine and the birth of full-fledged American imperialism. It is impossible to say how Thoreau would have reacted to the changes that occurred in the years immediately following his death, yet based on the written record that he has left us, there is little reason to think that his view of the modern state would have been fundamentally altered, especially in the light of the expansion of American imperialism.

But even if we could imagine a world in which the American state did not employ its force in order to protect the interests of slaveholders or merchants, I am not convinced that a person with Thoreau's convictions would necessarily be inclined to reconcile with the modern state. To appreciate why this is so, we must understand that I have staked my anarchist interpretation of Thoreau's political philosophy on more than a claim about how the above injustices shaped his conception of the duties that we owe to the territorial state. I have stressed that Thoreau objected to the American and Massachusetts governments on the basis of their form. In particular, I indicated that Thoreau maintained that it was desirable and "possible to take a step further towards recognizing and organizing the rights of man." By this I take Thoreau to be making a case for consent-based political organizations. In short, Thoreau maintained that the ideal society would be one comprised of voluntary associations. He gave voice to this ideal throughout his speeches and writings. To that end, when taken together, I submit that Thoreau's speeches and writings present a religious-ethical and sociopolitical vision that is consistent with anarchism as it has come to be understood.

Thoreau's vision has inspired a long line of anarchists, including Tolstoy, Kropotkin, Emma Goldman, Henry Salt, Herbert Read, Paul Goodman, Howard Zinn, and Noam Chomsky. My analysis in this chapter has brought to the surface the aspects of Thoreau's theory and praxis that have proven important for such persons. Interestingly enough, the fact that this is so points to the fact that not all is lost for persons not persuaded by my interpretation of Thoreau as an anarchist. It seems to me as though one value of my approach to Thoreau is that I have basically performed an anarchist reading of Thoreau that many others gesture at yet do not carry out in an extensive or systematic fashion.[92] In other words, on some levels I have read Thoreau's work in precisely the way that persons who find Thoreau's vision conducive with anarchism (must) read his work. Juxtaposing *A Week*, *Walden*, and essays such as "Resistance to Civil Government," has allowed me to illustrate the way in which religious-ethical and political theoretical themes intertwine and permeate Thoreau's thought. Finally, connecting Thoreau's political essays to some of his texts that are not always interpreted in political philosophical and theoretical terms has put me in a position to identify premises that might serve as ground on which to defend or construct an anarchist ethic.

Because Thoreau did not devote much energy to articulating a constructive vision of community, vehemently criticized "institutional religion," and based on his thoroughgoing emphasis on individual autonomy, many anarchists, social theorists, and political philosophers maintain that it is impossible to found a flourishing, diverse community based on Thoreauvian ideas. I am not sure that this is true. But rather than turn to Thoreau's ideas with an eye toward resolving this issue, having made explicit the themes and ideas extant in Thoreau's thought that have informed the formation of an emergent religiously motivated anarchist tradition, we will gain more by turning to Dorothy Day, a more conventionally religious person, who weaves together a constructive vision with elements—such as autonomy, asceticism, and revolutionary withdrawal—remarkably and perhaps surprisingly similar to those developed by Thoreau.

# 2

# Love in action: Dorothy Day's Christian anarchism

*No honest and serious-minded man of our day can help seeing the incompatibility of true Christianity—the doctrine of meekness, forgiveness of injuries, and love—with government, with its pomp, acts of violence, executions, and wars. The profession of true Christianity not only excludes the possibility of recognizing government, but even destroys its very foundations.*

LEO TOLSTOY, *The Kingdom of God Is Within*

## I

A religious conversion, says William James, is a conversion in which "religious ideas become the center of one's spiritual energy."[1] It is precisely the fact that conversions entail the centering of certain ideas that makes reflecting on conversion narratives so insightful. Conversion narratives ordinarily tell much about a given narrator's essential characteristics or about what the narrator *takes to be* his or her essential characteristics. Dorothy Day's religiosity and concomitant normative political commitments are best understood in relation to her conversion to Roman Catholicism, in 1927 at the age of 30, after being raised in a nominally Episcopalian household and living estranged from institutional religion for nearly a decade.

Day had difficulty identifying the factors that led up to and instigated her conversion to Catholicism. As she put it, "A conversion is a lonely experience. We do not know what is going on in the depths of the heart and soul of another. We scarcely know ourselves."[2] Yet, just as do most religious converts, with the passing of time and after reflection, she did attempt to situate the shifting contours of her religious faith in a larger narrative. Perhaps what separates Day from the typical convert is that she was a gifted writer, who spent probably the better part of her vocation as a writer representing to the public the character of her religious faith, her spiritual pilgrimage from Union Square to Rome, as she describes the shift or relocation in her first book-length autobiography. Throughout her life, Day continually interpreted and reinterpreted her past in the light of subsequent experiences and vice versa. This is especially on display in Day's book, *From Union Square to Rome*, a text that Day presents in the form of a letter to her brother John Day Jr, a communist. She offers John reasons for her turn from Union Square to Rome. That is, Day explains why she felt unsatisfied in the world of the nonreligious radical left, which she figuratively refers to as Union Square.

While Day's book-length autobiographical texts, *From Union Square to Rome* and *The Long Loneliness*, dwell the most on her conversion, nearly all of Day's postconversion writings, whether strictly autobiographical or not, explicitly or implicitly offer reasons for her conversion and share her sense of the meaningfulness of certain of her experiences in relation to the deepening of her religious faith. What Day gives throughout her writings might be referred to as an ongoing conversion narrative qua apologia. So understanding Dorothy Day's religious ethics and normative social philosophy begins with her spiritual autobiographical notes as they manifest in her vast body of writing. Day depicts her turn to Catholicism as a gradual blossoming of faith. Day's was very much a conversion that began and culminated with love.

Day begins her conversion narrative by describing her first awakening. It came in 1913, during her final year of high school. It was during that year that she encountered or read intently for the first time Upton Sinclair's *The Jungle* and Peter Kropotkin's humanistic and lyrical anarchist writings. These writers awakened her to the power of prose and to the nature of the social injustice around her. Masterful writers do this for us. They help us see our surroundings and ourselves in a different light. Sometimes they bring us to tears and leave us in a fit of anxiety: could life be meaningless or absurd? But at other times great writers call our attention to the beauty of smiles, flowers, and reconciling lovers. They transform us by transforming our perspective. The best literature demands our attention and puts us in the mood—in the frame of mind—to perceive things differently.

In her second book-length autobiography, *The Long Loneliness*, Day recalls how reading Sinclair's romantic realism in *The Jungle* transformed her many walks through Chicago's immigrant neighborhoods. In particular, Sinclair's stunning documentation of Chicago's Back of the Yards neighborhood and the plight of immigrant workers heightened Day's sensitivity to injustices in her hometown, a place that she had assumed she knew well. Even during her teenage years, Day felt that such injustice demanded a constructive response; she decided that she would respond through writing; she would be a leftist writer. Years later, she would quote from one of her favorite Dostoevsky stories, *The Insulted and the Injured*, in order to elucidate the character of her vocational aspirations and to explain in particular how her commitment to social justice informed her writing. Dostoevsky's story is about a young author whose first book is rather well received. What draws Day's attention is the reaction of the author's father to the powerfulness of the book. In a chapter, in *Loaves and Fishes*, that takes its name from the title of Dostoevsky's story, Day quotes the father's reflection on how his son's book had moved him: "'What's happening all around you grows easier to understand and to remember, and you learn that the most downtrodden, humblest man is a man, too, and a brother.'" Day goes on to say, "I thought as I read those words, that is why I write."[3] Day became a writer with the idea of "brotherhood" (the unity of humanity) and the suffering and injustice experienced by the downtrodden in mind: she wrote in the shadow of a profound contradiction that demanded correction.

Uncertain about the best means by which to pursue her vocation as a writer, Day decided to accept a scholarship to study at the University of Illinois at Urbana-Champaign. Never the keenest (formal) student, she was reluctant to matriculate yet grateful for the opportunity provided by the scholarship. She arrived on campus in the autumn of 1914. Immediately, Day immersed herself in the radical literature—anarchist, socialist, and communist—of the early twentieth century. Growing increasingly militant politically and rebellious culturally, she joined the socialist party, hoping to fulfill her desire to constructively channel her compassion. Also, she began to shy away from institutionalized Christianity, as did many socially conscious bohemians in the 1910s. Neither agnostic nor atheist per se, Day felt that religion was an "opiate of the people" that would "impede" her work as an activist and writer: "I wanted to have nothing to do with the religion of those whom I saw all about me. I felt that I must turn from it as from a drug. . . . I hardened my heart. It was a conscious and deliberate process."[4] So Day's initial conversion to leftist radicalism entailed movement away from religion, particularly Christianity.

For a season, she was satisfied. But forever restless and fitting for a radical activist born at the turn of the twentieth century, Day would leave college before completing the coursework for a degree. And no less appropriate, for a bohemian journalist with socialist commitments, with two years of college behind her, Day relocated to New York City. She would settle in Greenwich Village, America's bohemian enclave, then home to the likes of Eugene O'Neil and William Faulkner, and still a bastion of leftist political radicalism. It was a time of war, revolutionary fervor, and technological innovation. America would soon enter World War I; the Bolsheviks would soon sweep away the Tsar in Russia; Henry Ford's automated assembly line, introduced in 1913, would soon transform industry and society. These events and social developments defined the era in which Day came into herself as an activist. From the mid-1910s up until her conversion to Catholicism in 1927, Day would write for several nonreligious leftist publications, including the *New York Call*, the *Masses*, and the *Liberator*, and work with important organizations on the radical left such as the No-Conscription League and the Industrial Workers of the World (IWW or the Wobblies). Day had left Chicago and later the University of Illinois to become a writer and an activist. By most accounts, she had met with success. She had worked with Max Eastman. She had written a novel, *The Eleventh Virgin*. She had interviewed Trotsky. She had participated in boycotts and pickets and contributed to several important causes. Yet still, Day experienced an enduring sense of incompleteness or even emptiness.

Retrospectively, Day would characterize her sense of incompleteness in terms of her disappointment with the ideals prevalent among left activists. In particular, by the late 1910s to early 1920s Day felt that socialist and communist activists generally possessed what she regarded as a truncated conception of humanity and in consequence they misdiagnosed the problems confronting humanity. According to Day, communists and socialists were to be commended for being committed to social justice and for even loving the poor. Yet few of the activists with whom Day worked deemed it as imperative to love both oppressed workers (i.e. brothers) and exploitative capitalist employers (i.e. enemies). So she relates in *From Union Square to Rome*, "I will not deny that often the Communist more truly loves his brother, the poor and the oppressed, than many so-called Christians. But, when in word and deed the Communist incites brother to kill brother, one class to hate and destroy other classes, then I cannot feel that his love is true."[5] Day interpreted the unwillingness of most communists to love their enemies as the result of a failure to appreciate the radical interconnectedness of creation. And their refusal or inability to love their enemies made it difficult for Day to imagine how communist and socialist activists could enact the kind of social change that she regarded as necessary. This dissatisfaction left her searching for more. On Day's telling, this dissatisfaction spelled the beginnings of her ultimate turn toward God and the Roman Catholic Church (Catholic Church or Church). Moreover, her assessment of the short-comings of communism would lead her toward anarchism.

Around the same time that Day was growing dissatisfied with nonreligious leftist activism, she found herself in the throes of broken relationships, namely the one with her then partner, Forster Batterham, with whom she would eventually have a child. Experiencing an identity crisis wrought by a crisis of community, that is, the experience of relational crises, Dorothy Day carried around a heavy heart in the lead up to her conversion to Catholicism. On one level, it was a broken heart, in a broken world, that moved her to long for a more spiritually meaningful life. But negative experiences are rarely enough to inspire conversions like Day's, and it would in fact be inaccurate to say that it was simply a broken heart that led her to God or religion. Certainly political disillusionment and relational grief factored in. Yet, there were positive forces at play too.

To begin, during the mid-1920s, Day had begun to love the natural environment; she had begun to feel at peace and closer to the divine when in certain natural settings. In particular, there were the long walks, inspired by restless moods, along the Staten Island seashore, where Day had purchased a beach house (with the earnings from the sale of her novel, *The Eleventh Virgin*, to a Hollywood film production studio). The rush of the tide and the setting of the sun elicited in Day a sense of divine presence. In addition to this, after birthing a child, Tamar Theresa, in 1926, Day says that as she embraced her infant daughter, she was overwhelmed by feelings of inexhaustible love. In such moments, Day felt that her capacity to love was unbounded, yet she also felt in those moments that only "God" could properly receive such an outpouring of love. Beautiful and sublime, nature and Tamar Theresa inspired in Day a reverence for life and religious passion that ushered her along a path toward God.

A combination of painful and joyful encounters transformed Day's notions about love and its significance. On one hand, Day experienced love's absence: she experienced the absence of "true love" among nonreligious leftists and she suffered heartbreak in relationships, which provoked a yearning for a more complete love. On the other hand, Day experienced abundant love as an overwhelming force: being present in nature and in the presence of her infant daughter inspired feelings of love and a desire to worship. Ultimately, then, her preoccupation with love moved Day toward God in stages. Appropriately, the section in *The Long Loneliness* in which she announces and explains her final decision to convert is entitled "Love Overflows."

Love is undoubtedly the key term in Day's religious-ethical vocabulary, with her conception of it giving shape to her religious-ethical commitments and normative political vision. In *The Long Loneliness*, where Day presents her most detailed and articulate account of her reasons for converting to Roman Catholicism, she explicitly relates her idea of love to what might be referred to as the problem of disunion, which is the cause of what Day herself memorably terms *the long loneliness*. For Day, disunion—one human from another and humans from God—is the principal problem that human persons must surmount. To put it differently, Day contends that what it means to be human is to long for communion. She therefore asserts that the primary "longing of the human heart is for . . . communion."[6] Interestingly and importantly, the disunion-communion dichotomy undergirds or extends from Day's conception of the human person; human persons are constituted such that our hearts, "longing" to overcome disunion and *the long loneliness*, long for *communion*.

Day's elaboration on this thesis about the quest for communion brings together her reasons for converting to Roman Catholicism and points toward the anarchist position that she would subsequently develop. Above we saw that Day, in *From Union Square to Rome*, found communists' and socialists' understandings of love wanting. On Day's view, their conceptions of love were underinclusive. Continuing her habit of clarifying the character of her religious faith by contrasting it with the communist alternative, Day tells us in *The Long Loneliness* that "If I could have felt that communism was the answer to my desire for a cause, a motive, a way to walk in, I would have remained as I was. But I felt that only faith in Christ could give the answer. The Sermon on the Mount answered all the questions as to how to love God and one's brother."[7]

Few passages have been more important for radical activists in America than chapters five, six, and seven in *The Gospel of Matthew*. And no biblical passage was more important for Dorothy Day, as her mature political philosophy flows largely from her understanding of the implications of the Sermon on the Mount, with its love imperative, as will be evident shortly. For now, I would like to reflect on Day's invocation of the Sermon on the Mount's lesson on love in the light of her thesis regarding the yearnings of human hearts.

Day's invocation of the Sermon on the Mount sets the stage for her answer to what she identifies as the principal problem confronting humanity and one of the most illuminating passages in Day's corpus. To a degree, the entire narrative in *The Long Loneliness* leads up to the extended passage that I have in mind, a passage that Day begins with an ardent assertion: "Community is the answer to the long loneliness."[8] Several pages later, she reiterates and hones her point: "The only answer in this life, to the loneliness we are bound to feel, is community. The living together, working together, sharing together, loving God and loving our brother, and living close to him in community so we can show our love for Him."[9] Finally, exuding conviction, Day declares in the first-person plural: "We have all known the long loneliness and we have learned that the only solution is love and that love comes with community."[10]

Community, then, is the answer to the problem of the long loneliness and the above statements, when taken together, qualify Day's conception of community in a way that it is crucial to appreciate. In particular, the above statements reveal that what Day cherishes and commends, in the light of the Sermon on the Mount, is not merely community as such. Rather, it is the act(s) of loving in community. Day's understanding of love's relationship to community can be restated paradoxically: love creates community and community provides the context for acts of love. Over time, as she moved from Union Square to Rome, Day came to see the way in which loving other persons could create a community *made whole by the transformative power of God's grace*. It is in this way—that is, Day's understanding of God's active role in the temporal order—that Day's conception of love differs most substantially from nonreligious or even non-Christian conceptions of love. The implications of this difference will be clear in the next section. What should be evident already, though, is that it was Day's longing for a community created through love—or love sustained by community—that moved her to convert to Roman Catholicism. In accord with this, Day brings *The Long Loneliness* to a close with a simple but arresting testament to love that equals the best letters on Christian love in the English language. The passage's shortest sentence is probably its most telling: "The final word is love."[11]

To grasp the full theological or religious implications or meaning of Day's centering of *Christian* love, we must consider how Day deploys Catholic teaching (ideals, concepts, doctrines, and dogmas) in order to explicate her understanding of love's significance or function. With this in mind, I would now like to turn to a more substantial reflection on Day's religious faith as she comes to express it in explicitly Christian, especially Roman Catholic Christian, terms, so as to set the stage for an acute analysis of her political philosophy.

# II

Importantly, conversions can enhance communicative and interpretive capacity by multiplying the lenses and vocabularies that converts have on hand. Converts often creatively interpret or translate their preconversion principled commitments into the idioms or parlances provided by the traditions to which they have converted. In Day's case, her discipleship as a Catholic Christian was an ongoing process of negotiating her many pre-Catholic commitments with her understanding of her duties and responsibilities as a Catholic layperson. In other words, Day's life as a Catholic entailed explicating her pre-Catholic commitments in Catholic terms and interpreting Catholic beliefs and teachings in terms of her extra or pre-Catholic commitments and experiences. This dialectical process of mutual enhancement and interpretation resulted in a fascinating melding of radical leftist and Catholic ideals. Consistent with this, Day put to use Christian, particularly Catholic Christian, concepts in order to describe her developing sense that fundamental social problems confronting modern persons were in actuality, at bottom, religious problems.

That this is so is revealed by Day's invocation of general Christian and specifically Catholic ideals, concepts, doctrines, and dogmas, especially as they relate to questions about the nature of God, the human person, and reality generally speaking. Day's identification of a lack of community, a paucity of neighborly love, and the denial of God as central problems confronting humanity hints at the kind of social order that she would find ultimately satisfactory. The character of Day's religious ethics and the sources of her anarchism, then, are on display in Day's interpretation of Christianity and Catholic teaching.

In this section I reflect on four vital facets of Day's Catholic commitments (or four vital facets of Day's interpretation of Christianity and Catholic teaching) as they relate to the ideas of love and community, so that we can see how Day extends Christianity and Catholic dogma and social teaching in anarchist directions (and vice versa). While the four facets in question are interrelated, so that my analysis of them will overlap, it might be helpful to enumerate them in the order in which they will be presented. First, I will consider Day's characterization of the problem of disunion or separation in terms of the Christian idea of sin and discuss her thesis that it is love that bridges separation and thus overcomes sin. Second, I will discuss Day's employment of the doctrine of the Mystical Body of Christ, concentrating on the way in which Day invokes it in order to buttress her argument in favor of compassionate love and ultimately as a rejection of hatred and cruelty based on difference, especially in terms of nation or race. Third, I will comment on the significance of Day's appropriation of several themes or ideas presented in French personalist philosophy, as it is in the terms of French personalism that one can begin to grasp Day's postconversion conception of God, the human person, ultimate reality, love, and community. Particularly important, the conception of God and the person that Day enunciates, in the terms of French personalism, functions to elevate the importance of human agency and underwrites her criticisms of centralized authoritative entities such as the modern territorial state. Finally, I will discuss the way in which Day brings the above facets together through her argument about the ethical implications, for all practicing Catholics, of the Catholic counsels of perfection, which will reveal that Day's religious-ethical commitments have a strong perfectionist quality and give a prominent role to certain moral absolutes (or categorical imperatives). The significance of this, for our purposes, lies in the fact that Day's moral perfectionism, when combined with moral absolutism, motivates an anarchist ethic.

Sin is a central category in Christian thought and so perhaps it is unsurprising that the idea of sin factors into Day's rendering of Catholic Christian ideas in a way that it is crucial for us to understand. In practice, Day offers little by way of extensive commentary on the idea of sin—particularly regarding its origin or nature. But the idea is always in the background and is one of the more important keys to understanding Day's conception of the Christian love ethic, as, in many respects, Day's conception of love and sin can only be understood in relation to one another. I have already indicated how love is related to the problem of the long loneliness. On some levels, the phrase "the long loneliness" is merely a special way of naming or describing sin or the nature of sin. Similar to many Roman Catholic and Protestant Christians, Day regarded disunion or separation, particularly a turning away from God, to be the cause, effect, and incident of sin. Such Christians regard sin as disobedience or unfaithfulness to God, divine law, or moral law and, in practice, disobedience or unfaithfulness to God, divine law, or moral law—which is technically an act of sin or sinning—separates or disunites human persons from one another and separates the disobedient agent from God.

To understand Day's conception of sin we must only keep in mind the primacy that she gives to love and recall love's function or effect. Remember that Day offers love in community as the solution to the long loneliness and the problem of disunion. Sin, in this frame, constitutes a failure or refusal to love. We can therefore say that, for Day, love constitutes something of an antidote to sin. This is a simple but profound correlation. By conceiving of sin as a failure to love, Day is able to register her sense of love's importance as a theological and religious-ethical category. Christians have recourse to no more meaningful negative terms than sin and its relative, hell. So it is ordinarily revelatory to trace a given person's invocations of these terms. Day suggests that because the final consequence of sin or sinning is hell, a failure to love leads to hell. She quotes Georges Bernanos to make this point: "Hell is not to love anymore."[12]

Day's juxtaposition of hell and love is important mostly for its implicit positive dimension: If the cessation of love is hell, then it would appear that love is redemptive; love redeems in that it overcomes disunion or separation—a multitude of sins.[13] To this end, Day intimates,

> Love and ever more love is the only solution to every problem that comes up. If we love each other enough, we will bear with each other's faults and burdens. If we love enough, we are going to light that fire in the hearts of others. And it is love that will burn out the sins and hatreds that sadden us.[14]

Although Day never explicitly announces that "Heaven is to love," she does identify "the kingdom of God" as a place where persons would love completely and perfectly. In this way, she belongs to a contingent of twentieth-century American Christians who posited the beloved community as a normative ideal to be sought after as a matter of religious devotion. To appreciate the multiple bases on which Day maintains that striving for the beloved community is a religious-ethical duty, we should consider in turn her construal of the Catholic doctrine of the Mystical Body of Christ, her invocation of personalist philosophy, and her understanding of the Catholic Counsels of perfection.

Paradoxically, Day posits the unity of creation and at the same time presents disunion or separation as a problem confronting human persons. This assertion of the unity of creation, which is at the core of Day's religious ethics and normative political vision, is an ontological or metaphysical claim about ultimate reality.[15] In order to communicate this conviction, Day broadly interprets, perhaps idiosyncratically, the Catholic doctrine of the Mystical Body of Christ, a doctrine derived from several Christian scriptural texts, especially Paul's *First Letter to the Corinthians*.[16]

According to Day, all human persons belong to and are united through the Mystical Body of Christ.[17] This mystical body transcends time and space, so that, through it, each person simultaneously attains an identity with Christ, saints, and sinners. In Day's own words, "We [Catholic Workers] think of all men as our brothers then, as members of the Mystical Body of Christ. 'We are all members, one of another,' and, remembering this, we can never be indifferent to the social miseries and evils of the day. The dogma of the Mystical Body has tremendous social implications."[18] And a few years later she says, "We are those who are sinned against and those who are sinning. We are identified with Him [Christ], one with Him. We are members of His Mystical Body."[19]

Day's interpretation of the doctrine of the Mystical Body of Christ and the theory about reality that she derives from it are important for several reasons. To begin, by positing the interrelatedness of persons in Christ, Day is able to assert that what we do to or for another human being, we do to or for Christ, so that to act unjustly or lovingly in relation to a particular person is to do the same to Christ. Second, because all persons share an identity with Christ, all persons suffer with Christ. Finally, because each human person shares an identity with saints and sinners alike, all persons suffer with one another, and so have reasons to be concerned with the actions of other persons. Crucially, Day extends the doctrine of the Mystical Body of Christ in a way that profoundly elevates the stakes of human agency and motivates a concern for social evil and misery, so that persons "can never be indifferent to the social miseries and evils of the day." The way in which Day approaches and construes the doctrine of the Mystical Body of Christ is indicative of how Day weaves other Catholic teachings and practices into her life. As Mel Piehl notes in *Breaking Bread*, Day's invocation and application of Catholic doctrines, allowed her to integrate "sacramental notions with seemingly secular concerns."[20]

Day's texts are replete with examples of her subtle interweaving of the sentiment embodied in the doctrine of the Mystical Body of Christ with ostensibly sociopolitical concerns. In most cases, this interweaving is done in order to commend love and community and to condemn sin and disunion. And, the effectiveness of Day's writing is the fruit of her ability to express her response to social phenomena and relate the phenomena in question back to a principle that moves her. To study Day's corpus is to witness her at work reinterpreting Catholic faith in the light of her experiences, and those experiences in the light of the reinterpreted principles of her faith. This proclivity manifests clearly in Day's frequent allusions to and invocations of the doctrine of the Mystical Body of Christ. Three examples should suffice to demonstrate how this is so and show why the doctrine was so important for Day's religious ethics.

The example that I begin with is perhaps the one in which it is most clear that the idea inherent in the doctrine of the Mystical Body of Christ actually informs Day's interpretation or description of social reality. Meditating on the dictates of Christian love, Day attempts to convey the powerful effects of love in action and to make evident the significance of the unity of humanity. She does this by defining compassion—which is best thought of as an aspect of love—and connecting it with the doctrine of the Mystical Body of Christ. Day relates,

> Compassion—it is a word meaning "to suffer with." If we all carry a little of the burden, it will be lightened. If we share in the suffering of the world, then some will not have to endure a heavy affliction. It evens out. What you do here in New York, in Harrisburg, helps those in China, India, South Africa, Europe, and Russia, as well as in the oasis where you are. You may think you are alone. But we are members one of another. We are children of God together.[21]

In the above, Day does not use the term "the Mystical Body of Christ." Instead, she employs Catholic doctrinal content in order to put into words the value and nature of compassion. As Day sometimes employed the term "compassionate" as a verb, we might say that, in the above, she invokes the doctrine of the Mystical Body of Christ so as to encourage "compassionating" or compassionate action. Importantly, compassion, as an aspect of love, overcomes disunion, and so paradoxically, it is inspired by both the unity and disunion. We are one, says Day, and can alleviate suffering in the world, if we will only suffer with one another, if only we will be conscientious about how what *we do here* affects others.

Perhaps no example better illustrates the depth of Day's compassion than her reflection on a stint that she did in a Washington DC jail after participating in a women's suffrage picket in 1917. Day would repeatedly refer to this jail experience throughout the rest of her life. Such experiences affirmed her belief in doctrine of the Mystical Body of Christ and in turn shaped how she would interpret and describe her experiences.

With the suffragist movement in full swing, movement participants had decided to stage a protest outside of the White House. Day had joined the suffragists in their demonstration because she found their agitation inspiring. Yet she had never been interested in electoral politics or parliamentarian reform—Day never cast a vote in a political election. But while Day did not identify with the suffragists' objectives as such, her participation in the protest was fateful.

Jail terms have often been a source of radicalization. This is true of Thoreau, Kropotkin, Gandhi, Norman Thomas, Rustin, Bertrand Russell,

Dostoevsky, Angela Davis, and countless others. It also proved true for Day. Two things impressed her. First, Day was repulsed by the violence that she witnessed in jail, with the way that the prison guards treated prisoners. Second, Day was struck by the kinds of persons who were in prison. To begin, Day found prison to be full of persons overwhelmed by sadness and even despair. Then, there was the fact that in modern society, particularly modern American society, there is an arbitrariness about who ends up in jail, although it is in fact largely the dominant class, in terms of race and economic class, that determines the legal rules, so that class and race largely predict who goes to jail. The criminal justice system is a window into an unjust social system and peering through that window profoundly affected Day's impression of modern society.

In *From Union Square to Rome*, Day speaks of the way in which her time in jail instigated what for the lack of a better term I will call a quasimystical experience. Only, to be clear, she did not lose herself in God per se. Rather, she suffered with others—she empathized and "compassionated" with human persons—and experienced an erasure of boundaries between herself and others. The dire conditions in the jail and the isolation left her to reflect on the human predicament. Such reflection thrust her into *communion*, which is in many respects a state of being compassionate. She intimates,

> I suffered not only my own sorrow but the sorrows of those about me. I was no longer myself. I was man. I was no longer a young girl, part of a radical movement seeking justice for the oppressed, I was the oppressed. I was that drug addict, screaming and tossing in her cell, beating her head against the wall. I was that shoplifter who for rebellion was sentenced to solitary. . . . I was that mother whose child had been raped and slain. I was the mother who had borne the monster who had done it.[22]

A psychologist or psychiatrist might say that Day's extreme identification with others signaled a mental breakdown. But Day would never reduce experience to the sensational response to material phenomena, and so she would cull the experience for spiritual edification and illumination. This experience, I want to suggest, informed Day's understanding of Catholic doctrine, particularly the doctrine of the Mystical Body of Christ and the idea that persons are one in and through Christ, and thus participate in the sufferings of others.

In jail, Day confronted squarely how suffering marks the human condition. Such confrontation is difficult and Day recognized specifically the psychological risks associated with loving in such a sorrowful context. The act of love expressed in a broken world threatens to break the lover's heart, psyche, or spirit. But loving under such circumstances is more than simply potentially tragic. It is also a practical challenge. The question is, and it is a serious one, in the personal domain as well as in the public, how we muster the courage and the strength to love in the light of our vulnerability and our collective problems. According to Day, in practice this is precisely where faith and liturgy must meld with hope and grace to provide the persons in question with the capacity to love. The Catholic Church's liturgical tradition provides persons with the spiritual resources and practices to make God's grace operative. This grace in turn gives persons the strength to love in the particular way that is necessary for communion between or among individuated persons and God.[23] So God's grace saves—through love and the sacraments—the faithful from the hopeless abyss.

With her faith in the power of God's grace, Day maintains that there rests no middle ground between indifference and identification. There is a religious-ethical imperative to confront reality and identify with suffering persons; we are called to love one another; we are one in Christ. By confronting pain and hardship that other persons suffer, we evade indifference or complacency in the face of social suffering, and we avoid (willed) complicity in suffering and injustice. And, for Day, compassion includes a concern for the immediate sorrow or suffering among persons and consists of a concern to alleviate the suffering and the cause(s) of the suffering that inspires the compassion in the first place. Thus, even while one identifies with both perpetrators of injustice and the subjugated, one's ultimate concern is to eradicate the injustice.[24] Gandhian philosophy greatly influenced how this orientation toward victims and perpetrators would be understood by many mid-twentieth-century activists, including Day. First, liberation is posited as something that liberates both the oppressed and the oppressor. Second, love for both the oppressed and the oppressor conditions the means that may be employed in order to effectuate liberation. Normative proponents of nonviolence predicate the value of nonviolent means largely on the way in which such means are said to avoid or minimize harm to oppressors. Therefore, to identify with either oppressed or suffering persons in the way that Day suggests is to be prompted to question social practices that are unjust or result in unnecessary suffering. This is clearer with the third example that I would like to discuss.

I noted above that Day repeatedly returned to her 1917 jail experience. Consistent with this, she reflects on the experience in *The Long Loneliness*. That account differs slightly from the one in *From Union Square to Rome* in that Day construes compassion or identification with the suffering of others in a way that links it directly to social justice. That is, in the account that follows, Day's empathy and compassion are directed in more stridently political terms, as she explicitly calls into question the fairness of the so-called justice system. As Day alludes to double standards and hypocrisy, in a way, the whole social order is put on trial:

> I lost all feeling of my own identity. I reflected on the desolation of poverty,
> of destitution, of sickness and sin. That I would be free after thirty days

meant nothing to me. I would never be free again, never free when I knew that behind bars all over the world there were women and men, young girls and boys, suffering constraint, punishment, isolation and hardship for crimes of which all of us were guilty. . . . Why were some caught, not others? Why were some termed criminals and others good business men? What was right and wrong? What was good and evil? I lay there in utter confusion and misery.[25]

Day's compassionate and emotional response to the injustice and suffering and hypocrisy that she perceived in early twentieth-century America is unsettling. It has been nearly a century since she experienced that misery in jail and almost six decades since she published *The Long Loneliness*. But the questions that Day asks remain important ones, ones that continue to haunt many Americans, myself included.

One of the things that keeps many persons from being distressed or disturbed by other persons' suffering or oppression, in the way that Day was, is that they find it difficult to feel a sense of compassion for persons with certain skin colors, persons engaged in certain professions, persons who eat certain foods, speak in certain languages or with certain accents, worship certain gods, wear certain clothes, engage in certain kinds of sexual intercourse. Day invoked the doctrine of the Mystical Body of Christ in order to combat what we might call "indifference rooted in difference" and interpreted the doctrine's significance in the light of a context in which hatred motivated by nationalism, racism, classism, and sexism was rampant. So, although she does not explicitly refer to the doctrine in the three passages that I have just presented, I want to suggest that the doctrine shaped how she understood compassion and identity, and so shaped how she would ultimately describe her experiences, including the fateful jail term.

So with the doctrine of the Mystical Body of Christ, Day found a powerful way to express her belief in the interrelatedness of creation and a way to commend love and community in the face of the unjust conditions of twentieth-century American society. And she also managed to relate compassion to the doctrine of the Mystical Body of Christ in a way that allows her to characterize compassion as a religious-ethical value or virtue. She thus suggests that persons have a religious-ethical duty to be compassionate because "we are members of one another" and "children of God together," thus framing racism and indifference rooted in difference as contradicting Christian ideals. Christian activists have often made such claims about the implications of Christian love for human interaction. What is unique with Day, once again, is how she brings her normative vision together by construing and applying the doctrine of the Mystical Body of Christ in a way that heightens the significance of human agency and hence personal responsibility and sociopolitical action, particularly love in action.

The full significance of and reasons for Day's emphasis on love in action and personal responsibility are perhaps best understood in the light of her appropriation of French personalist ideas, as it is in the terms of personalism that Day asserts that each person has a personal responsibility to love in order to create community with God. Day began her study of French personalism after becoming acquainted with Peter Maurin, the itinerant ascetic French Catholic immigrant with whom Day would cofound the *Catholic Worker* in 1933. French personalist philosophy emerged as an alternative to Marxism and existentialism—which personalists understood to be committed to materialism and nihilism respectively—and became increasingly important during the 1930s with Emmanuel Mounier's publication of the journal *Esprit*. In some respects French Catholic personalists such as Mounier and Jacques Maritain merely reformulated standard Thomism in a distinctively modern vernacular in order to counter certain negative tendencies—moral relativism, individualism, and materialism—that they regarded as prevalent in modern philosophical thought.[26] By the mid-1930s Day often drew from the language of French personalist philosophers such as Mounier, Maritain, and the Russian immigrant Nicolas Berdyeav, as the three offered Day language with which to express her view that God is love and the idea that it is through acts of loving that one actualizes one's self, creates community, and brings the presence of God into one's life. In the end, the personalist elements that Day appropriates are quite basic.

Day believes, with Maritain, Mounier, and Berdyeav, that the spiritual and the material are inseparable, which allows Day to explain how God is active in history and to give an account of the divinity or spiritual essence of the human person. More to the point, the idea of the inseparability of the spiritual and material allowed Day to argue for the positive value of human action in the temporal order. As such, Day drew inspiration from Berdyaev's assertion that "Christianity does not depend on constant miracles, but very much on the creative, even daring, activity of Christians in the world, working together with God's grace."[27] In addition to a belief in the inseparability of the spiritual and the material, Day insists that the universe is (essentially) personal and that God is the *ultimate* person. Moreover, according to Day, God is the ultimate *loving* person. Day, on the basis of her encounter with personalist philosophy, asserts that the personal God is the creator of human beings who, because created in the image of God, must be regarded as individual *persons*. This last point is what makes personalism important and distinctive and is a point that Day develops in profoundly important ways. For, it probably would not be going too far to say that a personalist conception of personhood underwrites her entire normative vision in that it informs or represents her theological anthropology.

There are at least two noteworthy aspects of Day's conception of personhood. First, for Day, persons by definition exist primarily or even solely in relation to other persons. Persons are relational beings. Persons cannot be disunited (from other persons and still be persons). Persons were made for and are meant for communion. Second, Day insists that personhood implies freedom (of the will). And to exercise freedom (of the will), persons must assume personal responsibility for their actions. To recognize the dignity of human persons is to recognize and respect the fact that they have this (God given) freedom of the will. Day brings these two aspects of personhood together in a way that is especially important. On Day's view, love in action is the means by which human persons commune; and, community is the theater of love; and to fully realize one's personhood entails acknowledging the personhood of other persons and treating them in accord with this; therefore, persons have a responsibility to create and preserve community and by extension a duty to love.

Day's enunciation of personalism is distinctively theological both in that she posits a divine personal creator and insofar as she contends that the ultimate actualization of personhood is realized in relation to God. According to Day, for human persons, being in relationship with God—the ultimate person—represents communion at the highest level. God created a world in which loving—which is always interpersonal—brings human persons into communion with one another and with God. And, for Day, love brings God and human persons together in a special way, as human persons can love God only by loving other human persons. Drawing from several biblical texts, especially 1 John (4.40), and positing what has been referred to as the "anthropological experience of God," Day intimates that "we can only show our love for God by our love for our fellows."[28]

This familiar Christian theory about how human persons relate to God is especially important for our purposes because it shapes Day's normative sociopolitical vision—it means that her political vision is a religious vision. To greater and lesser degrees most religionists' political visions are extensions of their religious visions, as religionists typically assert the necessity of certain social conditions as preconditions to the full expression and exercise of their religiosity. In Day's case, social conditions are important because they structure human interaction and thus determine the possibility of communion with God: persons must live in community in order to love one another and by extension God; only in this way, says Day, can human persons reasonably hope to approximate fulfillment in the temporal order.

Many religionists offer similar understandings of reality and such an understanding is often the stuff that theocratic visions are made of. Day, however, eschews theocratic politics by several means and none was more important than her view that the universal dignity of the human person means that all persons must be treated as though they are free, responsible persons. (We could even say that all persons possess a right to autonomy. This right we might call an "enabling right."[29] It is an enabling right because it is a right that a person must have in order to achieve self-actualization.) Because, according to Day, love in action must always be a free exercise of the will, persons should not be forced to belong to a community and they certainly cannot be forced to love. Love, then, or at least Day's conception of it, moves her beyond theocratic ethics. Indeed, rather than a source of a theocratic vision, the ideas above, when taken together, inform Day's anarchism.[30] Crucially, for Day, freedom and love go together. They stand together against coercion and violence. It is easy to see how such ideas might become a source of anarchism. One only has to give them primacy and insist on never violating the principles that they are thought to entail. Day assumes precisely this posture, as we will soon see.

As we have already seen, Day's religiosity had a rare intensity to it. And to Day, religious faith and religious practice are inseparable. Indeed, to have (a certain) faith is to be committed to (a certain) practice. Day's conversion to Catholicism meant a complete devotion to God, which entailed rigorous spiritual discipline. She bears witness by attempting to embody Christian ideals, in particular love. With Day, religious fidelity and spiritual discipleship involve questing for moral perfection. In many respects, Day's emphasis on moral perfection is simply an extension of her emphasis on (personal) responsibility.

Day's special concern for moral perfection motivates a turn to one of Western Christianity's richest spiritual traditions and thus one of Christianity's most exacting moral regimens, the pre-Reformation radical Gospel tradition and the Catholic counsels of perfection.[31] The pre-Reformation radical Gospel tradition is so called because its adherents literally interpreted certain passages from the Christian Bible, especially the New Testament, and attempted to make the principles that they derived from their literal interpretations of those passages the basis of their day-to-day activities. The Christian "martyrs" (i.e. Christian witnesses) of ancient Rome are often pointed to as the early members of this tradition and early to late medieval Roman Catholic mystics, ascetics, and monks kept the radical Gospel tradition alive. Indeed, it was a contingent of medieval monks who were inspired by and derived from a literal interpretation of Jesus's comments in the New Testament Gospels about how to "be perfect."

The counsels consist of three vows of perfection: perfect chastity, perfect charity, and obedience (living in community). These three vows were preserved in Catholic practice by Francis of Assisi and the earliest mendicant orders in the first part of the thirteenth century. Historically, within the broader Catholic Church, the counsels, as opposed to precepts, have generally been regarded as supererogatory; whereas precepts are regarded as binding for all members of the Catholic Church, the counsels of perfection are taken to apply only to persons with special vocations. Yet Day maintained—in the face of criticism from other Catholics—that all persons could and ought to seek perfection and strive to adhere to the counsels: "We have been criticized for holding up the counsels of perfection as norms of human conduct. It is sad that it is always the minimum that is expected of lay people."[32] On Day's view, only by means of a literal interpretation of biblical texts could one truly comprehend the Gospel. Moreover, she believed that literally interpreting the Sermon on the Mount and attempting to live in accord with the norms that it holds out sets one on the path toward righteousness or perfection: "I know it seems foolish to try to be so Christ-like, but God says we can. Why else His command, 'Be ye therefore perfect.'"[33]

Striving for moral perfection is crucial for Day because, as I have already suggested, human spiritual fulfillment and the realization of the kingdom of God—the beloved community—hinges on human action. And, as we might expect, Day regards the task of becoming a loving person as the most important aspect of the ethical quest for perfection. There are many bases on which one might criticize Day's insistence that persons seek perfection. Christian critics of this kind of perfectionist ethics have often contended that perfectionists are committed to an unrealistic conception of humanity or social life. Along these lines, ethical stances similar to Day's are commonly dismissed as naïve or regarded as a sign of naiveté. Yet, in truth, the religious radical who puts love first in the way that Day does has rarely been naïve. In Day's case, her commitment to social justice and sensitivity to social suffering rendered her too aware of the distance between her ideal and the status quo to be guilty of naiveté.

William D. Miller perfectly captures the tone of Day's ethical strivings in the title that he bestowed on his wonderful historical study of Day and the Catholic Worker movement—*A Harsh and Dreadful Love*. Rarely do titles radiate so much light on the subject matter. That title was, of course, borrowed from a line in another one of Dostoevsky's stories from which Day frequently and faithfully quoted. Invoking the memorable words of Fr Zossima (from Dostoevsky's *The Brothers Karamazov*), Day would often relate: "Love in practice is a harsh and dreadful thing compared to love in dreams. Active love is labor and fortitude."[34]

That Day had no illusions about the struggles that come with endeavoring to live out the Christian love ethic is apparent in nearly all of her descriptions of its demands. According to Day, love constitutes an attitude or disposition in relation to another person that takes intrinsic interest in that person's well-being. Love is kind. Love is patient. Love is longsuffering. It is thus maximally gentle and peaceful and by extension minimally coercive. In *From Union Square to Rome* she intimates:

Love is the best thing we can know in this life, but it must be sustained by an effort of the will. It must lie still and quiet, dull and smoldering, for periods. It grows through suffering and patience and compassion. We must suffer for those we love, we must endure their trials and their sufferings.[35]

Day appreciated both the fact that love is harsh and the fact that the quest for perfection could be daunting. She realized that the goal that Christian perfectionists seek after can sometimes seem ethereal. And there are always temptations to give in to despair or to abandon the love ethic as unviable for human persons. She also understood the fact that the problems that we face are grave and intractable: racial hatred, starvation, economic exploitation, war, and so on. As well, the human population is large, the earth immense, and the problems seemingly infinite; thus we might be tempted to make general problems the center of our attention; in that case most causes will appear to be lost causes.

Day resists these temptations by calling for an ethical posture centered on the concrete particular at particular moments. The greatest moralizers share with the great teachers and great coaches a gift for isolating fundamentals in order to make complicated tasks or problems manageable. The prophetic Christian moralist as exhorter is always an instructor. To that end, Day provides instructions to the Christian disciple who is endeavoring to adhere to the love ethic. In other words, Day recommends a way to approach ethical action. Day's response to this problematic establishes her as one of the most important commentators, Christian or otherwise, on ethical striving in the contemporary world.

Breaking ethical action down to the fundamentals, she shifts the focus from the general to the specific and from the abstract to the concrete for practical reasons. By doing this, by personalizing normative ideals, she brings such ideals to a level where "the possible" is made tangible. Ethical life consists of specific acts in accord with particular principles. For an individual person to comply with (i.e. assume responsibility for) particular ethical ideals or principles is always plausible. Day, in light of the facts of modern social life, pushes for the same kind of reclamation of responsibility that Thoreau, Tolstoy, and Gandhi advocated for. What we must do, says Day, is stress the implications of irresponsibility and responsibility. Our social criticism must be a call for personal responsibility—individual action amid a collectivity in the midst of a complicated scenario. Further and perhaps most significantly, it is imperative that we appreciate the fact that ethical action is action in time, meaning action at a particular moment. So again, while the quest for perfection is a struggle, Day insists that the focus remain on the individual person and the possibility of perfection. An acknowledgment of the power of human action or particular acts, mediated by divine grace, must be at the heart of our ethics.[36] Day thus writes,

> One of the greatest evils of the day [even] among those outside of prison is their case of futility. Young people say, What good can one person do? What is the sense of our small effort? They cannot see that we must lay one brick at a time, take one step at a time; we can be responsible only for the one action of the present moment. But we can beg for an increase of

love in our hearts that will vitalize and transform our individual actions, and know that God will take them and multiply them, as Jesus multiplied the loaves and fishes.[37]

Day suggests, then, that the challenge to "Be ye perfect" is a challenge for persons to *become* perfect *by* being perfect. Being is becoming in that every particular act is constitutive of the actor, so that action brings to life a new being. Becoming is in actuality being or an effect of being in the sense that one becomes through acts at particular instances in time and space. You *are* what you *did* insofar as what you *did* shapes what you *are doing* and *will do*. One seeks perfection, which suggests an orientation toward the future, by being intently engaged in particular moments—moment by moment—and in particular interpersonal encounters—encounter by encounter. Day insists that persons interested in becoming perfect can do so by seeking to be perfect. To be perfect means adhering to Gospel norms and ideals at particular moments. When someone asks for your coat, at that moment you have been presented with an opportunity to be *and* become perfect. According to Day, you should thus give them your coat along with your shoes. This, she once said, was foolishness in Christ. This is the way to be perfect, the way toward perfection. Day proposes concentration on the minute against the larger background as a means by which to generate hope. Hope is the fruit of doing. So understood, the seemingly impossible demands made by Christian love (commandments) become palpable.

Day's preoccupation with the particular, perhaps paradoxically, is married to a concern with the ultimate end, communion, which is both occasioned by and indicative of religious-ethical perfection. (Thus, perfection constitutes both the means and the end.) It is in this way that Day's rigorous religiosity represents an example of moral perfectionism.[38] Her ethics can be defined as perfectionist in that she believes that persons have a religious-ethical duty to cultivate a capacity to love and she seeks to promote institutions that establish and maintain the conditions for the maximization of interpersonal loving-kindness. In this sense she is committed to a teleological ethics: she posits a *telos* (i.e. an end) that moral action ought to be calibrated so as to attain.

It is commonly believed that teleological ethics must be consequentialist ethics. Yet this is not the case. Therefore, we must be careful not to assume that Day's ethics, if perfectionist, must also be consequentialist. While value maximizing ethical orientations can be consequentialist, it is not necessary for them to be so. Perfectionist moral theories, which are teleological, can include a proposition for moral agents to seek some end or telos, without being consequentialist, as moral perfectionists do not have to define the rightness of moral acts merely in virtue of the consequences of the acts, as do act-utilitarian moral theorists, for instance.

In addition to the above, it is crucial to appreciate that embracing a brand of teleological ethics does not commit one, on the basis of principle, to rejecting deontological commitments, where deontology is taken to include categorical imperatives that entail acting in accord with some moral principle, rule, or duty (the right) independent of consequences (for the good).

On my view, perfectionism is compatible with both deontological and consequentialist ethics. Consistent with this, perhaps we might say that Day is committed to a version of perfectionist deontological ethics or deontological perfectionism. Importantly, Day commends the promotion of love and institutions that facilitate the development of personhood, yet her interrelated conceptions of love and personhood presuppose certain categorical imperatives or unconditional duties.[39] For example, as will be clear shortly, Day suggests that a consistent Christian conception of the human person, as explicated in terms of personalism, entails an absolute prohibition against coercion, since, according to her, love and coercion are incompatible. So Day's brand of moral perfectionism entails striving for greater levels of loving-kindness and the promotion of community. Day evaluates social practices and institutions based upon the degree to which they promote community and loving-kindness among persons. Institutions must encourage personal responsibility and this responsibility implies resistance to institutions and practices that impede the expression of love.

Significantly, for Day and other Catholic Workers, the assuming of personal responsibility is nearly always equated with radical social action that is designated with the terms revolution or revolutionary. Consistent with this, she relates that taking personal responsibility means "beginning with oneself, starting here and now, not waiting for someone else to start the revolution."[40] For Day, recognition of one's essential nature—a person created by a personal loving God and meant for communion—prepares one for responsible action and this responsible action makes it possible to establish and realize the kingdom of God. In her words, "the new social order as it could be would be if all men loved God and loved their brothers because they are all sons of God!"[41] So Day issues a Christian-inspired prophetic call: Love God and your neighbor. Do it now. That's the beginning and the end of the revolution.

This can actually be stated in Thoreauvian or Transcendentalist terms: Day posits self-reform (or moral reform of the self) as tantamount to social reform. Since Day seldom invoked Thoreau or any other nineteenth-century American activists, for that matter, it is difficult to say for certain the degree to which persons such as Thoreau or William Lloyd Garrison directly influenced her. Nonetheless, Day's ethics share an unmistakable and remarkable affinity with Thoreau and several other nineteenth-century religious radicals. Mel Piehl suggests this much in his wonderful study on Day and the Catholic Worker movement. According to Piehl, the Catholic Worker's "social activism, egalitarianism, and concern for individual liberty . . . revealed its American provenance," so that at times "the movement resembled nothing so much as a Catholic version of the American tradition of perfectionist utopianism and religious revivalism that went back to the early nineteenth century and before."[42]

One dimension of moral perfectionism that I have endeavored to highlight in this section is the emphasis that Day, as a perfectionist, places on moral agency. It is probably this emphasis on moral agency and its revolutionary implications that most clearly connects Day with nineteenth-century religious radicals. Importantly, Day and Thoreau emphasize moral perfection and responsibility in a way that leads them to adopt similar attitudes toward political authority. In a word, they value moral freedom or moral autonomy so much so that they are led to reject as illegitimate most forms of political organization. As I argued in Chapter 1, Thoreau adopts an attitude toward authority and the territorial state that is best described as anarchist.

I have thus far bracketed the question of precisely how Day's religious commitments connect with anarchism. This I have done in order to keep our attention focused on her religiosity. But even while so far in this chapter I have concentrated on Day's religiosity, for the most part, I have considered only the aspects of her religious beliefs that I regard as relevant to her political philosophy or at least our consideration of her anarchism. In many respects, the crucial parts of Day's anarchism have already been presented in that, as Mark and Louise Zwick note, Day's "nonviolent anarchism is the assumption of personal responsibility and love in a world of objects and impersonal structures."[43] In the following sections I will break down how this is so.

# III

By around 1930, Day had already embraced an anarchistic ethic. Yet newly converted, and still trying to get her bearings in her new world, she had yet to settle into a community or social organization. From 1929 through 1932 she spent time between New York City and Mexico City, writing occasional editorial and news pieces for the Fellowship of Reconciliation, the ecumenical pacifist organization, and *Commonweal*, a leading liberal Catholic weekly. Day's stint with *Commonweal* proved surprisingly pivotal to her later career as a lay Catholic activist. *Commonweal*'s editor George N. Shuster represented what we might call a well-connected Catholic. As an editor of a leading Catholic paper, his contacts included American Catholics from coast-to-coast and of all walks life. It is to George Shuster that the world owes Dorothy

Day's friendship and collaboration with Peter Maurin, a French Catholic itinerant ascetic. Shuster had encouraged Maurin to be in touch with Day, as they—Day and Maurin—"thought alike."[44] Born in France in 1877, Maurin was a lay Catholic amateur social philosopher who believed in the literalness of the Christian Bible no less than Day. Maurin and Day met in 1932 and would launch the Catholic Worker movement a year later.

The first issue of the *Catholic Worker* appeared in 1933. It was May Day and the Great Depression showed few signs of abating. Selling papers for a penny per copy, Day had found a way to continue her vocation as a writer and satisfy a longing to be involved in a spiritually inclined, politically radical project. She and Maurin had envisioned a paper that would provide a Catholic (religious) alternative to the *Daily Worker*, the leading American socialist paper of the period. Up to that point there had been no radical paper targeting America's growing Catholic population. Through the *Catholic Worker*, Day and Maurin hoped to spread the Gospel of the Church; in particular, they would provide commentary on Catholic social teaching, as indicated in the papal social encyclicals, in order to advocate for workers and publicize distinctively Catholic proposals as to how to deal with the crisis of modernity—economic depression and oppression, statist repression, militarism, racism, spiritual decadence.

The paper's name signaled at once a leftist orientation and a possible conservative one. In truth, the Catholic Worker movement combined traditionalism and radicalism that defied categorization and baffled critics on both the left and right. But it was mostly persons who hoped that, despite the name, the paper would take a moderate approach who would be disappointed again and again during the years that followed the *Catholic Worker*'s emergence. Indeed, Mel Piehl is correct to call the Catholic Worker movement "the first major expression of radical social criticism in American Catholicism."[45]

Catholic Workers were committed to anarchist and pacifist criticism of the social order and particularly criticism of the modern social order from a Roman Catholic Christian perspective. From 1933 through the 1970s, Day creatively connected orthodox Catholic teaching with radical leftist ideas, and built a case for strong anarchism on the basis of her conception of love and the personal responsibility that it entails, such that, in general, her criticisms of the modern social order, particularly the inherently coercive practices of the centralized territorial state and capitalistic materialism, flow directly from her normative conception of love.

# IV

Dorothy Day was neither a political scientist nor a social theorist. And it would be going too far to assert that she provided a systematic analysis of the modern social order. Nonetheless, a careful survey of Day's work does yield a basic theoretical or descriptive account and criticism of the modern social order that takes as its primary objects the territorial state or states and the capitalist economy or economies. Day criticizes the territorial state for its operational mode (centralized, impersonal, and underinclusive procedure), its effects on social life (it undermines mutual aid and personal responsibility), and for the ends (protection of capital) that it seeks. She criticizes capitalist practices for being excessively materialistic, exploitative, and oppressive.

Perhaps the most distinctive aspect of Day's anarchism is the fact that it is in part motivated by her particular criticisms of the centralized character of the modern territorial state. It is widely accepted among contemporary social theorists that the modern territorial state is a centralized bureaucratic organization. The *modern territorial* state is differentiated from other kinds of political organization based on the fact that a modern territorial state divides earth into political geographic units with borders, regulates the movement of human bodies across earth, and asserts authority to regulate, with violence if necessary, the behavior of persons, that is, political subjects, who occupy the terrain over which a given state claims as its territory. Modern territorial states are notable as well for the fact that they are comprised of bureaucratic offices, departments, and agencies charged with regulating an array of social practices and activities.

In the context of the United States, since the mid-nineteenth century, the American state has steadily increased in size and scope. But the most exponential growth, over the shortest span of time, came arguably during the period spanning the mid-1930s with the emergence of New Deal social security and welfare programs, through the establishment of clandestine national security agencies during the Cold War, and the implementation of racial justice and urban reconstruction programs during the Lyndon B. Johnson and Richard Nixon presidencies of the 1960s.

By the latter part of the twentieth century, most if not all territorial states, including the American state, had begun attempting to regulate nearly every aspect of human life. In the American context, the modern American territorial state has grown exponentially for reasons that have to do with the competing ideologies proffered by left and right wing liberal actors respectively. Since the turn of the twentieth century, liberal Democrats have tended to contend that Americans need a strong centralized (federal-level) state in order to protect the economic interests of the poor, working, and middle classes; they propose a welfare state. Liberal Republicans have tended to contend that the state is needed for protection from social deviants and foreign aggressors; they propose a military state. No matter the causal factors, it might be said that Americans reside in a national security social welfare state.

Day's normative political commitments led her to regard this unfolding of the modern territorial state and the expansion of federal governmental power and authority as a horrifying development. To be sure, the twentieth century hosted a large cast of critics of the welfare state; some couched vicious racism in terms of antigovernment rhetoric that endures one decade into the twenty-first century; others genuinely objected to social welfare provisions on the basis of free-market oriented classical liberalism. Therefore, we understand little of import about Day simply by knowing that she found the welfare state problematic. It is her reasoning that is of the essence.

In general, Day identifies two problems with the territorial state that are important to discuss. First, the territorial state, as it endeavors to monitor and regulate human behavior, has a tendency to "encroach" on almost all areas of social life, negatively impacting the social institutions and practices that are necessary for flourishing communities. Second, as a hierarchical centralized (bureaucratic) political decision-making entity, the territorial state employs coercion in order to enforce its decisions. On one level, these two objections are merely two ways of saying the same thing: the territorial state does not respect and thus does not promote personal responsibility and the moral freedom or autonomy that responsibility implies.

Of the criticisms of the state that Day presents, the one that she mentions most often is the fact that territorial state social welfare initiatives have usurped local and individual aid initiatives. According to Day, the rise of the welfare state, in response to social dislocations caused by unjust inequalities resulting from technological innovations and population increases, population increases that themselves led to extensive unemployment and underemployment, undermined community. The rise of the welfare state undermined community by displacing local and community-based voluntary and mutual aid societies, replacing them with centralized and so impersonal bureaucratic agencies, which has the ongoing effect of engendering persons' increased reliance or dependence on the territorial state.

So, according to Day, territorial state intervention, to meet authentic needs in the face of a depressed economy during the 1930s, only exacerbated and compounded existing social problems. For, the amplification of state power(s), in order to meet welfare needs during one crisis, always becomes a reason for future interventions; and these periodic interventions entail a steady increase of territorial state powers and functions that serves to convince persons that it is essential for the territorial state to intervene; this in turn spawns among persons a declining sense of mutual responsibility (for one another as members of the Mystical Body of Christ), which is problematic, for Day, in that, as we saw in our reflection on the idea of the Mystical Body of Christ and personalism, self-actualization is predicated on assuming personal responsibility and in recognizing the unity of humanity. In the face of these developments, Day cries, "It is strange and terrifying business, this all-encroaching state, when it interferes to such a degree in the personal practice of works of mercy."[46] By interfering with the personal practice of works of mercy, the territorial state impedes persons' efforts to put love in practice, so that the territorial state undermines the ability of persons to live in accord with the dictates of the Sermon on the Mount.

Day's postconversion discipleship can be understood, at least in part, as an effort to warn others of the dangers of giving over to the territorial state the responsibility to care for one another. As do most prophetic social critics, she appeals first to those who profess to care: "If every family that professed to follow scriptural teaching whether Jew, Protestant, or Catholic," would put love in practice, "there would be no need for huge institutions. . . . Responsibility must return to the person with a hospice and a center for mutual aid, to the group, to the family, to the individual."[47] Huge institutions tend to deflate our sense of responsibility, even though most people get the sense that many such organizations—nursing homes, psychiatric wards, orphanages, prisons—are ineffective precisely because they are impersonal. Day complains repeatedly that "the system is all too big, too ponderous, too unwieldy."[48]

Against this backdrop, she appeals to decentralization, a central norm in her political thought. "Everything," pleads Day, "needs to be decentralized into smaller institutions."[49] On Day's view, the principal way to reestablish responsible modes of being would be to break things "down into smaller units that are workable according to man's nature."[50] Breaking things down into smaller units would awaken persons to their mutual dependency, and by extension underscore the importance of persons acting responsibly. Ultimately, a move away from centralized bureaucratic institutions, Day says, would spell the "beginning of an order in which men could be conscious of their dignity and responsibility."[51] Day and other Catholic Workers advocate "a personalism which takes on ourselves responsibility for changing conditions to the extent that we are able to do so."[52] It is with this interest in taking responsibility that Catholic Workers established houses of hospitality, or Catholic Worker houses. These houses of hospitality provided a space where "the works of mercy could be practiced to combat the taking over by the state of all those services which could be built around mutual aid." The houses of hospitality represent an effort to "take care of those in need rather than turn them over to the impersonal 'charity' of the State."[53]

From Proudhon, Kropotkin, and Tolstoy to George Woodcock and Paul Goodman, most anarchists have given primacy to the fact of universal human dignity and have stressed the indispensability of persons recognizing that they are responsible for and dependent on other persons. Indeed, it is Proudhon and Kropotkin who established mutual aid as a vital term in the anarchist pool of ideals. Day's special contribution to anarchism is the way in which she managed to so articulately relate the anarchist ideal to an ethic of compassion and care. Few examples could better convey Day's penchant for melding anarchism with this ethic than her subtle effort to define anarchism in her piece "The Scandal of the Works of Mercy." Day writes, "Anarchists that we are, we want to decentralize everything and delegate to smaller bodies and groups what can be done far more humanely and responsibly through mutual aid."[54]

Day's explication of anarchism in terms of humaneness, responsibility, and mutuality was intended to instruct through irony. During the 1930s and 1940s, anarchists were widely depicted as nihilistic, reckless purveyors of violence. It is against this backdrop that we must understand Day's suggestion that an anarchist ethic is motivated by compassion, an interest in personal responsibility, and a concern with how institutional arrangements affect human personality and sociality. Her point is that, rather than it being anarchists who are irresponsible or callous, it is actually the territorial state's agents and agencies—large and hierarchical entities—that are inhumane, impersonal, and destructively irresponsible. According to Day, it is precisely for these reasons that anarchists reject the territorial state and hope to establish a social order based on mutual aid.

Day's objection to the existence of the territorial state on the basis of its undermining of mutual aid and personal responsibility differs from Proudhon and Kropotkin, of course, in that Day's objection is an extension of her Roman Catholic commitments. Personalist ideas, the doctrine of the Mystical Body of Christ, and moral perfectionism are implicit in Day's commendation of decentralized institutionalized practices. That Day construes the value of decentralization in the way that she does evinces the importance of her conceptions of God, the human person, love, and community for her normative political vision, revealing the special way in which Day's anarchism is religious or has religious values as its source.

Now, in truth, it is quite complicated to say precisely how certain aspects of Day's anarchism relate to her Catholicism and vice versa. To be sure, Day often explicitly pointed to the compatibility of her anarchist emphasis on decentralization with Catholic social teaching. For example, she often invoked the Catholic doctrine of subsidiarity, an idea that proved particularly amenable to anarchist interpretation, so as to support her decentralist project. Yet Day's invocation of the doctrine of subsidiarity actually puts on display both how intertwined Day's Catholicism was with her anarchism and how complicated it is to tell the one from the other.

The Catholic doctrine of subsidiarity emerged from interpretations of ideas about the proper relationship between government and nongovernmental social institutions presented in Pope Leo XIII's encyclical *Rerum Novarum* in 1891. The clearest statement of the idea was probably presented by Pope Pius XI, who maintained that, "It is a fundamental principle of social philosophy, fixed and unchangeable, that one should not withdraw from individuals and commit to the community what they can accomplish by their own enterprise and/or industry."[55] Although the principle of subsidiarity as presented in Pius XI's encyclical is ostensibly compatible with an anarchist position, Catholic popes who have invoked the doctrine have hardly meant to commend anarchism per se and few Catholics who endorse the principle of subsidiarity take it as a path to anarchism. This includes French personalists Mounier and Maritain, who both endorsed a version of the principle of subsidiarity yet explicitly rejected anarchism. It also includes many members of the 1930s "Catholic consensus" who gave their wholehearted support to Franklin D. Roosevelt's New Deal policies with the idea that they were being faithful to the spirit of Pope Pius XI's encyclical in which the idea of subsidiarity is most clearly delineated. Since most Catholic social thinkers maintain or assume that the territorial state is necessary for the procurement of at least some goods, the doctrine of subsidiarity is typically understood as a principle specifying the proper scope of the territorial state's authority.

Day pushed the doctrine of subsidiarity to its limit. She does this in at least two ways. First, Day refrains from specifying which responsibilities might be delegated upward, as she had a profound faith in the capacity of individual persons to cooperatively manage the most vital aspects of social life without assistance from above. In addition, and related, Day maintained, on moral grounds, that individual persons must come to mutual agreement about which organization(s) or at what level within an organization important decisions will be made or which agency will fulfill certain functions.[56]

This concern about decision-making processes points to and connects with the second aspect of Day's criticism of the centralized bureaucratic character of the modern territorial state that I alluded to above. While the above consideration of her criticism of centralization might give the impression that Day rejects the territorial state simply because it fails to promote mutual aid, love in action, or personal responsibility, in actuality Day objects to the territorial state's exercise of power and assertion of authority on a more basic level than that. Deeming its operational mode inherently problematic, she rejects the legitimacy of the territorial state on the basis of its centralized and so necessarily underinclusive and impersonal decision-making process or procedure. To understand exactly how Day arrives at this position, it is essential to appreciate (1) how Day's conception of love relates to coercion and (2) her assumptions about the centrality of coercion to the practices of the territorial state.

According to Day, because territorial states—including representational democracies—are centralized bureaucratic organizations, they by definition have hierarchical and exclusive decision-making processes, which locate authority to decide with a select group of persons.[57] Furthermore, in political philosophical terms, we can say that territorial state political officials are granted authority, understood as a right, to coerce; the right to coerce in practice amounts to a right to force persons to perform or refrain from performing certain acts.[58] Since modern territorial states do not govern or rule with the consent of the governed, as a general matter, territorial state officials assert authority over persons who have not consented to the authority of the state. Day concludes in the light of this that in practice, through the territorial state, a segment of society forces its will on another segment of society. (Again, even in democratic territorial states, the decision-making process is exclusive, so that some persons can be said to be ruled by others.) This description is important insofar as the repudiation of coercion is a key part of Day's normative political philosophy.

As I indicated earlier, Day's Christian-inspired conception of the person is incompatible with theocratic politics. (This is because of Day's conception of love and love's centrality to Day's idea about how one fully expresses personhood.) By noting how Day's conception of love precludes a theocratic vision, I meant to signal the fact that when carried into the political domain, Day's conception of the person and idea of love have significant political philosophical implications. To reiterate, Day's idea of the universal dignity of the human person, inspired by her interpretation of the Gospel and a central component of her personalism, entails an absolute rejection of coercion, so that Day's ideal society—the beloved community—can reasonably be described as a society without coercion.[59]

Coercion, for Day, especially in the sense that is relevant to political philosophy, always operates on the basis of the threat of violence. Violence in this sense is the act of subjecting a person to physical—and the psyche is undoubtedly physical—harm or the threat of such harm in order to force a person to perform some act or set of acts that a given person would not perform but for the fact of the inflicted harm or violent threat. To be sure, coercion and violence are terms that can be defined more or less broadly and how they are defined undoubtedly shapes whether or not it is possible in practice to avoid coercive or violent action. And like most contemporary proponents of nonviolence, Day was (1) conscious of the fact that there are varying degrees of coercion and violence and (2) aware of the implications of how we define coercion and violence. Day insisted that we refrain from using the fact that in practice it is difficult to realize a given ideal as a reason to outright discount it. In addition, Day, following other nonviolent theorists, maintained that persons committed to the principle of nonviolence must always refrain from intentional killing and always use the least harmful, nonlethal means available in order to accomplish a given just end. Most people recognize that it makes a difference whether we use guns or speech to make our points. So, although persuasive speech—as opposed to unpersuasive speech—and direct action methods do perhaps have a coercive element, they most definitely do not have the same effect as whips, electricity, clubs, or bullets, and thus constitute a categorically different kind of coercion, if we want to classify nonviolent direct action as coercion at all.

Two interconnected concerns ground Day's position on coercion. First, according to Day, coercion, or the act of coercing, is antithetical to love as action, so that one cannot engage in an act of coercion and at the same time perform an act of love. Therefore, the coercer and coerced are both diminished by the coercive encounter. Finally, Day maintains that to be coerced is to be denied moral freedom or autonomy, which is precisely why Day maintains that Christian love precludes recourse to coercion.[60]

Day's clearest articulation of this point comes in a passage in which she defines pacifism and anarchism in terms of love, and suggests that love entails a refusal to coerce or exercise authority over other persons. Day relates, "Pacifism and anarchism, when you get down to it, mean that we try always to love, rather than coerce, 'to be what we want the other fellow to be,' to have no authority over others, to begin with that microcosm man, or rather, with ourselves." This concise statement sums up Day's entire political philosophy. Pacifism and anarchism both entail a commitment to love; and love, as an ethical norm, prohibits coercion. Anarchism and pacifism, then, are at least superficially identical, on Day's view, as they stand for a repudiation of coercive means to ends, a refusal to wield "authority over" others. Ultimately, Day's normative conception of love is combined with her description of the territorial state and expressed in the form of a syllogism: coercion is wrong; the territorial state coerces; thus persons (committed to avoiding wrongful action) must not support or cooperate with the territorial state.

It is vital to take careful note of the grounds on which Day builds her case for anarchism. She bases her anarchism on a principle of nonviolence. Further, notice that an idea of moral autonomy or freedom is inherent in the principle of nonviolence as Day explicates it. This is significant because it points to an unmistakable yet underappreciated dimension of Day's ethics: Day embraces a strand of voluntarism.[61] Voluntarism, of course, is a theory about the essential role of voluntary action in moral and social life. Implicit in the conception of voluntarism that is important for political philosophy is an idea about the place of coercion in social and political life. Social critics and theorists often juxtapose coercion and voluntariness of action. An excellent example of how coercion and voluntary action are often mutually defined is presented in the work of medieval Catholic theologian Thomas Aquinas, probably the most important Roman Catholic thinker for the largest number of Roman Catholics in the twentieth century (including French personalists).

In his *Summa*, Aquinas asserts that "just as it is impossible for a thing to be at the same time violent and natural, so it is impossible for a thing to be absolutely coerced or violent, and voluntary."[62] Here, Aquinas presents what has probably become the standard Catholic understanding of the nature of moral autonomy or freedom: voluntary action and coerced acts are mutually exclusive.[63] Day more or less accepts this understanding of the concepts in question.[64] Yet formal definitions of principles seldom explain the whole of a given normative political philosophical position, and merely accepting

Aquinas' definition of voluntary action makes one neither a voluntarist nor an anarchist. So, to be clear, the point here is not that Aquinas commended voluntarism or opened up a pathway toward anarchism. Instead, the fact that Aquinas has spelled out a conception of voluntary action that has been developed in strikingly different ways highlights the distinctiveness of Day's Catholicism.

In ethics, what counts most is the priority, place, or weight that is given (or not given) to this or that value or principle. To that end, in order for Aquinas' understanding of voluntary action to become a basis for voluntarism as such and by extension anarchism, one must privilege or give priority to voluntary action or moral autonomy. Day, of course, does precisely this, which distinguishes her from Aquinas and others. Again, Day claims that coercion is *absolutely* prohibited (by love) and she concomitantly attributes absolute value to moral autonomy or voluntary action. In a word, Day stresses the importance of moral autonomy or voluntary action to the point that it becomes a source of anarchism.

Voluntarism as I am using the term should probably be qualified with the term *political* so as to make clear the fact that voluntarism in the sense that I am employing it is not a doctrine about the metaphysics of the will per se. *Political* voluntarism, to repeat, is a claim about the place of consent and so coercion in the sociopolitical sphere. And, I assume that in the fullest sense, (voluntary) consent and coercion are mutually exclusive. Indeed, voluntary consent renders coercion superfluous and effectively employed coercive means makes it impossible to realize voluntary consent in a particular case. For Day, and many other anarchists, it is imperative that persons, especially adults, relate and associate on the basis of mutual consent. Specifically, persons, as moral beings or agents, should not be coerced into belonging to any particular organization. Association should be voluntary. In particular, participation in or contribution to the practices of political organizations or governments should be voluntary. Stated negatively, one does not have a moral obligation or moral duty to participate in practices that one does not regard as morally appropriate or valuable to society for practical or principled reasons. And one certainly does not have a moral obligation to defer to commands of other persons. This principle registers a respect for the dignity of the person and protects moral autonomy.

Now, clearly this means that in some cases persons will refuse to participate in practices that many or perhaps even most other persons regard as essential to the common good. In such cases, the persons who *do* participate in or regard the given practices as valuable might accuse the "resisters" of failing to discharge a moral duty or fulfill a moral obligation. Anarchists such as Day can in some instances agree with this kind of accusation, assessment, or judgment. Yet what Day cannot do, given her brand of anarchism, is suggest that the resisters be violently forced to participate in or contribute to the practices in question. To employ violence or coercion in this way would be to violate the moral autonomy of the resisters, which would mean violating a fundamental component of Day's anarchism. In light of the above, I would contend that Day bestows a value on voluntary participation that is constitutive of political voluntarism.

Let me try to clarify this matter about what gives rise to political voluntarism with a hypothetical case. Let us grant that coercion is only necessary, as a practical matter, to the degree that a given person, person 1, wants some other person, person 2, to perform (or not perform) some act that person 2 does not in fact want to perform. Say that there are two persons—person 1 and person 2—who find themselves more or less in this situation. Person 1 can respond in multiple ways. I will note four. Person 1 might (A) simply accept and respect person 2's preference and nonperformance of the act in question; (B) offer an argument or range of (persuasive) reasons, exclusive of the threat of force, for action in accord with the command or request; (C) physically harm or threaten to physically harm person 2 or an associate of person 2, if person 2 refuses to perform the said act; or in certain cases (D) employ physical force in order to force person 2 to perform the given act. For the purposes of political voluntarism, it is scenarios C and D that are of concern in that in those cases a coercive factor is introduced.

So what exactly is the issue between nonviolent anarchists such as Day and persons who reject anarchism or political voluntarism? In short, it is the question as to whether any person or persons, particularly persons organized into a political unit, ever have a veritable moral reason to *physically* force other persons to perform any act or acts that such persons, for moral reasons, do not want to perform. Some say that force is sometimes morally appropriate, both in intra-group and out-group relations. Day, of course, embraces a moral principle that entails the absolute prohibition of options C and D. Persons, including persons organized as political entities, never have a right to use force. In this way, Day universalizes the Anabaptist claim that Christians do not have "a right to the sword." Persons (and certainly Christian persons), if they are to act in accord with right/love, must operate strictly on the basis of persuasion and mutual consent. Thus person 1 does not possess a right to force performance or violently punish nonperformance. In the above scenario, from Day's perspective, if person 1 chooses option C or D, then person 1 is morally wrong in that person 1 has failed to respect the moral autonomy of person 2 (the resister). Again, Day rules out coercion because she believes that it is antithetical to the dictates of Christian love and the idea of moral autonomy that it implies.

Notice that nothing that I have said about Day's commitments bears on whether she can maintain that persons have moral obligations or duties outside the context of consensual or voluntary relationships. Rather, persons are free to sin, as Christians often put it. Persons who find the behavior of others problematic must give special concern to nonviolent ways to encourage cooperation. And, to be sure, Day conceded that it is difficult to even imagine how a society could or would operate on the basis of consent and without coercion. But she maintained that this must remain the ideal guiding our actions and our deliberations about how to best shape our relations. We should attempt in practice to make certain that all of our associations are as voluntary as is possible. For Day, this was a religious duty.

Day's commitment to anarchism and the important role that voluntarism plays in her ethics can be gleaned from the following:

> The word anarchist is deliberately and repeatedly used in order to awaken our readers to the necessity of combating the "all-encroaching state," as our Bishops have termed it, and to shock serious students in to looking into the possibility of another society, an order made up of associations, guilds, unions, communes, voluntary associations of men, on regional instead of national lines, where there is a possibility of liberty and responsibility for all men.[65]

On the basis of the value that she attributes to liberty and responsibility, Day encourages persons to seek alternatives to the territorial state and to "look into the possibility" of a social order comprised of "voluntary associations." And to voluntarily associate is, of course, to associate by consent. Importantly, voluntary associations should be decentralized social organizations, as decentralized organizations are thought to facilitate participation thereby eliminating (in theory yet perhaps only minimizing in practice) the necessity of employing coercive means to regulate behavior. Decentralization, then, is an essential value for Day because she posits a decentralized social order as one in which love—and the principles or ideals that it implies (nonviolence and moral autonomy or personal responsibility)—will be most effectively promoted and protected.

Since Day's conception of love, with its concomitant idea of moral freedom or autonomy, leads her to embrace a strand of voluntarism, it should be evident that her ethics share an affinity with the American revolutionaries and radicals that I discussed in Chapter 1. Following Staughton Lynd, I noted that there has been a tendency among American revolutionaries and radicals to assert moral freedom as the primary political philosophical value and to conclude that such a political philosophy requires establishing a society comprised of voluntary associations. There are compelling reasons to regard Day as a full-fledged member of this group of American revolutionaries or radicals. That a Roman Catholic Christian can be said to belong to this tradition might have seemed odd or doubtful to the nineteenth-century Unitarian reformers who found even Congregationalism stultifying and too amenable to various forms of (nonvoluntarist) authoritarian organization.

Yet, the fact that a Roman Catholic can belong to this tradition should hardly surprise us, at least if we recognize and appreciate the way in which what we refer to as the Protestant Reformation was in actuality a Roman

Catholic affair. It should also not surprise us if we keep in mind the degree to which what we call modernity, particular in relation to the principles of toleration and consent, has profoundly transformed European and American institutions, the Roman Catholic Church included, and the way that Catholic clerics and laypersons understand the role of authority and the individual in social life. Day joined a Catholic Church quite different from the Church in its earlier emanations. In particular, the Church's ecclesiastical hierarchy in Day's time differed remarkably from the pre-Reformation period. The Church's move toward tolerance began in the nineteenth century with the abolition of the Church's claim to temporal authority or power, that is, secular political authority, was formalized with the 1849 Constitution of the Roman Republic, and culminated with the Lateran Treaty of 1929, just two years after Day's conversion. With the signing of that treaty, the Roman Catholic Church ceased to be a state-supported religion in Italy, and assumed a less formal political role in society.

By the 1930s, the Catholic Church had repudiated coerced belief and the employment of violent means to punish sin or heresy. The Church had become a voluntary association, in the sense that, as a practical matter, individual persons could refuse to join or decide to leave the Church and church authorities would only have persuasive speech as recourse against a person's decision about church affiliation. In the light of this, Day could assert that there is "tremendous freedom . . . in the Church, a freedom most cradle Catholics do not seem to know they possess. They do know that a man is free to be a Democrat or a Republican, but they do not know that he is also free to be a philosophical anarchist by conviction."[66]

Day regarded this freedom as a license for her preference for voluntary associations and the fact that she commends voluntary associations is pertinent to the question of how to classify the variety of anarchism that she espouses, as it reveals that she does not reject all forms of political organization per se. To be sure, one might define the *political* so that the idea of coercion and violence are a necessary part of it. In that case, we would have to say that Day rejects *political* organization as such. While many theorists, including some anarchists, define the political in precisely these terms, doing so makes it difficult to adequately understand the normative commitments of proponents of nonviolent anarchism. That is, it obscures the character of the normative political philosophy of persons such as Day. In particular, it makes it difficult to appreciate that anarchism is often presented as a form of political organization (or government). On my view, at least in theory, coercion and violence are not necessary characteristics of politics or political organization.

Indeed, as with Thoreau, Day's anarchism can be interpreted so that she is understood as arguing that a particular form of political organization (or government)—that is, anarchy—is preferable to other forms of political organization.[67] In particular, Day proposes an anarchist order, with voluntary associations, as an order that ought to replace the (inherently violent and coercive) representative democratic order because voluntary associations make "liberty and responsibility" possible, and liberty and responsibility are preconditions to the actualization of personhood and the realization of community among persons and between humanity and God. According to Day, an anarchist social order provides a way to formally register respect for human dignity as she understood it. Therefore, we can say that, for Day, only political organizations or institutions that operate on the basis of explicit universal consent *and* replace coercion/violence with cooperation and persuasion can be morally legitimate.

It should be clear why Day contends that representative or constitutional democracy is inconsistent with the idea of moral autonomy that she embraces. As I noted in the introduction, only consensus or unanimous direct democracy, where all laws governing a given society were consented to by each person subject to those laws, is compatible with the idea of moral autonomy that most anarchists present, Day included. Any other political authority lacks legitimacy from the perspective of persons committed to the idea of moral autonomy (again, as I have presented it). What this reveals is the way in which Day, as an anarchist, regards questions of legitimacy as inseparable from questions of justice. Importantly, the fact that territorial states are illegitimate means that they are also unjust, insofar as they employ violent and coercive means in order to force persons to perform certain acts. And by extension, the fact that territorial states lack legitimate authority means that persons are under no moral obligation to comply with their laws and commands. We could even say, then, that Day's anarchism *is* a *form* of government or at least a political philosophical norm that restricts the means (procedure) through which an entity can govern, that is, make decisions of a political nature.

The above analysis brings to the fore why or how it is helpful to differentiate between anarchists who reject government as such and those who contend that some form of government might be morally acceptable. As I indicated in the "Introduction," some anarchists maintain that all promise making is morally prohibited and thus rule out *all* types of political organization. Day does not take this track. In fact, she regarded the practice of promising and contracting as vital to the perpetuation of certain voluntary associations and regarded voluntary associations as central to a flourishing communal life. In consequence, Day belongs to the collection of anarchists who have proposed replacing one sociopolitical form with another, not dispensing with political organization per se.[68]

# V

So far I have concentrated mostly on Day's claim that the centralized and coercive character of the modern territorial state generates practices that implicitly and explicitly violate human dignity or aspects of human personhood. But Day rejects the authority and legitimacy of the modern territorial state on multiple distinct yet connected grounds and so, if we are to adequately understand Day's anarchism, we must give attention to (1) Day's theory about how the territorial state is related to capitalistic economic practices and the role of violence in the capitalistic social order and (2) her constructive proposals about how persons should attempt to move beyond the territorial state and the capitalistic economic order. The following analysis of Day's criticisms of capitalism will lay the ground for a consideration of her positive prescriptions and reveal that Day advocates for the abolition of the state via nonviolent means, namely through the creation of decentralized cooperatives and communes, and is therefore best classified as a *strong* anarchist, one who rejects the idea that there are general political obligations and additionally maintains that individual persons have a moral duty to oppose and actively seek alternatives to the territorial state.

Day is unrelenting in her criticisms of capitalist economies. Her principal criticism of capitalist economic practices is directed at the way in which such practices involve exploiting persons qua workers and transforming persons qua employees into instruments employed by employers merely as a means to financial gain. Day tellingly follows socialists and communists: workers are paid slave wages and thus are little more than slaves. For Day, chattel slavery and wage slavery are merely points on a continuum. Moreover, with the division of labor and the emergence of modern means of production, and the ownership of the means of production by a minority class of persons, most persons are given stultifying work, and forced to perform dehumanizing tasks, under dehumanizing conditions. In addition, capitalist economies (1) create economic crises marked by extreme deprivation and (2) establish and sustain unjust wealth inequalities, particularly in terms of access to land. This gives rise to an economic system revolving around usury and to a situation in which a multitude of persons are slaves of debt.[69]

But that is not all. Day also complains that capitalist economies, with the advent of the advertising industry, attempt to generate superfluous needs that in turn distort human desire in a way that undermines personality or persons' psychological states, and undermines community. In *Loaves and Fishes*, Day observes that "newspapers, radio, television, and battalions of advertising men (woe to that generation) deliberately stimulate our desires, the satisfaction of which so often means the deterioration of the family."[70] As a general matter, according to Day, capitalism creates conditions under which persons are unfulfilled and insecure, thus leading to anxiety, interpersonal violence, pervasive thievery, vicious competition, and other ills. Life in capitalist societies has been and is diminished, especially from a Christian spiritual perspective. Indeed, capitalism (along with the emergence of the territorial state) has created a spiritual crisis by denying the primacy of the spiritual.

The capitalist's logic, taken to its (fullest logical) conclusion, can be understood as the assertion of material possession(s) as an end in itself. We might say that instead of positing possession of material goods as an ultimate end, the capitalist moralist (i.e. capitalist economist) posits pleasure as the chief end, and wealth as a means to that end. In either case, from Day's vantage, capitalism is underwritten by or underwrites a materialist perspective, thus producing materialistic subjectivities. So, Day rejects capitalist practices, on the basis of the features that I have enumerated, because these practices constitute the denial of the dignity of the human person and represent idolatry insofar as the capitalist worldview is materialistic.

These criticisms of capitalist economic practices connect with Day's political commitments in that, according to Day, capitalism's sustenance is contingent on the existence of the modern territorial state. A consequence of the exclusiveness of the territorial state's decision-making process and its centralized power structure is that the powers that the territorial state makes available to certain classes of people are employed in a way that serves narrow (class) interests to the detriment of the persons excluded from power. In practice, all territorial states are controlled by wealthy and technical elites (technocrats) who are able to collectively impose their will(s) on the majority of persons, especially the poor, through the state apparatus. And the territorial state's existence has facilitated the unequal distribution of natural resources, including land, and the state protects the property of the dominant class through its legal regime, that is, its violent or coercive enforcement mechanisms. Day minces no words,

> Class war does exist. We cannot deny it. It is here. Class lines are drawn even here in America where we have always flattered ourselves that the poor boy can become president, the messenger boy, the head of a corporation. The very fact of the necessity of national security laws, old age and unemployment insurance, acknowledges the existence of a proletariat class.[71]

Day's reference to national security laws is especially notable. These laws give shape to the territorial state's national security apparatus, which consists of the armed forces, clandestine intelligence agencies, and an armaments industry, with its research and manufacture units. In the American context, clandestine intelligence agencies such as the Central Intelligence Agency (CIA), the Federal Bureau of Investigation (FBI), and the National Security Agency (NSA) engage in a range of operations, including assassination, sabotage, spying, and black propaganda. The CIA, of course, has been known to topple governments and corporations said to threaten the security of the United States of America and kill persons who allegedly pose a threat to international stability. The FBI operates domestically, and has sabotaged a series of grassroots activists, organizations, and social movements in the

American context. It is difficult to say what else these clandestine agencies have done and are doing. And it is just as difficult to accurately describe the character of the armaments industry, as so much happens under a shroud of secrecy. However, what is indubitable is that most armaments research and manufacture companies, such as Boeing, Raytheon, and Lockheed Martin, are not technically a part of the territorial state proper, yet they conduct research and produce weaponry by means of financial resources provided by the territorial state's national security apparatus. Day refers to this horrifying configuration variously as the war economy or the military industrial complex, borrowing Dwight Eisenhower's often used term. According to Day, the "whole modern economy is based on preparation for war."[72] Day may go too far here, as there are certainly economic practices that are not necessarily based on war. Yet the national security apparatus and the modern economy (or economies) do intertwine in ways that make it difficult to ascertain where the one ends and the other begins.

Under capitalism, economic considerations and the economic interests of the dominant class dominate decision-making processes about how to use state power. And police power, preparation for war, and actual war are employed (i.e. exploited) both to mobilize populations (1) in a way that reinforces the strength of territorial state agencies and actors and (2) in order to forward the economic interests of select social classes. With respect to the American domestic sphere, Day presents the American territorial state's violent intervention in favor of capitalist-managers against workers in the labor-capital disputes and strikes from the 1880s through the early twentieth century as examples of the territorial state's role not merely in defending the private property (in terms of accumulated wealth, in the form of land and money) of the dominant class, but as an entity organized so as to protect and pursue the special interests of an elite clique to the detriment of large segments of society.[73] On the international front, according to Day, America and other territorial states have been and are engaged in militarism as an extension of colonialist and imperialist projects that originated in the needs of capitalist economies in terms of natural resources, consumer markets, financial markets, or cheap labor.

Related to all of this, territorial state actors have repeatedly shown themselves to be indifferent to questions of morality and justice—from violent crackdowns on labor demonstrations in 1930 to Hiroshima and Dresden. Day found the events leading up to World War II particularly elucidative. Worldwide, capitalists and politicians were mostly indifferent to the suffering of the Jews in France, Poland, and Germany during the Nazi reign. But they were not simply indifferent; for, capitalists and state officials, even in purportedly democratic states, collaborated with and supported Hitler throughout the 1930s in order to protect financial interests and to check the power of the Soviet Union. For many, few historical events have seemed to demonstrate the necessity of the state and the importance of coercion and violence more than Nazism, the Holocaust, and World War II generally speaking.

Yet, according to Day, it was precisely the emergence of the modern territorial state and the concentration of power that came with it that made the Holocaust possible and even likely. (This is especially so given the territorial state's call for blind obedience to its authority and its claim to have the right to conscript persons into the military.) Moreover, and more to the point, the very racist sensibilities and economic interests that gave rise to the territorial state are social facts that render the territorial state complicit in the social evils that its defenders have claimed that the state is needed in order to counteract. Day's charge is incisive: "The modern States which built up a Hitler, which did not depopulate concentration camps and gas chambers by providing living space, giving asylum or by imposing economic sanctions, are monstrosities."[74] The Holocaust, according to Day, did not demonstrate the necessity of the state; it demonstrated its inadequacy. By pointing out that American governmental officials had not been willing to combat Nazism when it first arose, Day calls into question the revisionist accounts of the 1930s and 1940s. On Day's view, territorial states not only possess too much power and claim too much authority for themselves. They also consistently and incessantly engage in and facilitate unjust practices. They are vehicles of evil that totalize the social sphere and complicate or at least attempt to complicate everyone in their unjust practices.

Day concluded that the modern territorial state, with its bureaucratic centralization and rationality, its protection of resource inequalities (i.e. the private property of the wealthy elite), and its military industrial complex, constituted a hindrance to community and communion, a detriment to interpersonal love and mutual aid. This is because of what Day understood such love to rule out. It rules out nationalism. It rules out racism. It rules out the use of violence. It rules out hatred. It rules out usury. It rules out capitalizing or profiting from the misery and labor of others, as do capitalist money lenders and employers. These things, which love rules out, sow discord and division and separate human persons, one from another. In particular, territorial state practices undermine love and render persons remote from one another and thus God. Territorial state practices are fundamentally impersonal and divisive, so that they contradict truths inherent in Christian revelation. That is, territorial state practices implicitly and explicitly deny the unity of humanity, the dignity of individual persons, and the primacy of love that is implied by the idea that persons are all members of the Mystical Body of Christ.

It was the fact that territorial states engage in practices that are antithetical to love that left Day in agreement with Tolstoy. For Day, Christian love, properly understood, requires going beyond the territorial state (and the capitalist economy), since the territorial state is a coercive and violent entity that sustains and perpetuates an arrangement marked by exploitation and oppression. To Day, Christian love implies anarchism; indeed, it entails *strong* anarchism. Because the territorial state is unjust and makes us agents of injustice and the causes of suffering, persons should attempt to replace it with some other type of political organization.[75] To that end, Day and other Catholic Workers advocated "a complete rejection of the present social order and a non-violent revolution to establish an order more in accord with Christian values."[76] In announcing a commitment to abolishing the territorial state through nonviolent means, Day belongs to a significant line of anarchists who have advocated and continue to advocate for nonviolent rather than violent revolution.

Popular perception notwithstanding, nonviolent anarchists probably outnumber anarchist proponents of violent revolution. Part of this has to do with the conditions under which anarchist thought has developed. Anarchism emerged in tandem with the rise of Marxist variants of communism and socialism and has been regarded as an alternative to Marxist political theories and revolutionary strategies. Consequently, anarchists have tended to reject hierarchical centralized organizations, including political parties and the territorial state, as a means by which to realize the ideal society. As David Graeber has argued, because the rejection of Marxist communist revolutionary strategies has fundamentally shaped the development of anarchist theory in general, anarchism can properly be regarded as a philosophy of means: "Marxism has tended to be a theoretical or analytical discourse about revolutionary strategy; anarchism, an ethical discourse about revolutionary practice."[77] Anarchist discourse about practice has focused on the morally acceptable and practically efficacious means through which to realize ideal ends. Anarchist social theorist Murray Bookchin in his classic work, *Post-Scarcity Anarchism*, states well the general anarchist idea of the inseparability of means and ends: "There can be no separation of the revolutionary process from the revolutionary goal. A society based on self-administration [i.e. inclusive administration] must be achieved by means of self-administration."[78]

Because anarchists have asserted the inseparability of means and ends, many anarchists have gravitated to nonviolent theories of social change, so as to give an account of how it is possible to enact noncoercive or nonviolent social change. In consequence, anarchist thought converges at critical points with pacifist thought, even if not all anarchists have been pacifists. Quakers and other Christian pacifists were among the principal early theorists of nonviolent social change. For Christian pacifists interested in participating in the social sphere without endorsing or employing violence, a critical challenge was establishing how in practice one could be socially or politically engaged and remain a faithful (nonviolent) Christian. In early nineteenth-century America, opponents of slavery began to argue that certain kinds of nonviolent action or resistance could transform the social order. At least since the nonresistance of William Lloyd Garrison in the 1830s, religious radicals have consciously theorized the revolutionary implications of principled noncooperation with unjust or evil actors.

Thoreau, to repeat points made in Chapter 1, was influenced by and contributed to the theory of nonviolent social change. Recall that Thoreau posited the possibility of a "peaceable revolution" being effectuated by a coincidence of refusals (to serve or support unjust institutional practices). Nonviolent theories of social change developed from the mid-nineteenth century and were nearly fully developed by the time Day reached maturity. In the American context, nonviolent activists drew inspiration from Thoreau's "Resistance to Civil Government," Tolstoy's *The Kingdom of God Is Within* (1893), Richard Gregg's *The Power of Non-Violence* (1934, Gandhi's activism in South Africa and India, and the thought and praxis of radical pacifist A. J. Muste. With such inspiration, Americans in the early to mid-twentieth century had begun to propose noncooperation and withdrawal of support from existing authorities as the means by which to make revolution.

Day, of course, was also influenced by and contributed to the development of nonviolent theories of social change. Enunciating a position not too different from Garrison, Thoreau, Tolstoy, and Gandhi, Day contends that in order to abolish the territorial state, persons must only withdraw their support from it, which is to refuse to contribute to its unjust practices. Day suggests that taking personal responsibility entails noncooperation with or the withdrawal of support from both the territorial state and capitalistic enterprises. On her view, the territorial state and the war economy survive only because there are everywhere persons *willing* to serve in the military, work in the armaments industry, pay taxes, and so on. What is needed, say Day and Catholic Workers, is persons willing to refuse cooperation: "Refusal to pay taxes, refusal to register for conscription, refusal to take part in civil-defense drills, non-violent strikes, withdrawal from the system are all methods that can be employed in this fight for justice."[79] To refuse service is to *will* a revolution.[80]

As we might expect, Day links habits of consumption to the maintenance of the military industrial complex and the capitalist social order and thus politicizes or moralizes the question of consumptive habits in a way that brings Thoreau to mind. In an especially telling passage in *Loaves and Fishes*, Day maintains that responsible persons must "avoid being comfortable through the exploitation of others" and insists that persons "can [at least] avoid physical wealth as the result of the war economy."[81] As I indicated in the first chapter, Thoreau regarded asceticism or voluntary poverty as an indispensable part of liberation in the context of modern capitalistic economies. Day follows Thoreau: "There may be ever-improving standards of living in the United States, with every worker eventually owning his own home and driving his own car; but our whole modern economy is based on preparation for war, and this surely is one of the great arguments for poverty in our time."[82]

Day commends voluntary poverty for several reasons, two of which I will mention. First, from a strictly moral vantage, it is commendable to evade complicity in exploitative and oppressive economic practices; indeed, it is probably only by embracing voluntary poverty that one can avoid committing certain wrongs, given the fact that in modern societies most commodities are produced and most wealth is accumulated by exploiting and defrauding the destitute, the involuntarily poor.[83] Voluntary poverty is also important as a type of withdrawal or refusal in that it can have palpable practical consequences. In short, the (politically conscious) voluntarily poor person is essentially engaged in a perpetual boycott and a permanent strike, such that voluntary poverty can be revolutionary.

To be clear, while I have thus far presented Day's prescription to modern social injustices in mostly negative terms, a key aspect of Day's thought and praxis was the emphasis that she gave to positive or constructive alternatives to the status quo. In a fashion once again comparable to Thoreau, Day encourages persons to develop alternative social arrangements through radical experimentation. In many respects, Day prescribes negative action primarily in service of the positive: persons are encouraged to withdraw from certain social practices so as to undermine those practices and thus create space for the emergence of new institutions and novel forms of political organization. Revolution, then, consists in a radical transformation of social practices that includes political and economic matters.

Integral to Day's normative project is the idea that activists should develop alternative economic practices. She regarded the establishment of decentralized local-based economies as particularly promising:

> We are beginning the farm as humbly as we began *The Catholic Worker* which started with no staff, no headquarters, no mailing list and no money. But this small beginning is part of our propaganda. St. Francis says you cannot know what you have not practiced. From now on when we write about the land movement as a cure for unemployment we will be writing about a small group of people who are on the land. . . . This experiment, written about from month to month, should be of interest to groups of families, to the unemployed, to the college graduate who comes out of school and does not know which way to turn.[84]

Day's radical experimentation constitutes an attempt to put ideals (love) into practice and to write about the experiment in order to inspire others to initiate their own experiments, so that the deed (experimentation) is both itself propaganda and the source of propaganda. Day envisaged the emergence of farm communes and cooperative economic endeavors that would eventually usurp capitalistic practices, thus rendering them unnecessary.[85]

In the long term, small villages, with surrounding farms, would replace the overcrowded capitalist metropolis. In such villages, the "means of production and distribution" would be worker-owned, thus eliminating "a distinct employer class."[86] Wealth would be collectively and more or less equally distributed (yet not necessarily collectively owned or controlled). And labor would be as united as is possible.[87] Doing away with the employer class, says Day, would lessen the need for repressive mechanisms prevalent in capitalistic social orders ruled by territorial state actors. Therefore, for Day, economic experimentation constitutes an extension of the refusal to contribute to the territorial state's political processes. One withdraws in order to create cooperatives. In fact, according to Day, the revolution itself can be "accomplished by decentralized co-operatives." This, says Day, would be "revolution from below."[88]

Day regarded a nonviolent revolution from below, effectuated through decentralized cooperatives, as a way to generate social change through means that would prefigure the beloved community, and thus be not only consistent with the dictates of Christian love, but also be an expression of it. As should be clear, Day embraced strong anarchism, as she both denied the legitimate authority of the state and advocated its elimination. It should also be clear that religious reasons informed her rejection of the territorial state and capitalist economies. And Day is in good company. Agrarian idealism has been espoused by Russians Tolstoy and Kropotkin and American Southern Agrarians, such as Allen Tate and Robert Penn Warren. And in the midst of urban decay and the emergence of massive permanent unemployment across the globe during the twentieth century, it is easy to appreciate why radical communitarians have proposed an agrarian return as the solution to contemporary social problems. Uninhabited land abounds. Farming, said Day, is dignified work, if there is any. With a return to the land, unemployment and food crises would be solved at once. We should also keep in mind the crime and social fragmentation that has plagued poor people displaced from the land and thrust into crowded inhospitable urban jungles across the world in recent decades, from Rio de Janeiro to Mumbai, before we dismiss Day's vision.

However, a few questions remain. In particular, after reflecting on Day's criticisms of the modern social order and her prescription, one is probably left with questions about the viability of her program. Does not Day overstate the chances of realizing a nonviolent revolution from below? I will address this question in a roundabout way. At various points in this chapter I have described Day's anarchism in a way that suggests that she shares much in common with certain right-libertarians and with democratic socialists. It might be edifying to ponder exactly how Day is similar to or different from certain right-libertarians (who posit the existence of the territorial state as an impediment to economic freedom, innovation, and growth) and democratic socialists (who criticize capitalist economies). This may appear to be an odd direction in which to carry my analysis of Day, yet taking up the question about how Day's normative political philosophy compares with certain strands of right-libertarianism and democratic socialism will allow us to consider pertinent aspects of the larger American political-ideological landscape and at the same time shore up our understanding of Day's anarchist commitments.

# VI

Students of American political philosophies, theories, or ideologies will probably be unsurprised by the fact that, as a political philosophical matter, it is quite difficult (and perhaps impossible) to differentiate a (consistent) right-libertarian from Day. And there are good reasons for this difficulty. To begin with, from the mid-nineteenth century up to present, many anarchists on both the political left and the right have used the term libertarian synonymously with the term anarchist. Right-libertarians, at least *radical* right-libertarians, belong to what Murray Rothbard has referred to as the Old Right, and the Old Right emerged in response to New Deal policies and the rise of the welfare or managerial state. According to Rothbard,

> [T]he Old Right was born and had its being as the opposition movement to the New Deal, and to everything, foreign and domestic, that the New Deal encompassed: at first, to burgeoning New Deal statism at home, and then, later in the '30s, to the drive for American global intervention abroad. Since the essence of the Old Right was a reaction against runaway Big Government at home and overseas, this meant that the Old Right was necessarily, even if not always consciously, libertarian rather than statist, "radical" rather than traditional conservative apologists of the existing order.[89]

Crucially, major contributors to the Old Right—Ludwig von Mises, F. A. Hayek, and Frank Chodorov, for instance—were repulsed by any suggestion that they were conservative.[90] Chodorov, for his part, once quipped, "As for me, I will punch anyone who calls me a conservative in the nose. I am a radical."[91] Chodorov was clearly no absolute pacifist, yet he and other members of the Old Right were staunch critics of American imperialism, which placed them closer to leftists such as Day than is often appreciated.

The Old Right's decline was precipitated by the emergence of the Cold War; for, as the politics of the Cold War took shape, the political right realigned around national security issues, and in the process the libertarian mantle was (ostensibly and ironically) taken over by anti-Soviet interventionists, that is, war hawks, of the New Right. Whereas members of the Old Right had opposed militarism, members of the New Right, such as Barry Goldwater or William F. Buckley Jr, trumpeted the need for a strong American military, to counter the Soviet Union and the communist menace, and framed this as a defense of liberty and freedom. Even though anti-imperialist and antistatist libertarian activists have often eschewed identification with the Republican Party, and either opted to align with the Libertarian Party or altogether rejected electoral politics, often-enough such activists have entered into alliances with the Republican Party, given its historical anti-interventionism (pejoratively derided as "isolationism"), antifederalism, and antitaxation stance.

The synthesis or attempted synthesis of libertarianism with conservativism and the alliance of certain libertarians with the Republican Party led to the development of conservative-libertarianism, which has obscured the character of right-libertarianism. In practice, right-libertarianism is often reduced to conservative-libertarianism.[92] But, importantly, the Old Right and *radical* right-libertarians should be distinguished from *conservative* right-libertarians and the New Right that is so often identified with the contemporary Republican Party.

Keeping the distinction between radical right-libertarians and conservative-libertarians in mind is actually easier to do when the focus is on certain political philosophical principles, particularly normative conceptions of political authority and obligation. So, once again, it is imperative to acknowledge that there are in fact right-libertarians, such as Walter Block and Roderick T. Long, who are consistent antiauthoritarians and anti-imperialists. Long's social thought represents an illustrative example. Equating anarchism with libertarianism, Long refers to himself as a "market anarchist" and a right-libertarian. As a substantive matter, he maintains that he is committed not to eliminating government as such, but only to abolishing any centralized governmental entity that is controlled by a small segment of society. In Long's words, "anarchy is a situation in which government is extended to include everybody . . . [This] diffused legal system is preferable on pragmatic grounds because anarchy multiplies checks and balances: handing all power over to a single monopoly agency [i.e. the state] is too risky."[93] Long, then, more or less presents a case for decentralized government by explicit and universal consent.

Radical right-libertarians such as Long espouse political philosophical commitments that overlap at important points with the vision that Dorothy Day embraced. This fact has potential practical political implications or implications for a possible social movement. Indeed, there are reasons to believe that there will likely be a major anarchist or libertarian social movement in America and beyond in the coming years. And if there is a widespread anarchist/libertarian social movement in twenty-first-century America, it will likely consist of a reshuffling of the political-ideological landscape such that left- and right-libertarians (and this includes various kinds of anarchists) unite around a mutual opposition to centralization and authoritarian institutions. For this to happen, the similarities will have to be made clear and explicit. It will be critical too for the differences to be confronted, analyzed, and debated. In practice, the viability of any coalition between right- and left-libertarians will likely hinge on economic-related questions, and it is on the economic front that the differences between Day and right-libertarians are most on display.

Crudely speaking, left-libertarians are generally libertarian-socialists whereas radical right-libertarians are generally libertarian-capitalists. Indeed, because so many right-libertarians are unmistakably procapitalism, a large number of contemporary radical right-libertarians in fact self-describe as anarchist-capitalists (anarcho-capitalists) or market anarchists. Day, of course, sides with the leftists, including left-libertarians, with respect to economic issues. Day thus embraced a theory of the emergence of the territorial state that many radical right-libertarians disagree with.[94] And Day doubted that capitalism could be sustained outside of the context of the modern territorial state, with its concentration of power in the hands of wealthy elites and technocrats. Finally, Day and radical right-libertarians such as Walter Block or Roderick Long take different stances with respect to the question of the *moral* permissibility of practices such as usury. Indeed, Long and other radical right-libertarians assert that persons have a right to private property and understand this right to include a right to sell or alienate one's labor power and the right to purchase persons' labor power or employ others as workers.[95]

The differences are unmistakable. Yet, it is unclear what follows (especially as a political philosophical matter) from this moral disagreement about capitalism or economic rights. To appreciate why this is so we have to keep in mind Day's conception of the means by which a revolution can and should be accomplished. Because Day's commitment to nonviolent revolution is an extension of her commitment to love or moral autonomy, her criticisms of capitalist economic practices would not necessarily stand in the way of a person with her commitments from collaborating with radical right-libertarian proponents of capitalism. This owes to the fact that Day and radical right-libertarians share a commitment to noncoercive institutional practices; and they both assert that an ideal social order is one in which coercion is nonexistent and where governmental or political entities operate based on the universal consent of the relevant population of persons. Thus, radical right-libertarians, no less than anarchist proponents of nonviolent revolution, would have moral reasons to rely on purely nonviolent means as a way to abolish the territorial state.

Ironically, in practice, left anarchists such as Day might encounter greater difficulty in entering into sustained coalitions with leftist progressives, including democratic socialists, than with radical right-libertarians. This is because such leftists typically take the fact of centralization for granted. The late Michael Harrington and Cornel West are two leading leftists of this type. Michael Harrington served as an editor for the *Catholic Worker* in the

1950s. His departure from the Catholic Church influenced his decision to part ways with the Catholic Worker. And Harrington decided to leave the Catholic Church in part because of his conversion to Marxist socialism. By the late 1950s, Harrington regarded anarchist politics as impractical. Centralization was unavoidable in the postindustrial social order. After reaching this conclusion, Harrington would go on to give a great deal of his energy to lobbying government, that is, seeking to influence the legislative process. Harrington was aware of the limitations of this approach; yet he regarded Lyndon B. Johnson's Great Society programs as promising—even if limited—developments, developments that could over time result in a socialist state, or the socializing of the state.

Cornel West, a close collaborator with Harrington during the 1970s and 1980s, shares much in common with Harrington. Importantly, if anarchists, especially Christian anarchists, are to unite with democratic socialists, then it would be with someone similar to West, in that he is a prophetic Christian and because he is sympathetic to the libertarian cause. West favors a form of "democratic and libertarian socialism" that provides mechanisms that engender universal "participation in the decision-making processes of those major institutions which guide and regulate our lives." This emphasis stems from West's Christian conception of the role of the human person in social life. According to West, it is an egalitarian mandate: "all human creatures are made in the image of God and thereby endowed with a certain dignity and respect that warrants particular treatment, including a chance to fulfill their capacities and potentialities."[96] Yet, significantly, West stops short of endorsing libertarian decentralization and thus joins contemporary democratic socialist critics of decentralists.[97]

In general, most democratic socialists assume (1) either that centralization is inevitable or desirable and (2) that radical reform is an effective way to promote social change and social justice. These two assumptions motivate a politics that centers in many respects on seeking control of the territorial state apparatus. Consistent with this, West has concentrated his energies on two things in the political sphere. First, West has supported efforts to cultivate interracial grassroots activism with the hope of catalyzing a social movement that forces the state to transform its practices in the areas of criminal justice, foreign policy, treatment of the poor, and its relationship to the business elite—holding elites accountable to the demos. In addition, West has supported progressive politicians at various levels, hoping to put into political office persons committed to progressive politics. One gets the sense that West believes that large-scale social change and movement in the American context revolves around the electoral process, particularly at the national level. West thus belongs to a tradition of radical activists that includes William Jennings Bryan, Eugene Debs, Norman Thomas, and Ralph Nader, although West has never accepted a party's nomination of him as a candidate for political office.[98] In the following chapter we will see that, during the last part of his career, Bayard Rustin anticipated West, becoming toward the end of the 1960s one of America's most vocal critics of decentralist projects. He and other leftists predicate their rejection of decentralist projects such as Day's on practical reasons. On their view, Day's program is unrealistic and bound to fail. At best it will have no impact. At worst it will sap energy from more productive activist projects. I mention this only in order to point to an issue that will have to be addressed if there is to be a sustainable coalition between social democrats such as West and strong anarchists of Day's mold.

Day recognized the challenge presented by democratic socialists as a serious one, yet she stopped short of conceding the inevitability of centralization. Instead, she conceded only that realizing the nonviolent revolution from below would be an arduous and slow process. This is no trivial issue, as it is impossible to generate significant social change or sustain a social movement unless the persons involved see some prospect of progress. Acknowledging this potential *motivation problem*, Day once issued a warning to young activists: "We have a big program but we warn our fellow workers to keep in mind small beginnings."[99] So, we might say that, on Day's view, the major difficulty with her prescribed action is that it requires more patience than many social justice activists possess. Appropriately, Day responds to what I am calling a motivation problem with a theory of social change. Implicit in Day's theory of social change are both a religious conception of time and, at least ostensibly, a nonreligious theory of perpetual (nonviolent) revolution. I say ostensibly nonreligious in that Day's theory of revolution is best understood in relation to her Christian conception of time (and grace).

Day mentions her "sense of time" explicitly during an interview with biographer Robert Coles in a response to a question about whether or not she could be properly described as overly idealistic. After reflecting intently on the question, which she had heard many times before, Day interrupted the silence with a telling response: "Sometimes when people call me a utopian, I say no, I just have a different sense of time than many others have."[100] Day's sense of time differs from others in at least two related ways.

First, she explicates a Christian vision of time that is often referred to as a realized eschatology. The "eschaton" is often taken to refer to the end of time or the final period of time. To articulate a realized eschatology is to assert that there is no fundamental division between time and the period beyond time. Along these lines, taking solace in St. Catherine's notion that "'All the way to heaven is heaven,' because He had said, 'I am the way,'" Day announces that "time and eternity are one."[101] The conception of time that Day adduces in response to the democratic socialist challenge relates back to our earlier consideration of Day's perfectionism. It is a sense of time that is inflected with a religious sensibility, making it impossible to understand Day's movement through space over time without reference to her religiosity.

I indicated earlier the way in which Day understood personal responsibility to require a radical concentration on the concrete present—particular acts at specific moments. Recall that Day suggests that in order to become perfect, one must concentrate on being perfect. A more just social order, contends Day, begins with *each* of us devoting ourselves to imaginative and creative means by which to transform ourselves into instruments of justice. The fact that an ideal seems difficult or impossible to attain does not rule out its viability as an ethical norm. The ideal—an anarchist social order—is a possibility if only we will pursue it incessantly. The realization of this possibility—the beloved community—is contingent upon each person assuming moral responsibility for his or her actions at all times. One must lay one brick at a time, and hope that others lay theirs. We as individual persons must perform "daily duties, simple and small, but constant."[102]

This relates to the second way in which Day's sense of time differs from others. Day, perhaps paradoxically, takes a longer view of history than many others. She maintains that individual persons and communities can transcend time through a faith that unites them with ancestors and descendents. She relates,

> We are communities in time and in a place, I know, but we are communities in faith as well—and sometimes time can stop shadowing us. Our lives are touched by those who lived centuries ago, and we hope that our lives will mean something to people who won't be alive until centuries from now. It is a great "chain of being," someone once told me, and I think our job is to do the best we can to hold up our small segment of that chain.[103]

To understand how all of this relates to the question of the practicability of Day's decentralist project we must appreciate the essential aspects of the alternative theory of social change that Day and other nonviolent activists and theorists, especially anarchists, have been articulating for nearly a century.

Such activists and theorists have made two moves worth noting. First, as I have already suggested, they have pressed for a reconsideration of the types of acts that qualify as veritable means through which to effectuate revolution. Second, they have offered reconceptualized notions of how (time as a unit should be employed) to measure the effects of the chosen revolutionary means. This can be stated more simply. Many nonviolent and anarchist theorists and activists regard certain acts or actions as revolutionary that others are inclined to discount as revolutionary (or political); and these theorists and activists maintain that the larger social consequences of revolutionary action is difficult to assess immediately and so the immediate evaluation of revolutionary action should focus on the degree to which the chosen means prefigure the sought after end.

David Graeber aptly captures the essence of the meaning that revolution has for many radical nonviolent and anarchist theorists and activists in his essay, "The New Anarchists," where he suggests that we should "stop thinking about a revolution as a cataclysmic break" and instead focus on what constitutes revolutionary action. According to Graeber, "Revolutionary action is any collective action which rejects, and therefore confronts, some form of power or domination and in doing so, reconstitutes social relations." He continues,

> Revolutionary action does not necessarily have to aim to topple governments. Attempts to create autonomous communities in the face of power . . . would, for instance, be almost by definition revolutionary acts. And history shows us that the continual accumulation of such acts can change (almost) everything.[104]

In Day's case, a Christian conception of time (or temporality-logic) shapes what might be called a nonviolent revolutionary view of sociopolitical action and so undergirds a conception of perpetual revolution. With something like Graeber's view of revolution in mind, Day lauds the patience that inspires the doing of small things. This is how the revolution will be continued. The territorial state and centralization may be inevitable for *now*. But radical social action—withdrawal, refusal, experimentation—in the now interrupts the status quo and over time can change everything. As Thoreau said, "Revolutions are never sudden."

What differentiates Day from many other nonviolent and anarchist theorists and activists is that Day's anarchist vision of a beloved community was religious all the way down. This should be clear by now. Yet to make it clearer, we can conclude our analysis of Day by returning to Day's conversion narrative. In a passage in *From Union Square to Rome*, where Day is attempting to explain to her brother John Day why Marxist communism is misguided, Day targets a central tenet of classical Marxist communist social theory and posits the indispensability of religion to the realization of the beloved community: "Communism is a good word, a Christian word originally, but to expect to achieve a state of society in which all is held in common, where the state will 'wither away' through state socialism, maintained through a dictatorship of the proletariat, this is impossible for a reasonable person to believe. It is only through religion that communism can be achieved."[105]

Day regarded religion as indispensable to social justice movements not simply because many oppressed persons are religious and so will be averse to contributing to movements that are militantly atheistic or antireligious. Instead, Day has in mind the role that religious practice itself plays in engendering the strength to strive after and struggle for freedom and social justice. And, in truth, Day does not have in mind just any religion. According to Day, the Catholic Church is the principal vehicle of the Holy Spirit in the temporal order and the Church's sacraments keep the Christian disciple spiritually nourished and so able to see beyond the shadow of time and place. More to the point, Day had her doubts about whether it is possible to maintain what William James referred to as the strenuous mood without the sacramental ritual life provided by the Roman Catholic Church and its priests. So, in the end, Day's response to the challenge posed by democratic socialists—and to the motivation problem—is clearly a religious one.

It is not clear whether a large number of non-Catholic Christians, non-Christians, or atheists would find Day's expression of perpetual revolution compelling, given how tied up it is with her idiosyncratic theological assumptions, which raises a vital question for students of religion, ethics, and politics. Is Day's normative vision inclusive enough to be viable in a pluralistic society? I will not discuss this issue in depth in this work, yet I will say that I do not think that a Catholic Christian anarchist such as Day will, in practice, have problems accounting for how to deal with the problem of tolerance or inclusion. But even if Day can give an account of how non-Catholics can be included in decentralized anarchist social orders, Day's conception of the role of the Catholic Church and its priests raises other issues. In particular, can anarchism become the predominant or even a prevalent form of political organization? If Day's view of the essential role of the Catholic Church in social life is correct, then it must be asked, can non-Catholic anarchists cultivate the habits and the qualities of character necessary for the sustenance of an anarchist social order?

Day never addressed this issue directly and it is difficult to say precisely how she would respond to it. Yet, I suspect that she would suggest that we cannot know what is practical until we have actually put love in action, which is precisely why, in Day's radical imagination, experimentation and faith must combine. For Day, experimentation is a religious duty in that it is our responsibility as persons to live in ways that makes possible the emergence of the beloved community. It is an experiment precisely because a certain uncertainty circles our quests for revolutionized social relations. In *Loaves and Fishes*, Day intimates that Catholic Worker houses were home to a

> slipshod group of individuals who were trying to work out certain principles—the chief of which was an analysis of man's freedom and what it implied. . . . We were trying to overcome hatred with love, to understand the forces that made men what they are, to learn something of their backgrounds, their education, to change them, if possible, from lions to lambs. It was a practice in loving, a learning to love, a paying the cost of love.[106]

Day was concerned to understand what a Christian must become and what a Christian must do. Her answer was radical. A Christian must become love and must love beyond the state. This is a profound responsibility that Day would have us take up. And it is daunting, for me, to even think about what it would mean for me to truly put love in practice. Yet even if we find the idea of displacing and replacing the territorial state as untenable or impractical, we should not avoid asking the ethical questions. What must I do? Who must I be and become? Given the horrors and the oppression that mark our social milieu, what is unacceptable is the idea that we can do no better than the status quo. We can do better and we must. Day reminds us of this. We will not do better until we take up these questions with her urgency and reclaim moral responsibility. We do well, then, to give Day more of our attention than we have, even if her prophetic witness is unnerving in what it asks of us.

Reflecting on Dorothy Day's life has given rise to a series of questions that a person might pose to herself or himself. Should I be a Christian? Should I be a Catholic Christian? What are the moral obligations that one takes on as a Catholic Christian? What are the dictates of Christian love? Is it possible to live up to the Christian love ethic? Does Christian love imply absolute pacifism? Does absolute pacifism imply strong anarchism? These are profoundly important questions for any human person who has been presented with them, but especially pressing for the person who answers yes to any or all of them.

In the next chapter, I would like to reflect on a person who answers in the affirmative to more than one of the above questions. Specifically, I will consider issues related to the above questions via a descriptive ethical case study of the religious-ethical and sociopolitical philosophy and practice of African American public intellectual and social activist Bayard Rustin. Reflecting on Rustin's life will shed surprising light on the above concerns and thus the question that animates this work as a whole. What are the sources of anarchism and the implications of anarchism for other moral values and ethical commitments?

# 3

# The dilemma of the black radical: Bayard Rustin's ambivalent anarchism

*Let your life be a counter friction to stop the machine.*
HENRY DAVID THOREAU

*We need in every community a group of angelic troublemakers. Our power is in our ability to make things unworkable. All we have is our bodies. We need to tuck them, tuck them in places so that the wheels don't turn.*
BAYARD RUSTIN

## I

Strom Thurmond introduced Bayard Rustin to greater America in 1963. The seasoned white supremacist, hoping to delegitimize the March on Washington by smearing Rustin, its principle organizer, took the senate floor, calling Rustin a "draft-dodging, communist, pervert." Rustin survived the senator's onslaught, overseeing perhaps the most influential political gathering in American history. But for all of Rustin's work at the center of American social movement organizing and his influence on American social and political history, he has been aptly called "Brother Outsider."

Rustin's homosexuality meant that for much of the modern civil rights movement he was relegated to the margins, the shadows. But in an ironic twist, Rustin's marginal status as an openly homosexual black male has recently thrust him into the center of contemporary academic and activist circles, with queer theorists and queer liberation activists leading the charge to recover Rustin's story. With a 10,000 page FBI file, Rustin's most influential years might rest in the future.

As a contributor to nearly every major American leftist movement from the mid-1930s through the end of the 1980s, Rustin's life defies facile definition. Raised in a black Quaker household in West Chester, Pennsylvania, Rustin entered the world on March 17, 1912, just as Teddy Roosevelt waged the last competitive third-party presidential campaign; Rustin's last hours came in August 1987, just as Ronald Reagan ended his second term as president and completed his effort to roll back the New Deal. There is hardly a leftist cause that Rustin, as a full-time activist, did not contribute to during the period running from 1932 to 1987.

By his mid-twenties, a self-styled Gandhian Quaker, Rustin had immersed himself in the antiwar and communist movements. In 1936 Rustin joined the Young Communist League, an organization that accepted as members "all proletariats" between the ages 14 and 30. And Rustin found himself living in the hotbed of black intellectual and political life when he moved to Harlem in 1937. In Harlem, Rustin made two acquaintances that would transform his life. To begin, Rustin met A. Philip Randolph who later appointed Rustin as principal organizer of the March on Washington Movement during the 1940s and the March for Jobs and Freedom in 1963. During this time Rustin would also befriend A. J. Muste, who became director of the Fellowship of Reconciliation in 1941 and added Rustin to his staff soon after. Involved in two organizations that had long utilized mass protest and organized civil disobedience to challenge the status quo, Rustin helped bridge the work of Muste's FOR and Randolph's Brotherhood of Sleeping Car Porters.

From 1941 through 1952 Rustin worked as FOR's youth secretary and then led its race relations efforts; he followed that with a stint with the War Resisters League. During this time he became intimately involved in the civil rights movement, organizing several major initiatives and demonstrations, including serving as a founding member of the Congress for Racial Equality and the Southern Christian Leadership Conference, and serving as an "adult" adviser to the Student Nonviolent Coordinating Committee. And as is widely known, he was a longtime adviser to Martin Luther King Jr, leading some to refer to Rustin as the mastermind *behind* the modern civil rights movement. Toward the end of the 1960s he directed the A. Phillip Randolph Institute, a position funded in part by the American Federation of Labor, giving him an opportunity to concentrate his efforts on economic justice.

During the course of his career, Rustin worked alongside Norman Thomas, Evan Thomas, Eleanor Roosevelt, James Farmer, George Houser, Bill Sutherland, Michael Harrington, Ella Baker, Bob Moses, Stokely Carmichael, Staughton Lynd, and Walter Reuther, just to name a few. Internationally, for most of the 1940s and 1950s Rustin was the face of the burgeoning civil rights movement. He traveled to India to meet with Nehru in 1948; he worked with Nkrumah in Ghana in the early 1950s. Later, in the early to mid-1980s, he spent time in South Africa with figures such as Desmond Tutu and Poland with Lech Walesa as activists in those places organized Gandhian styled nonviolent revolutions.

Those familiar with Rustin's activism may find surprising my assertion that he can be classified as an anarchist. Asserting that Rustin was an anarchist is likely to be rejected altogether by those who remember Rustin for his insistence on the importance of a strong state for the liberation of the marginalized and oppressed. Dissimilar from Henry David Thoreau and Dorothy Day, Rustin did not publicly denounce the state as such. He did not reject electoral politics. He did not take up a Federalist position. Rather, he devoted the better part of his middle to late career as an activist lobbying the American federal government in one form or another, seeking the passage of new legislation. Thus it would appear at first an error, some great confusion to attach the appellation anarchist to Bayard Rustin. He was many things: black in the Jim Crow era, Communist in the Age of McCarthy, gay before Stonewall, and a pacifist in the age of fascism, Nazism, and the Cold War. But how could he be an anarchist?

To answer this question we must simply appreciate that, while many aspects of Rustin's activist career are open to question, there is no doubt about his status as one of the world's leading radical pacifists and proponents of nonviolent direct action some three decades before Randolph called on him to organize the March on Washington in 1963. Rustin's commitment to radical pacifism is crucial for our purposes in that, if I am correct, it has as its implication an anarchist ethic. Specifically, in my view, *radical* pacifism entails an acceptance of *strong* anarchism. A person can be a strong anarchist without being a pacifist, yet an absolute pacifist must reject the modern territorial state, and so should be categorized as some kind of anarchist.

Pacifism comes in many varieties, yet as a general matter pacifists are opposed to political violence, particularly the practice of war. There are *absolute* and *nonabsolute* pacifists. *Nonabsolute* pacifists reject war as a social practice and sometimes reject all organized violence, including that employed by domestic police; but nonabsolute pacifists may allow for the private use of violence in order to fend off unjust attackers. Many nonabsolute pacifists describe themselves as *contingent* pacifists. Contingent pacifists essentially maintain that most but not all wars are wrong. *Absolute* pacifists, on the other hand, regard all intentional killing as wrong, even objecting to the personal-private employment of violence in cases where a person is being unjustly attacked. So contrary to contingent pacifists, absolute pacifists assert that war is always wrong.

Pacifism comes in both pragmatic and principled versions. Contingent pacifists are ordinarily *pragmatic* pacifists whereas absolute pacifists are typically *principled* pacifists in that they base their pacifism on (a priori) principles. Pragmatic pacifists do not argue that war is wrong because it is always morally wrong to intentionally kill individual persons. Rather, pragmatic pacifists assert that war should be opposed because war represents an *ineffective* way to realize the ends that are ordinarily presented in order to justify recourse to war. Nuclear pacifists, that is, pacifists who argue that war is obsolete in the light of the proliferation of nuclear weaponry, are probably best described as pragmatic (contingent) pacifists: their rejection or acceptance of war is *contingent* on certain material conditions, conditions that if altered would in turn necessitate a changed stance vis-à-vis the moral acceptability of war.

The majority of pacifist activists during the period just prior to and just after World War I were nonabsolute pacifists—progressive reformers who concentrated their activism on building coalitions of pacifists and striving to create a permanent international congress to mediate and arbitrate disputes between territorial states so as to avoid war.[1] This group included John Dewey, Jane Addams, and Jessie Wallace Hughan. Reform-oriented organizations established between 1915 and 1920 include the Women's Peace Party-New York Branch (1915) and the Women's International League for Peace and Freedom (1919). These organizations belonged to the Outlawry Movement and participated in advocacy for treaties such as the Kellogg-Briand Pact, which made war illegal and was a precursor to the United Nations system of international law.

We can hardly understand leftist activism in contemporary America if we don't appreciate the importance of the contingent of *radical* pacifists who emerged from the period of promise and upheaval that marked the first decades of the twentieth century. Several factors radicalized a segment of the peace movement during the 1920s and 1930s. First, the devastation wrought by World War I convinced many that reforming the territorial state system (i.e. the Westphalian system)—a system that arose with the Peace of Westphalia and culminated with the Treaty of Paris and Vienna Congress that coincided with the defeat of Napoleon in 1815—would be insufficient. Abolishing the system would be the only way to save "humankind." The increased connection between the socialist and pacifist movements during the period between 1915 and the late 1920s also affected pacifist activists. In particular, socialist and pacifist criticisms of colonialism and attribution of the cause of World War I to the "Scramble for Africa" led to analyses that linked the violence of the territorial state to racism and capitalism. Third, the Bolshevik Revolution in Russia excited revolutionaries and reformers, pacifist and socialist alike. The overthrow of the Russian Tsar confirmed a belief that had moved many activists during the end of the second decade of the twentieth century—the belief in the possibility of the radical transformation of society. For the first time since perhaps the American and French revolutions (of the 1770s through 1790s) it seemed manifestly clear that the social world could be remade. In such a context, reformers became radical revolutionaries. This brings us to the final major radicalizing cause that warrants mention. Anticolonialism in India captivated the world. Mohandas Gandhi's *satyagraha* and concomitant nonviolent direct action inspired pacifists from London to Chicago.

Radical pacifists, as Scott H. Bennett points out, are typically absolute pacifists who oppose "all wars or armed social revolution, support . . . both peace and social justice . . . [and advocate for] nonviolent social and democratic 'socialist' revolution."[2] With roots in the radical reformation, the American abolitionist movement, and socialism, radical pacifists maintain that only by radically transforming the social structure can war and injustice be eliminated, and they have insisted that individual persons are in fact capable of instigating social reconstruction. Following Garrison, Thoreau, Tolstoy, and Gandhi, radical pacifists maintain that evil social structures are only able to survive because so many people unconsciously cooperate with the rulers whose interests it is to preserve the structures. Noncooperation is proposed as a way to awaken one's fellows and as a way to deprive the state of the support that it needs in order to sustain its unjust practices. With the Indian example appearing to confirm the truth of Thoreauvian and Tolstoyan theories of social change, radical pacifists turned to advocacy for and exercise of nonviolent protest, resistance, and direct action, including political and civil disobedience.

The significance of radical pacifism during the late 1940s can hardly be overstated. Founding the Congress of Racial Equality (CORE) and conducting nonviolent direct action campaigns and training throughout the country, radical pacifists set the stage for the mass movement that emerged during the mid-1950s.[3] James R. Tracy describes them in *Direct Action: Radical Pacifism from the Union Eight to the Chicago Seven*:

> The radical pacifists who founded CORE operated in an American reform tradition that espoused faith that if a small group of people— or even an individual—behaves in a utopian fashion, the results could be revolutionary for the entire society. This reform tradition stretched back at least to the colonial Quakers and included Garrisonians and Thoreau, whose example radical pacifists often cited to support their actions.[4]

Speaking about the same group, D'Emilio intimates that Muste and FOR associates such as Jim Farmer, Glen Smiley, and Rustin belonged to a "new breed of pacifist" that helped redefine pacifist activism. This group turned wholeheartedly "to the example of Gandhi and the anticolonial movement he had spawned." According to D'Emilio, "Rustin was in the vanguard of this new confrontational approach that adapted Gandhian nonviolence to attacking racism in the United States."[5]

During the buildup to World War II Rustin, then a youth secretary with the FOR, traveled the country spreading the radical pacifist message and endeavoring to combat white supremacist oppression and militarism with Gandhian methods. FOR and its secular counterpart, the WRL, the nonreligious pacifist organization that emerged after World War I as an alternative to the religious Fellowship of Reconciliation, constituted a leading institution on the left wing of the peace movement. Under A. J. Muste's leadership, FOR organizers worked to forge a Christian radicalism that confront head-on the triple evils of modernity—capitalistic exploitation, militarism, and racism. What separated Muste's understudies from other radical leftists during our period was not simply a concern to combat the just mentioned evils or even the decision to pursue change via extrajudicial methods. Leninists, Social Gospel reformers, black separatists, suffragists, and others crowded the left toward the end of the Great Depression. Muste's concern to infuse American radicalism with a Gandhian ethos distinguished him from other notable activists and his encouragement of Rustin's interest in Gandhi proved remarkably important for Rustin's formation, and is an important factor as we endeavor to make political philosophical sense of Rustin's early activism and ethical commitments.

That so many persons have been designated Gandhians—Kwame Nkrumah, Martin Luther King Jr, Cesar Chavez, Lech Walesa, Desmond Tutu, Aung San Suu Kyi—makes it difficult to say exactly what being a Gandhian entails. That said, there are critical elements of Gandhian social philosophy uniting this disparate collection. Most important of course is the commitment to nonviolent resistance to social evil. And vital to this commitment is the mutual concern for self and others that implies love for enemies and underwrites the commitment to nonviolent action.[6] It is the Gandhian's concern with the oppressor and the oppressed alike that informs the insistence on nonviolence or un-harmful (a-himsa) action. The Gandhian hopes to act in a way that does not harm but does in fact move persons who support oppressive practices. Gandhians hope that their acts of nonviolent resistance to evil will move members of the oppressed and oppressive classes to refrain from complying with oppressive social institutions and practices. In short, Gandhians aspire to convert their opponents, to transform their hearts.

From the mid-1930s up to the mid-1960s Rustin adopted an ethos of love-inflected sacrificial political ethics and embraced Gandhian philosophy in the fullest sense. This is crucial because insofar as one is committed to Gandhian ethics in this way, one will refrain from employing violence to accomplish one's social and political objectives, even indirectly by calling on the territorial state for support. More to the point, I want to suggest that a Gandhian is disposed to embrace commitments that would if generalized dissolve the territorial state. In fact, insofar as a Gandhian is an absolute pacifist, it would seem to me that a Gandhian must be an anarchist of one variety or another. This crucial fact about Gandhian ethics provides a key to comprehending Rustin's career as an activist. As we move along, it will be clear that Rustin is unable to reconcile his commitment to radical pacifism and Gandhian nonviolence with his commitment to economic justice in the postindustrial era. Through the 1940s and 1950s, though, Rustin harbored no doubts about the viability of radical pacifism.

During this period Rustin and other radical pacifists, influenced by Gandhi, concentrated their efforts on combating two particular social evils: white supremacist oppression and militarism. With respect to these two issues, radical pacifists were willing to risk death, thereby living out the sacrificial ethical ethos exhibited by Indians in their confrontation with the British Empire. Reflecting his embrace of Gandhi's philosophy of nonviolence, in "The Negro and Nonviolence," Rustin announced that "Nonviolence as a method has within it the demand for terrible sacrifice and long suffering, but as Gandhi has said, 'freedom does not drop from the sky.' One has to struggle and be willing to die for it."[7] Rustin goes on to explain how his Quaker, Christian ethical commitments relate to his role in society and to state his view that self-reform is a precondition to social reform:

> The primary function of a religious society is to "speak truth to power." The truth is that war is wrong. It is then our duty to make war impossible first in us and then in society.[8]

Rustin echoes other American activists who have preached self-reformation as the precondition to social reformation and thus belongs to the tradition of radicals that emphasizes living and speaking in fidelity to one's notion of the truth. Striving to "be the change that he wished to see," and speaking "truth to power," in November of 1943, Rustin refused to register for the draft that had been instituted in preparation for the American entry into World War II.

Rustin charted an anxiety-ridden path toward draft resistance. Pacifists, especially radical pacifists, have often targeted the state's conscription laws as a way of striking out against the authority of the state as such, as conscription laws epitomize the character of the state's claim of authority over persons in that the state asserts a right to command individual persons to kill and be killed on its behalf. By the time he wrote his "Letter to the Draft Board," Rustin had been a wholehearted pacifist activist for eight years. And as a Quaker since 1936, Rustin had the option of declaring himself a religious conscientious objector and reporting to a Civilian Public Service Camp in lieu of military service.[9] Two factors motivated his decision to defy the Selective Service Act of 1940. To begin, at the time Rustin subscribed to a radical norm of nonviolence, one that put a premium on avoiding complying with immoral, unjust, and oppressive practices to the fullest extent possible. In practice evading complicity entailed adhering to a standard of noncooperation. This noncooperation had two intermingled components: (1) Refusing to cooperate with authorities, when the commands in question required commission of unjust acts, served as prophetic witness against those authorities; and (2) it had the potential of disrupting the smooth functioning of the unjust system (i.e. the machine). In addition to the imperative of noncooperation, and perhaps related to it, Rustin had reservations about taking advantage of the religious exemption to military service since that policy discriminated against nonreligious objectors.

The United States has a long history of religious exemption from military service. Indeed, the First Congress of the United States considered providing constitutional exemption from military service for religious reasons, although ultimately no such exemption was included in the Bill of Rights. Nonetheless, the Draft Acts passed during the Civil War and the two World Wars provided exemption for religious conscientious objectors. The Selective Service Act of 1917 (1917 Draft Act) (P.L. 65–12, 40 Sec. 76) extended exemptions to persons belonging to a "well-recognized religious sect or organization [then] organized and existing and whose existing creed or principles [forbade] its members to participate in war in any form." It was understood at the time that this only meant exemption for members of the historic peace churches—the Quakers, Mennonites, and Brethren. Most radical pacifists, anarchists, and atheists objected to the narrowness of the exemption. In the famous Selective Service Draft Law Cases of 1918 (245 US 366, 1918) the Supreme Court held that the privileging of persons belonging to pacifist religious sects did not violate the Establishment and Free Exercise (nondiscrimination) clauses of the First Amendment. Defendants in one of the draft cases, anarchists Emma Goldman and Alexander Berkman, convicted for "conspiring to impede registration," asserted that the 1917 Draft Act constituted a law "respecting the establishment of religion," "prohibiting the free exercise thereof," "establishing inequality." While the challenge to the narrowness of the exemption provided for in the 1917 Draft Act was immediately unsuccessful, Congress did widen the exemption in subsequent years.[10]

Advocacy by the American Friends Service Committee, FOR, and others led to broadened exemption in the 1940 Selective Service Training and Service Act (Selective Service Act). No longer would it be necessary to belong to a pacifist religious sect; a person could be granted exemption from military service insofar as the person's opposition to war was rooted in "religious training and belief." Nonmilitary public service would be accepted as an alternative to combat. And remarkably, religious conscientious objectors during World War II were sent to Civilian Public Service camps (CPS camps) that were actually administered and managed by the peace churches themselves, with government aid. While ostensibly a conciliatory arrangement, it incensed a wing of the radical left, namely active members of the War Resistance League. The Selective Service Act, though different from previous acts, still denied nonreligious objectors exemption from military service. Resistance to war by nonreligious objectors meant jail time. Then executive of FOR A. J. Muste supported the church administered CPS camps and encouraged religious conscientious objectors to take advantage of the exemption provided by the Selective Service Act. This compromise with the "system" provoked many radicals, including David Dellinger and Evan Thomas, the brother of Norman Thomas, to resign their FOR membership. Dellinger and Thomas dismissed the religious exemption as unjustifiably discriminatory and regarded working in the civilian work camps as contributing to the war.

Rustin did not resign his post at FOR, yet he did opt against taking the religious exemption. Based on his philosophy of nonviolence and the norm of noncooperation, in solidarity with radical pacifists of the day who resented that nonreligious grounds were not accorded the same deference as religious bases, and under the influence of War Resisters League members John Haynes Holmes and Evan Thomas, Rustin wrote to the draft board articulating his decision to violate the Selective Service Act of 1940. He would go to prison rather than cooperate with the "propagation of evil."

Although Rustin did not seek formal religious exemption from the draft per the exception specified in the Selective Service Act, he resisted conscription on religious grounds and his "Letter to the Draft Board" is a textbook statement of religiously motivated denial of state sovereignty.[11] In the letter, he furnishes scripturally derived, spiritually mediated, religious reasons for his disobedience.

To begin, Rustin professed that his vocational calling contradicted the state's claim upon him; second, he asserted that his Christian beliefs entailed the rejection of nationalism, intentional killing, and the sovereignty of the modern nation-state insofar as that entity depended upon the practice of war; and finally, making a ethically informed practical claim, he contended that war constitutes an irrational means by which to create social order and cultivate friendship between persons.[12]

According to Rustin, in cases where one is called by God to do something that conflicts with a command issued by political authority, one has a moral and religious duty to follow the dictates of God's will against the demands of government officials. In his words,

Today I feel that God motivates me to use my whole being to combat by nonviolent means the ever-growing racial tension in the United States; at the same time the State directs that I shall do its will; which of these dictates can I follow—that of God or that of the State? Surely I must at all times attempt to obey the law of the State. But when the will of God and the will of the State conflict, I am compelled to follow the will of God. If I cannot continue in my vocation, I must resist.[13]

In this statement Rustin expresses the religious ethical basis of his decision and asserts that he must disobey the command of the state. Quite simply, Rustin rebuffs the state's claim on his life. Crucially, we should observe that here Rustin is not making an argument against war. Instead, his argument at this point goes to whether an individual has a moral duty to obey a given command of the state, irrespective of the content of the command. In particular, Rustin denies that the state may interfere with his religious vocation: he would not be able to combat racial tension if he were to follow the will of the state. Especially interesting, in the text just quoted, Rustin rests his draft resistance solely on his personal (subjective) religious experience: "I feel that God motivates me." Rustin passionately intimates that God "motivates *him*" to use "his whole being" to combat racial tension. It is maximally personal, private, or subjective insofar as one can only know for oneself what God has called one to do. This constitutes Rustin's testimony on his relationship with God and a declaration of the implications of that relationship for his status as citizen or subject of the state.

The careful reader might have noticed an additional noteworthy point in the above passage. Rustin relates that he must at "all" times endeavor to obey the law. Rustin's inclusion of this proposition indicates that Rustin's disobedience is based not on an a priori rejection of political obligation, but on an a posteriori assessment of the situation. In principle, we might say, not only does Rustin not oppose "obeying the law of the State," he takes himself to have an obligation to do so. That said, it is not a deeply held commitment and the implications of this expressed obligation must be minimal. Indeed, the proposed moral obligation to obey has little bearing on Rustin's actions. And given his religious convictions and his conception of the territorial state, conflicting demands on his allegiance were perhaps inevitable. As I implied above, radical pacifists typically regard the territorial state as an entity that relies upon violence and nationalism for its maintenance. In this way radical pacifists typically follow Tolstoy. And Rustin in the 1940s was hardly different.

This becomes especially clear in the closing of his "Letter to the Draft Board," where Rustin appeals to what we might think of as public or at least religious-communal norms. That is, Rustin provides scriptural, ontological, and pragmatic reasons to explain his disobedience:

> The Conscription Act denies brotherhood—the most basic New Testament teaching. Its design and purpose is to set men apart—German against American, American against Japanese. Its aim springs from a moral impossibility—that ends justify means, that from unfriendly acts a new and friendly world can emerge.[14]

He concludes with an emphatic declaration: "That which separates man from his brother is evil and must be resisted."[15]

As should be clear, the grounds that Rustin enunciates here are unlike those considered above. First there is an empirical/ontological claim built into a particular interpretation of the New Testament: the state's conscription act represents a denial of "brotherhood" (human connectedness) and thereby violates (or denies the truth of) New Testament teaching. It is not clear whether "brotherhood" is an already-present ontological fact (i.e. what Martin King Jr sometimes referred to "a fundamental dimension of reality") that must be acknowledged or an aspiration, a normative ideal that must be sought after. Either way, Rustin claims that the "design and purpose" of the laws of the state deliberately set persons apart on the basis of nationality and race. The territorial state (as nation-state) therefore "separates man from his brother."

Because the state makes war and war sows discord between peoples, by definition, on Rustin's terms, the state is evil and thus must be resisted. This connects to Rustin's statement on means and ends; Rustin challenges a premise that he takes to be implicit in the arguments for resorting to war. In basic terms, he repudiates consequentialism as a moral theory and rejects the rationality of war: ends do not, for Rustin, justify means and war cannot cultivate conditions of peace. In this concise line Rustin articulates a central thesis of radical pacifism, the inseparability of means and ends, combining practical and principled reasons for opposition to war.

We have before us a clear account of Rustin's radical pacifism and how it relates to his conception of political authority and obligation. His resistance was based on (1) religious experience and his feeling about God's desire, (2) scriptural teachings, (3) an ontological or normative claim about the oneness of humanity ("brotherhood"), and (4) a rejection of war as a viable way to bring about a morally desirable end.[16] These are related-yet-distinct reasons for disobeying the commands of the state and they can independently motivate distinct varieties of anarchism.

One might object at this point, doubting whether the refusal, the skeptic might say "mere" refusal, to obey draft laws is enough to warrant classifying a person as an anarchist. Several things can be said by way of answering such skepticism. But most importantly, I believe that this objection hinges in part on a certain understanding of what it means to be an anarchist and in part on a failure to carefully consider the character of the territorial state as a social institution. The former and the latter, of course, interrelate in significant ways, which is exactly why I have emphasized the value of analyzing sociopolitical activism in precise political philosophical terms.

In particular, I have suggested that when we speak of anarchism, we should focus on anarchism as a political philosophical thesis about political authority and political obligation. Further, I have suggested that there is a limited range of normative postures that one can assume in relation to the modern territorial state, particularly the state's claims regarding its own sovereignty and authority—sovereign authority. Keeping in mind the stipulated definition of anarchism that I have presented and concentrating on the territorial state's claims as to its own authority is essential to the task of wholly appreciating the political implications of Rustin's draft resistance and politically or morally motivated disobedience broadly speaking.

Radical pacifists have often commended this way of approaching an analysis of radical sociopolitical action. Consistent with this, my claim that we should employ stipulated definitions and keep in mind the character of the state is supported by World War I conscientious objector Evan W. Thomas in a letter that he wrote to sociologist Clarence Marsh Case discussing the political philosophy underlying the actions of World War I objectors. Thomas (using the term "philosophical anarchism" in looser or less precise terms than most contemporary theorists) argues that draft resistance "generally leads to philosophical anarchism." Thomas contends,

> Among the real "non-resistants" [sic] there is naturally a strong tendency to repudiate the agency of the sovereign state. This is a natural outcome of their philosophy of passive resistance, and where the individual is clear headed enough to think through the implications of his position and adopt a political philosophy it generally leads to philosophical anarchism in some form or another.[17]

To appreciate why Thomas's description is apt and applies well to Rustin we should consider the character of political and legal obligation as a general matter. At a basic level, there are perhaps only two ways in which one may comply with the law: one may comply with laws either based upon the source of those laws, that is, content-independent reasons for obedience, or based upon the substance of those laws, that is, content-dependent reasons for obedience. In the latter case, content-dependence, whether one complies with a law *depends* on the *content* of that law. Rustin's political philosophy entails a rejection of the idea that persons have moral obligations to obey the laws or commands of the state or political authority simply based on the source of those laws or commands. Rustin's "Letter to the Draft Board" betrays a content-dependent orientation to the law of the territorial state. Again, to reiterate, Rustin refuses to comply with the territorial state's commands for two distinct reasons. First, he refuses based on a contention about the responsibilities that flow from his vocational calling; so, he says, "If I cannot continue my vocation, I must resist." Second, Rustin resists the American territorial state because its practice of engaging in nationalistic wars violates what Rustin regards as universally applicable divine law or moral law.

In refusing to comply with the Selective Service Act, Rustin rejects the idea that one must adhere to a given law owing solely to its source (with the exception, perhaps, of the divine source). To be clear, this does not mean that one such as Rustin will always act in ways that violate the law. For there might sometimes be nonmoral (practical) reasons to obey given laws and one may adhere to the dictates of laws owing to one's own embrace of the moral principles informing a given law. But it is critical to recognize that in such a case one obeys not the law as such but acts in a way that does not contravene the law. That is, for the agent in question, from the first-personal perspective, the law is not itself a reason for action.[18] More to the point, a person who refuses to obey laws based simply on the source of the law denies that the political authority in question has a right to issue commands that an individual has a duty to obey.

A person who adopts this view denies the legitimacy of the political authority in question and denies that there is a moral duty to obey the law. On my view, these two overlapping yet different claims are sufficient grounds on which to classify a person as an anarchist, minimally speaking. Again, as has been noted in previous chapters, a person who only accepts these two claims is typically regarded as a *weak* (or philosophical) anarchist rather than a *strong* (or political) anarchist. Both the former and the latter deny that there is a moral duty to obey the law and so deny that the territorial state possesses legitimate authority. What differentiates the two kinds of anarchist is that strong anarchists contend that there is a duty to withdraw support from existing states while mere weak anarchists do not.

To make this distinction between weak anarchism and strong anarchism clearer, we can think about it in terms of how moral motives and moral intentions factor into a given agent's political disobedience. The motivational question is: on the basis of what reason or set of reasons does one not comply with the law or political command? The intentional question is: when one disobeys a law or a political command, for what end, or with what objectives in mind, does one disobey? In relation to Rustin's draft resistance, the intentional question goes to the issue of the aim or objective of the political disobedience. The interplay of the questions of motivation and intention inform or underlie most classifications of political disobedience into types and I believe that the strong anarchist and the weak anarchist are in part moved by the same motives while operating with different intentions. Strong anarchism can easily be defined in terms of a moral agent's intention(s): a strong anarchist is one who *intends* to undermine or eliminate the territorial state.

Several interrelated reasons support attributing strong anarchism to Rustin qua Gandhian pacifist and draft resister, even though he never claimed that he wanted to eliminate the territorial state as such. To begin, one purpose of an ethical case study such as this one is to clarify the social and theoretical implications of particular kinds of religiously and ethically motivated social action. Central to analysis of social action is the task of interpretation; and such interpretation is about explication and explanation. Engaging in second order reflection on social thought and action is instructive in part because, with the benefit hindsight and the time to reflect, it makes it possible to render explicit what was perhaps merely implicit for the actors in question. This is especially the case with respect to ethical norms. As Jeffrey Stout notes,

> There is more than one way of coming to a norm. The most obvious ways are by acknowledging it, explicitly through avowals or implicitly in action. But I can also be committed to a norm that follows from other commitments I have made. When I acknowledge a normative commitment, it directly implies other commitments, which I implicitly undertake, whether I am aware of it or not.[19]

With this fact about the nature normative commitment(s) in mind, to make sense of Rustin's ethics, it behooves us to consider both the philosophical and practical social implications of his explicitly held normative commitments.

Now, any conclusion that we draw about what is implied by Rustin's explicit commitments will be based on an interpretation and concomitant assertion or argument about the expected consequences of his intentional actions or the actions that he commended. (The persuasiveness or sufficiency of this interpretation will undoubtedly be predicated on the degree to which we are able to furnish reasons in support of the given interpretation.) Insofar as we are confident that a given explicitly held normative commitment implies some other commitment(s) and agree that the implication is clear, then there are grounds on which to attribute a given intention to the agent in question. In this way, we sometimes reach conclusions about what a given moral agent intended based on what we take to be the clear implications of that person's action or the action that the person commends.

In the present case, this points back to the above discussion about the nature of the territorial state as a social institution. Since we are here interested in whether Rustin's ethical commitments imply a rejection of a particular institution with a specific set of institutional practices, in order to make sense of the implications of Rustin's religious-ethical commitments, it is imperative that we consider them in relation to particular social practices and institutions, namely state practices.

The precise character of the modern state or state practices is undoubtedly controversial, which certainly complicates my analysis. Yet it is difficult to deny that a distinctive feature of the modern territorial state is its assertion of the right to force persons to kill other persons or to provide (monetary) means, in the form of taxes, to support institutionalized violence, that is, war. It is also clear that modern territorial states assert a right to designate persons as enemies who are susceptible to intentional physical harm and killing. I take these facts for granted and it should be evident that these features of modern state practice are critical for our analysis. As we have seen, Rustin maintains that there is a religious duty to strive to make war impossible (by defying the state). Insofar as one concedes that a distinctive mark of the modern state is its reliance on armed force, it should be easy to see why the universal acceptance of pacifism—with the war resistance and the tax refusal that it entails—would spell the end of the modern territorial state. That is, I would submit that in practice, if everyone were to follow Rustin's example, then the territorial state could not survive. As Paul Kahn points out in, *Sacred Violence*, his work on sovereignty and torture:

> The state . . . extends just as far as citizens are willing to die for the maintenance of sovereignty. Where the willingness to sacrifice ends, the border has been breached. The person who denies the state the right to demand sacrifice is, for this reason, cast as the enemy of the state. He has committed an act of treason from the state's point of view. He has effectively declared war on the state . . . for without the willingness to sacrifice the state cannot survive.[20]

Thus in rejecting war and *intending* to undermine territorial states' ability to execute their war plans, Gandhians and radical pacifist war resisters (implicitly) aim/intend to undermine the modern territorial state. It is in the light of this that Rustin's radical pacifism *implies* a rejection of the modern state as such and clearly involves creating friction meant to stop the machine, to put it in Thoreauvian terms. We can therefore say that Rustin's religiously motivated pacifism is a source of strong anarchism.

This is a strong claim, yet I think that it is a fair accounting of radical pacifism. And Rustin seemed to recognize this, which makes sense. He had, after all, closely read Garrison and Tolstoy, who both insisted that "Christianity, properly understood, does not merely deny the legitimacy of the modern state; it destroys its very foundations." Perhaps Rustin had Tolstoy in mind when he used to joke about how if you scratch a pacifist, then you get an anarchist. With this joke in mind, in the final analysis, Rustin determined that he could not in good faith be the kind of pacifist who had to be committed to the elimination of the state.

A virtue of the analysis in this chapter is that it makes explicit the radical implications of absolute pacifism and so brings to the surface the reasons that radical pacifism is a difficult position to maintain without contradiction, tension, or compromise. As we might expect, Rustin's commitment to an unconditional or absolute principle of nonviolence was constantly in tension with some of his other values. This is especially apparent in Rustin's activism for economic and racial justice in the American domestic sphere.

I have for analytical purposes separated Rustin's war resistance from his activism in other domains. At this point it is appropriate to turn to Rustin's justifications of political disobedience as a response to economic oppression and racial apartheid. In the following section we will see that Rustin maintains an exacting commitment to political disobedience, protest, or direct action (three terms that I will for the most part use interchangeably); and he argues for the use of direct action to combat racial injustice and the problem of militarism—the war economy, imperialism/neocolonialism, the Cold War arms race, and proxy wars.

Although Rustin clearly rejects certain claims about the legitimacy of the political authority of territorial states and the related political obligations that are said to arise in the light of that authority, a close analysis of his essays on political and civil disobedience in relation to racial and economic oppression reveals an important ambiguity or ambivalence in Rustin's thought. Similar to the moment in "Letter to the Draft Board," where he suggests that one must always endeavor to abide by the law, in some of his statements on political disobedience, Rustin suggests that his disobedience is aimed at improving "the nature of [the American] government." Further, Rustin often mentions the necessity of territorial state power for realizing just social conditions.

A tension lingers in Rustin's thought throughout the 1940s and 1950s. And the ambiguity extant in Rustin's thought is most evident when he is discussing the role of political disobedience as a means to combat economic and racial oppression. However, when combined with his radical pacifism, Rustin's argument that individuals have no duty to follow commands that contradict God's will and his contention that persons bear a duty to disobey the unjust directives of the state is consistent with a commitment to strong anarchism, even though Rustin sometimes suggests that disobedience should be in service of a standing state. So, as we turn to his essays and speeches about political disobedience in relation to economic and racial justice, we should bear in mind the fact that, during the period in question, Rustin was a (if not "the") leading proponent of Gandhian nonviolence and an uncompromising radical pacifist.

# II

Just as Rustin was heading to jail for his war resistance, he had been heading up the March on Washington Movement with A. Philip Randolph, in an attempt to bring Gandhian nonviolence to the United States so as to bring down racial apartheid.[21] Once released from prison in 1946, Rustin resumed his nonviolent praxis, rejoining FOR as a race relations secretary. Indeed, in April of 1947, approximately one year after being released from federal prison for his draft resistance, Rustin was arrested for his participation in the Journey of Reconciliation, a direct action campaign challenging segregated public transportation in the South that CORE spearheaded with the support of FOR and the WRL. Rustin would spend three weeks on a North Carolina chain gang for his defiance of Jim Crow laws during the Journey of Reconciliation.

Appropriately, an issue that Rustin addresses consistently during the 1940s and 1950s is the role of nonviolent direct action and political disobedience for activists concerned with combating injustice. As a general matter, in the relevant essays of the period, Rustin professes that an individual is under no obligation, religious or moral, to comply with the state when doing so contributes to injustice. Rustin explains the function of civil disobedience in the 1948 essay "Civil Disobedience, Jim Crow, and the Armed Forces":

> Civil disobedience against caste is not merely a right but a profound duty. Civil disobedience is urged not to destroy the United States but because the government is now poorly organized to achieve democracy. The aim of such a movement always will be to improve the nature of the government, to urge and counsel resistance to military Jim Crow in the interest of a higher law—the principle of equality and justice upon which real community and security depend.[22]

Rustin's is an exacting ethic: one has not merely a right but a duty to disobey unjust social arrangements—caste. And to be sure, Rustin's claim is hardly an instance of rhetorical flourish. When he asserts that civil disobedience is a duty, we most certainly understand that he is actually committed to the duty himself. We thus understand that in practice he stands against the claim that there is a (binding) moral obligation to comply with the law merely because it is law promulgated by the territorial state.

Notice as well the source to which Rustin attributes the duty to disobey caste. In the above, he bases the duty to disobey on "higher law" as such rather than on scriptural authority. Although he does not at any point make clear what the exact relationship of the higher law is to God's law, given the centrality of the idea of the "brotherhood of humanity" in Rustin's thought, we might assume that insofar as Rustin understands the higher law and God's law, as expressed in the New Testament, to give primacy to brotherhood, they share an identity. As such, to a degree, whether based on God's law or the higher law, the consequences are the same: an individual who cares to act rightly, from a moral vantage, must act in accordance with the principle of justice and equality, which is synonymous with the quest for "brotherhood." This can be stated in other terms. One can be said to have a duty to comply with the higher law; and the aspect of the higher law that is relevant is the principle of justice and equality. In practice this means that one must oppose caste (with one's whole being). Rustin's activism during the 1940s and 1950s targeted caste and division in various forms—racial, economic, social—and he insists that individuals have a duty to oppose caste, even unto death.

Rustin's anticaste ethos is instantiated in his explication of the relevant content of the higher law that he invokes. Notice that he refers to the principle of "justice and equality" rather than to the principle of "justice" and the principle of "equality." He seems to be suggesting that justice is equality. Equality is of course the positive state of affairs that Rustin juxtaposes with caste, that is, a hierarchically and horizontally divided society. Caste rends the fabric of community—it obstructs or opposes justice. Rustin's emphasis on social equality is a factor that conditions his normative political position and his understanding of the role of the state in society. This became increasingly important in Rustin's later years, as we will see shortly. But to an extent the effect of his conception of equality on his understanding of the role of the state is already on display in the above, where he asserts that the principle of justice and equality is the value that government ought to serve. And this principle of justice and equality is democracy. But when Rustin invokes the term democracy he is not talking about a form of government. For him, a government is not itself a democracy. Rather it is an entity that ought to cultivate democracy. This might appear an odd formulation, yet it registers an important nuance. It allows Rustin to contend that government should be an instrument for democracy. Thus government, for Rustin, is an instrumental value and thus subordinate to human needs.

Understanding that government is subordinate to the quest for justice and equality on Rustin's view is crucial in that it helps us appreciate his position regarding the objective of social action and the appropriate posture that an activist ought to take vis-à-vis the territorial state. Political disobedience, properly understood, is motivated by an interest in serving a higher law and that law is not identical with the positive laws of the territorial state. The individual's duty is to serve the principle of justice and equality, not the state. Rustin's rigorous ethical theory requires fidelity to the moral (higher) law even when the behavior in question violates the positive laws of the state. This is a commitment that he never abandons.

Throughout the 1940s and 1950s he emphasizes the practical indispensability of direct action and political disobedience and stresses the merely instrumental value of government and formal democratic procedure. His tone is perhaps at its sharpest in the 1956 essay, "New South . . . Old Politics." Invoking stridently militant rhetoric, Rustin announces that,

The fight for the ballot is integral to the revolt against oppression . . . [But] when the Negro comes back from the polls he must face problems that cannot be solved by voting. Northern Negros have had the right to vote for years without gaining economic or social equality. The same is true of most working [class] men, regardless of color. More often than not, reliance on voting in periodic elections has sidetracked them from using the more powerful weapons of direct action.[23]

Because the descriptive and evaluative terms that we invoke in our social analysis register a diagnosis and signal our prescription, it makes a difference whether we call for revolt or reform or describe certain hierarchical social relations as the just outcome of a fair process or the product and sign of oppression; it makes a difference whether we call for voter registration drives or advocate closing down cities, making democracy in the streets. Rustin's rhetorical moves in the above situate him squarely in the nonviolent direct action tradition, a tradition that casts aside principled arguments for formal democratic procedure such as voting. In accord with this, Rustin insists that the dispossessed ought to employ direct action or political disobedience in their revolt against oppression, in the effort to overcome racial and economic caste. Reminiscent of Thoreau, Rustin suggests that one must vote with one's whole being against oppression, not leaving the issue of justice to the electoral process. Specifically, Rustin presents principled grounds for rejecting the moral duty to obey the law and pragmatic reasons for political disobedience and direct action.

Our analysis thus far has made it clear that during the 1940s and 1950s Rustin rejects a reliance on formal democratic procedure, maintains a commitment to radical pacifism, and does not (yet) explicitly articulate a positive role for the state in the liberation of oppressed peoples. Given his radical pacifism and the other two just noted factors, again, it is reasonable to classify Rustin as a strong anarchist during the period between his draft resistance and the end of the 1950s. To be sure, drawing this conclusion would be more complicated if Rustin had renounced his radical pacifism before the 1960s. Since I have said that a strong anarchist must intend to undermine or eliminate the state, Rustin's suggestion, even if only in passing, that the objective of civil disobedience is to improve the nature of a given government might be taken as a rejection of any intent to undermine or eliminate the state. The fact is, though, that Rustin remained a strident radical pacifist during the phase that I have concentrated on thus far and in my view this position commits Rustin to strong anarchism.

Particularly important to my rationale on this point is my understanding of the importance of the respective theories of the state that orient the activism of radical pacifists. To bring the most relevant aspect of this theory to the fore, radical pacifists can be contrasted with nonpacifist leftists such as racial and economic justice activists. As a practical matter, I think that it is accurate to say that few radical pacifists believe that the territorial state can itself play a positive role in the elimination of the causes of war and injustice broadly speaking. Yet, racial and economic justice advocates often believe that the state can play a positive role. This is true of reformers and revolutionaries alike. We might say that radical pacifists are thus absolutely alienated from the territorial state whereas nonpacifist reformers and revolutionaries are often alienated yet not to the same degree. The upshot is that radical pacifists are committed to the elimination of the state as a way to eradicate certain social problems whereas radical racial and economic justice activists are often committed to the use of the state (apparatus) to eliminate social problems.

Now, one who takes the use of military force or the fact of political violence to be the major problem confronting humanity will likely either argue for the development of international mechanisms to limit the use of force or will seek to undermine (by way of grassroots activism) the state's ability to practice war. Either way, both the former and the latter are likely to regard the state in its present form as an evil institution that it is best to abolish. Persons who believe that racial injustice—particularly discriminatory racism—is the fundamental social evil or injustice will often regard the territorial state as a part of the solution. The same is true of a large number of democratic socialists who consider economic injustice to be a major problem. These latter two groups can envision the territorial state itself remaining more or less intact and the social conditions that they identify as problematic being eradicated or at least greatly improved, which differentiates such persons from radical pacifists in a way that is important for my concern to classify certain positions in political philosophical terms.[24]

Again, in the analysis of radical pacifism I noted that radical pacifists reject political violence, especially war; because war is so fundamental to the functioning of the modern territorial state, I argued that rejecting war means rejecting the modern territorial state; I have maintained that such a position is best regarded as strong anarchism. We will discover in what follows that Rustin no longer belongs to the radical pacifist contingent by 1965.

During the 1960s Rustin's political philosophy underwent a significant shift. Events pulled him increasingly into the civil rights movement, which eventually led him to downplay his radical pacifist commitments. For as his involvement in the civil rights movement takes center, and he begins to reflect at length on the social situation confronting African Americans, and the poor generally, he begins to make explicit and central the view that state power is necessary for the liberation of the oppressed. Ultimately, in approximately 1965, he renounced his radical pacifism and relinquished his position on the editorial board of the leftist journal *Liberation*, which he had helped Muste found in 1956. So by the mid-1960s Rustin did not advocate principles that committed him (even if only implicitly) to the position that an individual has a duty to seek the *elimination* of the state; during the later phase, then, it is inappropriate to categorize him as a strong anarchist. Yet, even after this shift, Rustin remains adamant about the fact that individuals bear no moral duty to comply with the state.

In the following sections, I turn to Rustin's social philosophy as it developed during the 1960s, allowing his draft resistance and his theory about the proper role of political disobedience for social justice activists to serve as a background for our discussion of his commitments during the 1960s and 1970s, with the goal of understanding the reasons for Rustin's shift and determining how a commitment to political disobedience should be classified, as a political philosophical matter, when not combined with radical pacifism. The major question going forward is: Can the later Rustin still be understood as holding views that imply a variety of anarchism?

# III

In 1956 the modern civil rights movement picked up momentum. The Montgomery Bus Boycott that began in late 1955 electrified activists from one corner of the globe to another. Mass protest had arrived as a tool of Negroes in the quest to get free. Rustin had been waiting for such a moment since the late 1930s when he enrolled as a full-time nonviolent freedom fighter. Having given so much of his energy to developing nonviolent direct action, it only made sense that Rustin would be among the most important outsiders sent down South by the WRL to support the work of the Montgomery Improvement Association. As it began, many hoped that the bus boycott would serve as a catalyst for activities elsewhere. Yet few anticipated that soon enough the names *Montgomery*, *Parks*, *King* would in fact take on world historical significance. Before long, the civil rights movement was shaking the foundations of the Southern social order. Before long, Rustin was organizing the March on Washington, and Martin Luther King Jr was accepting a Nobel Peace award. When Rustin ventured to Montgomery in 1956, he was a tested activist caught up in the whirlwind of revolt, as it is so often said of the central players in major social movements and revolutions—he was pulled from the margins to the center.

Much has been made of the transformation that Rustin underwent in the 1960s. Figures such as Bob Moses, Staughton Lynd, Tom Hayden, and David Dellinger have suggested that Rustin emerged as a part of the liberal establishment. His entrée into circles of power, it is said, undermined his radical impulse. His unbending support for Johnson and campaigning for Hubert Humphrey in 1968 are cited as evidence. And his apparent reluctance to protest against the Vietnam War coupled with his consistent criticism of the New Left, including leaders of Student Nonviolent Coordinating Committee (SNCC) and Students for a Democratic Society (SDS), is regarded as further proof. There is no doubting that Rustin underwent a shift. However, the question as to what caused the shift and what the substance of the shift entailed is an entirely separate matter.

The successes of the civil rights movement called into question several of the assumptions that had oriented Rustin's activism in the years leading up to the movement. It fundamentally transformed his sense of what was possible in America. In particular, having organized the March on Washington in 1963, Rustin regarded it as possible to build a progressive multiracial political majority that could revolutionize American society. In droves white Americans from all over the country flooded the Mall in Washington DC, standing side-by-side with Negroes, demanding the inclusion of Negroes as full-fledged American citizens. Add to this Lyndon B. Johnson's commitment to racial and economic justice. For the first time in his life, in the year after the March on Washington, Rustin began to believe that it would be possible to transform America via the formal electoral process. It appeared as though the visions of Tom Watson, Norman Thomas, and A. Phillip Randolph were finally possible: a multiracial electoral majority ushering in a socioeconomic revolution. This revelation greatly impacted Rustin's social and political philosophy.

Rustin had been at the forefront of radical pacifist activism for decades. During the 1930s through the 1950s his thought and actions exemplified those of an absolute pacifist. Particularly important, for radical pacifists, and thus ostensibly the younger Rustin, means and ends are so radically intertwined that reflecting on one means meditating on the other, so that to alter one's means betrays an implicit intent to change one's ends. And for Gandhian activists political action involved seeking to change opponent's "hearts." Rustin departed from the Gandhian pacifist fold as he gave more of his energy and attention to civil rights activism. Effectuating the desired social change would require giving more weight to the consequences of political actions and this would mean focusing on interests and not hearts. Action could only be recommended if it led to the realization of observable concrete objectives, and for Rustin it was imperative for political actors to avoid confusing means and ends. This increased concern for nearer term consequences of a given action indicates or signals Rustin's move toward a more pragmatic approach to social action. Rustin's stridently pragmatic orientation distinguishes him from many twentieth-century radicals and has led to the classification of Rustin as a political conservative. However, this is a label that does not quite work. As we will see shortly, even as he announced the need for a shift in the means employed by movement activists, Rustin called for revolutionary transformation of political economy and the democratization of the mode of economic production. Rustin was no conservative.

But let me be clear. I turn to this phase of Rustin's activist career neither to vindicate him nor his staunchest critics. As is so often the case, a portion of the truth rests on both sides of the line. Rustin biographers Anderson, Levine, and D'Emilio all wonderfully capture the debate that estranged Rustin from many leftists. My reasons for turning to this phase are multifold. First doing so will allow us to reflect on the implications of certain ethical principles for other ethical principles and values. As social circumstances change, strategic choices often bring into full view a host of tensions that were previously obscured. As one makes choices in the light of those tensions, often, what one values more or most comes to the fore.

With Rustin, events in the 1960s thrust to the surface several important tensions and analyzing Rustin's position as it developed during the civil rights movement, especially after the passage of the Civil Rights and Voting Rights acts, puts into focus the way in which holding certain values requires relinquishing others. Here the concern is with the implications of certain values in relation to pacifism and anarchism and the consequences of Rustin's shift for his normative conception of political authority or political obligation and the role of political violence in social life. Earlier, I argued that Rustin was a strong anarchist in what we might refer to as the early and middle stages of his activist career, owing to his embrace of radical pacifism. The task here is to come to terms with the reasons for and the political philosophical upshot of his abandonment of radical pacifism.

As we tend to Rustin's intellectual work during the 1960s and 1970s, we will be considering the moves that he makes against the background that has been provided by the analysis of Dorothy Day in Chapter 2. Day's anarchism flowed from her absolute pacifism and her concern about the deleterious effects that the rise of the territorial state as a centralized welfare bureaucracy had on human communities and for human persons qua moral agents. While it would be untrue to say outright that Rustin is unconcerned with the problem of bureaucratic centralization, it is certainly true that such issues are for him of secondary importance at best, which is a fact that a consideration of Rustin's call for a shift from protest to politics will make clear.

In arguing for a move from protest to politics Rustin is guided by three basic commitments: (1) his preference for class-based sociopolitical mobilization; (2) his belief in the necessity of a centralized state; and (3) his embrace of electoral politics. This can be restated in negative terms. Rustin rejected: (1) race-based politics; (2) a reliance on protest; and (3) localism, decentralization, or privileging participatory democracy. The adoption of positions (2) and (3) is significant in that Rustin's embrace of formal politics and a state-centered view of social change is inconsistent with strong anarchism. Yet, the fact that Rustin, even in his later years, did not reject the moral legitimacy of political disobedience means that it might still be instructive to describe Rustin as a weak anarchist.

I will conclude this chapter with a reflection on this undoubtedly controversial issue. In particular, I will argue the following: (1) One strand of anarchism, weak (or philosophical) anarchism, allows for some support of the state. (2) Advocating for perpetual political disobedience entails a commitment to (a strand of) anarchism, namely weak anarchism. (3) Rustin, in his late phase, explicitly noted the necessity of a strong state for the realization of certain desirable social changes. (4) But even in the later phase

Rustin retained a commitment to political disobedience. (5) Therefore, the later Rustin is probably best regarded as a weak anarchist. This issue is quite significant for students of African American studies, American religion and politics, social justice movements, descriptive ethics, normative ethics, and political philosophy. My sense is that weak anarchism is a conception of the individual's relation to the territorial state that jibes with the philosophical commitments of a larger number of persons than is typically appreciated. It behooves us to make explicit this rejection of a certain conception of political authority or legitimate political authority, and thus point, on the one hand, to why African American radicals might eschew strong anarchism yet revel, on the other hand, in the weak anarchist mode.

# IV

Rustin's shift must be contemplated in relation to the advancements made during the modern American civil rights movement. The Southern movement's two phases had proved effective: the mass protests for public accommodations that had begun in the 1950s and the voter registration drives in Alabama and Mississippi culminated in the 1960s, and by 1965 it was clear that key figures and decision-makers of the American establishment were committed to eliminating race-supremacist legal categories and delegitimizing racism at a formal political level. Lyndon B. Johnson signed the Civil Rights Act in 1964 and the National Voting Rights Act in 1965. The fourteenth amendment would now be enforced. Jim Crowism, challenged for at least seven decades, had finally been defeated. With this, the modern civil rights movement had reached its apex. The advancements that it produced transformed American society and in turn greatly impacted the structure of the black freedom struggle, especially the theorizing about how to proceed in the light of the altered situation.

The familiar questions of contemporary social movements moved to the fore, as activists contemplated and debated how to sustain the movement in the light of changes. Which class of actors would keep the movement alive? Did that class need allies? Would it be only blacks or poor blacks and poor whites? What would they demand? Would they seek land or jobs or reparations or formal political power? How would they go about acting? Would they vote or march or shutdown cities or take up guerilla warfare? These questions were at the heart of the strategy-debate that ensued just after the passage of the 1965 Voting Rights Act. Rustin participated in this debate, contributing several important essays, and it is to the ideas that he presented during this liminal stage of the black freedom struggle that I would like to turn. These essays (and this stage of Rustin's career) shed light on aspects of Rustin's social and political philosophy that are pertinent to my effort to interpret him as an anarchist.

Perhaps the most important question that emerged during this phase of the black freedom struggle was the role that race played in American society. The presumption that state-sanctioned exclusion (social, political, and economic) on the basis of race constitutes the gravest defect of American society guided many participants of the modern civil rights movement. Rustin explicitly rejected a race-based view of society and maintained that the focus on race that such a view entails undermines the possibility of building a coalition that is capable of instigating desirable social reconstruction. In general, Rustin's conception of race parallels that of American Marxists and communists, who have tended to adopt reductive views of race, and so regard racial consciousness as essentially false consciousness that negatively impedes upon the ability to judge the situation for what it in fact is. Many Marxists consider race consciousness and racism as facts that need to be eliminated; but overcoming the former and the latter is viewed merely as a precondition to the revolutionary praxis that will cultivate the relevant class-consciousness. On this view, economic class-consciousness is a precondition to authentic or truly revolutionary action.

That Rustin's conception of race resembles this basic Marxist account is reflected in the 1971 essay, "The Blacks and the Unions," where Rustin plainly states that economic class is more important than race: "The prominent racial and ethnic loyalties that divide American society have, together with our democratic creed, obscured a fundamental reality—that we are a class society and, though we do not often talk about such things, that we are engaged in a class struggle."[25] Continuing this line of argumentation, in "Affirmative Action in an Economy of Scarcity," Rustin criticizes activists who focus on racial discrimination:

> Everyone knows racial discrimination still exists. But the high rate of black unemployment and the reversal of hard-won economic gains . . . is a function of much broader economic failures; failures which, moreover, have left their mark on all Americans regardless of race . . . [As] long as inequality is treated as a product of racism [or racial prejudice], instead of economics, it will seriously direct the attention of society from difficult issues which must be tried.[26]

Rustin's disapproval of race-based views of society is rooted in his belief that such views "obscure reality" such that one is unable to formulate a plan of action that might improve material conditions.

Rustin's claim may not appear radical. But it was quite controversial at the time and Rustin's position on the role of race in American society distanced him from two camps at once. First, it distanced him from persons who thought that the civil rights movement had successfully removed the most important impediment to the inclusion of blacks into major American social and political institutions. In addition, it set him apart from persons who regarded the civil rights movement as primarily a black middle-class affair, both in terms of its principal leaders and in terms of its beneficiaries; according to this group, the civil rights movement did not address the major issues, namely social and cultural concerns, confronting the larger population of African Americans, especially the working poor and unemployed. James Farmer's trenchant criticism, expressed decades later, is characteristic of the latter group's perception of Rustin after the mid-1960s: "Bayard has no credibility in the black community. . . . Bayard's commitment is to labor, not to the black man. His belief that the black man's problem is economic, not racist, runs counter to black community thinking."[27]

This issue about whether to focus on race or class is so controversial in part because of the implications that it has for political praxis. As we might expect, Rustin's class-based view of society undergirds his evaluation of the civil rights movement. Because Rustin did not regard racism per se as the principal source or cause of social injustice, he did not regard the defeat of Jim Crowism as an ultimate victory. On Rustin's view, the judicial decisions from the late 1930s through the 1960s eliminated or at least undermined the basis for racism as a formal legal matter. The Equal Accommodations and Civil Rights acts consolidated the transformation at the legislative level. This constituted progress, to be sure. Yet blacks had not reached the Promised Land simply because they could vote or because they could sit on juries. Similar to his mentor A. Phillip Randolph, Rustin put a premium on economic matters.

In "From Protest to Politics," focusing on the relative importance of legalized segregation, Rustin relates that, as far as he is concerned, the formal (Jim Crow) legal order was "relatively peripheral both to the American socioeconomic order and to the fundamental conditions of life of the Negro people."[28] He adds,

> The Negro today finds himself stymied by obstacles of far greater magnitude than the legal barriers he was attacking before: automation, urban decay, de facto school segregation. These problems, while conditioned by Jim Crow, do not vanish upon its demise. They are more deeply rooted in our socioeconomic order; they are the result of the total society's failure to meet not only the Negro's needs, but human needs generally.[29]

Rustin recognized the import of the economic revolution that materialized following the postwar boom of the 1950s and saw early on that many blacks were becoming "superfluous labor" on a nationwide scale for perhaps the first time since the arrival of blacks in the New World. That is, many blacks were no longer being exploited as a class of cheap labor; they were being excluded from the productive process altogether. Africans arrived in the Americas as servants and slaves, experiencing economic exploitation from the seventeenth century through the mid-twentieth. But technological shifts and the movement of capital in the twentieth century had unleashed profound changes. The problem of economic marginalization had emerged, so that by the mid-1960s, blacks were experiencing unemployment at Great Depression-like rates. Addressing this problematic head-on, in "From Protest to Politics," Rustin observed, "This matter of economic role brings us to the greater problem—the fact that we are moving into an era in which the natural functioning of the market does not itself ensure for every man with will and ambition a place in the productive process."[30] With this concern in mind, he called for revolutionary changes to the system, arguing that American social institutions must be fundamentally transformed "to the point where social and economic structure . . . can no longer be said to be the same."[31] This revolution would entail basically three things: programs for full employment, the eradication of ghettos, and the construction of new schools.

Unlike Dorothy Day, who advocated for decentralization, Rustin's assessment of the economic situation leads him to assert that there is a need for centralized governmental action—government intervention—since combating the problem of economic marginalization would require a fundamental reorganization of American society. This commitment to centralized government intervention situates Rustin within the class of activists that has been referred to as the Old Left. Barbara Epstein's contrast of "activists of the thirties" (i.e. the Old Left) with "activists of the sixties" (i.e. the New Left) is elucidative. In *Political Protest and Cultural Revolution*, Epstein intimates that "Unlike the activists of the thirties, who gravitated to the issues of political and economic power, the activists of the sixties tended to gravitate to what seemed more fundamental issues of how social life as a whole should be organized, what ideas it should be ruled by."[32] Epstein's classificatory schema is based on an assumption about the formation of political identity along generational lines and is imperfect. After all, Rustin and Day were leading activists of both the 1930s and the 1960s. But if we focus on the substantive commitments of the groups that Epstein delineates, important light is shed on the issues that divided activists during the 1960s and 1970s.

As has already been suggested, Rustin was preoccupied with formal mechanisms of economic and political power (macrostructural institutions). This distinguishes him from new leftists who, at least as far as the standard account goes, eschewed the class analysis of the earlier leftists and generally shied away from developing concrete goals to orient political action. In accord with the standard account of the New Left, Rustin charged new leftists with lacking "programs"; they possessed no strategy for gaining economic or political power.

Rustin especially took issue with black power proponents (mainly "black separatists"), student activists (such as Students for a Democratic Society), and antiwar activists (i.e. the Weatherman Underground Organization) of the late 1960s and 1970s. Rustin perceived the disparate contingents to have in common a fixation on culture and an unyielding commitment to participatory democracy. Particularly relevant for our purposes is Rustin's criticism of the localism and decentralization preferred by participatory democrats.

In "The Failure of Black Separatism" [1970], Rustin complains that the period was one of great social confusion for activists. Activists were confused not only "about the strategies that should be [adopted], but about the very goals the strategies were supposed to bring" into fruition. Particularly problematic in Rustin's view was the fact that "progressive whites" and "black militants" had begun to doubt whether realizing "racial and economic justice would require expanding the role of the federal government." He criticized such activists for suggesting that "government has gotten too big and that what is needed to make the society more humane and livable is an enormous new move toward local participation and decentralization."[33] A long quote from "The Failure of Black Separatism" betrays Rustin's concerns and the spirit of his criticisms of participatory democrats:

> The new anti-integrationism and localism have been motivated by sincere moral conviction, but hardly by intelligent political thinking. It should be obvious that what is needed today more than ever is a political strategy that offers the real possibility of economically uplifting millions of impoverished individuals, black and white. Such a strategy must of necessity give low priority to the various forms of economic and psychological experimentation that I have discussed, which at best deal with issues peripheral to the problem and at worst embody a frenetic escapism. These experiments are based on the assumption that the black community can be transformed from within when, in fact, any such transformation must depend upon structural changes in the entire society. We need, therefore, a new national economic policy. . . . A successful strategy, therefore, must rest upon an identification of those central institutions which, if altered sufficiently, would transform the social and economic relations in our society; and it must provide a politically viable means of achieving such an alteration.[34]

In short, Rustin focuses on macrostructural analysis and recommends centralized top-down measures or a program of national planning. In other words, he proposes that centralized institutions be deployed in order to transform the entire society. That Rustin supports centralized national planning is an effect of what he takes to be the most pressing problem facing society, and by extension it is an expression of what he understands a viable solution to entail.

Rustin's normative support of centralization clearly distinguishes him from participatory democrats and other critics of the modern bureaucratic state. Indeed, Rustin's criticism of the New Left reveals that his conception of the major problems confronting the modern person or the contemporary American stands in stark contrast to Dorothy Day's. In the end, Day probably has more in common with new leftists ("activists of the sixties") than with Rustin. Whereas Day's spiritual ethos leads her to bemoan the fragmentation of community wrought by industrialization, urbanization, and bureaucratization, Rustin is nearly silent on these issues. And Rustin rarely speaks to the problems of existential crisis, anomie, social alienation, cultural decay—the psycho-spiritual problematic.

Consistent with this, Rustin does not propose spiritual renewal, cultural criticism and expression, cooperative local economies, or communal living experiments as viable means by which to improve society; he does not recommend localism or decentralization as solutions to major social problems. Quite the contrary, he dismisses focus on these values and practices as counterproductive to liberation—economic liberation. Just as persons who focused on race offered an obscured account of "reality," persons who emphasized localism and decentralization inadequately grasped the causes of social injustice and blocked the way toward improved conditions. According to Rustin, new leftists neglected the importance of the state to economic liberation; they did not focus their attention on the appropriate strategy-question: how can power be seized?

# V

Rustin provides his response to the above question in his 1965 essay "From Protest to Politics." Social change would come through formal political action. In short, Rustin thought that with the changes brought about by the direct action campaigns in the 1950s and early 1960s, protest had exhausted its efficacy and thus there was a need to turn to formal politics. Protest had been effective as a way to press for basic civil rights and formal political equality, but it could not be effectively employed in order to sufficiently transform the economic structure of the entire society. On Rustin's view, the capturing of formal political power, by the progressive left, constituted a precondition to the reconstruction of the socioeconomic order. To be clear, Rustin's turn to formal politics should not be taken as evidence of a conservative turn or as a reflection of a principled commitment to formal democratic procedure. Instead, Rustin's turn is best understood as flowing from his exacting commitment to social justice. His turn is primarily pragmatic.

To appreciate how this is so, we only need to ponder the debate that unfolded among Rustin, Stokely Carmichael (Kwame Toure), and Martin Luther King Jr. The three each believed that the defeat of Jim Crowism was important but insufficient. They all identified economic marginalization as the major problem confronting African Americans. More to the point, Rustin, King, and Carmichael all regarded the *intersection* of poverty and race to be the chief problem confronting African Americans. On this mark they were ahead of others. But they disagreed about the proper place of nonviolent direct action and the role of multiracial coalitions.

From the time that King emerged as a contributor to the Montgomery Bus Boycott in late 1955 to his death in 1968, he maintained that it would be impossible to achieve the total liberation of blacks in America without employing nonviolent direct action. As it was, blacks had limited options at their disposal. In short, they could either: (1) passively accept the status quo; (2) proactively advocate for racial segregation; (3) seek change, but (a) reject violence and nonviolent direct action; (b) accept violence; or (c) reject violence and embrace nonviolent direct action. A handful of black power proponents, such as H. Rap Brown, and even Albert Cleage, inspired by the Cuban and Chinese revolutions, and events in places such as the Congo, believed that blacks should consider revolutionary violence. King of course dismissed such calls as asinine. That left formal politics or protest. In *Where Do We Go from Here*, King's final book-length manuscript, he explicitly rejects a reliance on the formal political process:

> Many, especially in the North, argue that the maximum use of legislation, welfare and antipoverty programs has now replaced demonstrations, and that overt and visible protest should now be abandoned. Nothing could prove more erroneous than to demobilize at this point. It was the mass-action movement that engendered the changes of the decade, but the needs which created it are not yet satisfied. Without the will to unity and struggle Negroes would have no strength, and reversal of our successes could easily be effected. The use of the creative tensions that broke the barriers of the South will be as indispensable in the North to obtain and extend necessary objectives.[35]

By "visible and overt protest," King meant massive nonviolent direct action. On King's view, realizing social justice would only be possible if persons were willing to extend the application of nonviolent direct action. Rustin and Carmichael, of course, disagreed with King's prescription. To Rustin and Carmichael the time had come to downplay direct action. Its utility had mostly been exhausted. Rustin and Carmichael agreed that it was time to devise a strategy that focused on formal electoral politics. But at the same time, the two disagreed intensely about whether activists should focus on local electoral politics or national electoral politics or whether political organizing efforts should or should not be primarily interracial.

It was during this phase of the black freedom struggle, of course, that Carmichael starting talking about black power, a term which he is largely responsible for popularizing, even though it had been employed by others well before the 1960s. Central to Carmichael's black power program was the idea of black self-determination. The path to this self-determination was said to lie in local politics. In accord with this, Carmichael encouraged blacks to concentrate on building racial solidarity so as to be in a position to capture control of political districts—and cities—where blacks constituted a majority of the population. Since blacks could not rely on "well-meaning" white Americans, according to Carmichael, it made more sense to devote attention to shoring up black solidarity. In other words, he thought that it was impractical to rely upon the support of white Americans.

Rustin, however, argued that local politics were important but insignificant as a means by which to refashion the political economy. Again, only the federal government could restructure the economy along the lines that Rustin envisioned; and to capture control of the territorial state would require a national majority. So, while Carmichael maintained that blacks must close ranks and should start a black political party and make the most of the geographic concentration of blacks, Rustin insisted that multiracial coalitional politics was central. As Rustin put it in "From Protest to Politics": "The future of the Negro struggle depends on whether the contradictions of this society can be resolved by a coalition of progressive forces which becomes the *effective* political majority in the United States."[36] Rustin felt that "a coalition of Negroes, labor, liberals, religious organizations, and students" could "form a majority capable of democratizing the economic, social, and political power of America."[37] According to Rustin, it would be impossible to effectuate the necessary and desired social change in the absence of majority support: "The racial crisis . . . is not an isolated problem that lends itself to redress by a protesting minority. Being rooted in the very social and economic structure of the society, it can be solved only by a comprehensive program."[38] Blacks had no choice but to rely upon progressive and working class white Americans. From the vantage of African Americans, who comprised only a minority segment of the US population, majority support meant multiracial support.

So, to reiterate, whereas black power proponent Stokely Carmichael argued that a consolidation of racial solidarity was essential to the quest of liberation, Rustin insisted that only multiracial electoral politics could bring about the needed social change. King, of course, also argued that African Americans needed to formulate a plan to broaden the civil rights coalition to include poor and working class whites and Mexicans. Therefore, King and Rustin agreed on the importance of a multiracial coalition. Yet whereas King maintained that an interracial coalition should be mobilized for direct action, Rustin thought that such a group's energy should be directed to the national electoral process.

In many respects, the above comparative analysis could be a bit more nuanced. I could certainly say more about each of the three figures that

I discussed. Yet, the above analysis has made clear the point that is most important for the purposes of this chapter. It should be clear that Rustin's account of the social situation during the 1960s moved him to argue that eradicating injustice would require building a coalition (means to penultimate end) large enough to capture hold of the state (penultimate end) and refashion the political economy (ultimate end of sociopolitical action). According to Rustin, capturing formal political power, that is, the state, constituted a precondition to the reconstruction of the socioeconomic order. It should also be clear that what was at issue in the debate in question was the anticipated effectiveness of rival strategies for social change and not the moral acceptability of political disobedience. Significantly, Rustin's embrace of electoral politics was pragmatic and did not substantially affect his understanding of the moral duties that an individual owes to the state. I will return to this point in the next section. For now, it is important to appreciate that while Rustin's turn does not bear on his understanding of political obligation, the turn does reflect Rustin's evolving or evolved understanding of the relevance of Gandhian nonviolence and pacifism to political activism, so that Rustin's turn to electoral politics does have major political philosophical implications.

To appreciate these implications, we must first recognize the fact that Rustin's belief that state power would be needed in order to establish and enforce new socioeconomic practices means that he can be said to value the territorial state as an instrument of social change. Indeed, Rustin's emphasis on the need for governmental action and his concomitant embrace of electoral politics entailed a rejection of absolute pacifism and constituted a decisive break from his commitment to Gandhian nonviolence, since, as is widely accepted, a distinctive feature of the modern state is its reliance on violence. Radical participatory democrats and absolute pacifists eschew state-centered paths to social change for precisely this reason. The former group typically relies on a pragmatic premise: a centralized authority cannot in practice bring about a social order with the desirable level of social freedom and equality. The latter group rejects state-centered paths to social change on the basis of principle: the norm of nonviolence precludes the acceptability of the seizure of state power. By the mid-1960s Rustin was too concerned with the immediate consequences of prioritizing localism or peace for the marginalized to make them the fundamental values guiding his political engagement.

To understand exactly how Rustin's reordered commitments relate to Gandhian nonviolence it is crucial to recall the basic account of Gandhian thought that was presented in the first sections of this chapter. I noted there that Gandhians assert that at least one immediate aim of political protest ought to be to change collective sentiments, through minimally coercive *moral* persuasion, so as to make possible new institutional practices. According to Gandhians, persons' hearts and moral priorities must be changed in order to satisfactorily transform society or social institutions. As with Thoreau and the Transcendentalists, for Gandhians, self-reform is a precondition to meaningful social or political reform. For nearly three decades, from the mid-1930s up to the late 1950s, Rustin stood out as perhaps America's leading Gandhian. Yet, at some point during the 1960s, Rustin began doubting the viability of Gandhian theories of social change. By February of 1965, with the doubt in full bloom, Rustin was calling into question central Gandhian ideas. In particular, in the essay "From Protest to Politics," Rustin explicitly dismisses strategies based on appeals to conscience. Criticizing protest tactics that he found ineffective, Rustin announces, "hearts are not relevant to the issue; neither racial affinities nor racial hostilities are rooted there. It is institutions—social, political, and economic institutions—which are the ultimate molders of collective sentiments."[39]

Rustin's reassessment of the political value of Gandhian nonviolence and pacifism is each an effect of, indicative of, and best understood in relation to his evolving theory of social change. As we might expect, his more than three-decade-long career as a community organizer had a notable effect on his working theory about how social justice movements can be cultivated and sustained. It is fair to say that by the mid-1960s, Rustin had for the most part begun to regard social movements as essentially large-scale interest-group actions. And not unlike other community organizers, Rustin eventually decided that a community organizer could only reasonably expect to successfully organize directly affected parties—that is, the oppressed—and a small number of nonaffected empathizers. Along these lines, Rustin often depicted the civil rights movement as primarily a movement centered on African Americans' shared interest in combating white supremacist practices and racial oppression. On this interpretation, the movement's successes stemmed in large part from the fact that it was a movement comprised of persons with clearly identifiable mutual material interests. Acting in concert, civil rights movement participants were able to force political and economic power-holding elites to cease perpetuating certain unjust social arrangements.

With this view of the movement in mind, arguing against appeals to conscience, Rustin insisted that activists should endeavor to inspire large-scale social action by appealing to the interests of potential movement participants. This, of course, relates to Rustin's increasing preoccupation with building a multiracial working class coalition. As we saw earlier in this chapter, by 1965 Rustin thought that a multiracial coalition among working class persons could actually be brought together based on shared material interests. Rustin's faith in the possibility of organizing a multiracial coalition was predicated on his understanding of what he referred to, after the Marxists, as the "objective situation."

Based on his interpretation of the "objective situation," Rustin could contend that it was in fact unnecessary (and impractical) to appeal to conscience, since changed hearts were beside the point. What organizers and activists needed to do was to help people, namely workers, understand who their natural allies were. To Rustin it was clear. Persons suffering from economic deprivation, exploitation, and insecurity should, and could plausibly be expected to unite (around economic interests) in order to transform the entire social structure. And because inequality in the economic sphere is both the sign of unjust practices and constitutive of social injustice, the coalition to transform the socioeconomic structure would by definition be committed to social justice. Morality and prudence would coalesce.

In short, Rustin developed a view of the pertinence of material interests to social action that altered his sense of the relative importance of "changing hearts" and, quite naturally, this in turn conditioned the type of social action that he would prescribe. So, Rustin could maintain his commitment to Gandhian nonviolence as long as he believed that social action should focus on appealing to persons' moral sentiments; and as long as he believed that peace or nonviolence, as a political matter, was more important than racial and economic justice. Yet as his involvement in the civil rights movement increased, Rustin accorded less weight to peace and began to emphasize institutional change more than individual conversions.

In this way, Rustin biographer Jervis Anderson is correct to relate that Rustin's "role in the building of coalition politics had helped him to recognize that absolute pacifism was no longer effective."[40] Absolute pacifism was no longer effective in the sense that Rustin believed that absolute pacifism would remain a minority position and thus could not constitute a viable basis for a sustainable social justice movement. Rustin's involvement in the civil rights movement provided him with a new understanding of what social movements can attain and how they can attain it. Impressed with the scope, scale, and impact of the civil rights movement, Rustin had come to doubt pacifism's political value. He had spent decades trying to inspire a peace movement, yet with limited effect. Pacifism had proven a hard idea to sell—a bit too hard.

Since one can be an absolute pacifist without being a Gandhian, it is notable that Rustin simultaneously embraced commitments that entailed giving up both Gandhian nonviolence and absolute pacifism. This points to an issue that it is essential to be clear about. On its own, Rustin's altered understanding of the role of hearts and institutions entails breaking with Gandhian nonviolence, but it does not necessitate rejecting absolute pacifism.[41] Indeed, an absolute pacifist might agree with Rustin about the primacy of institutions (over hearts) yet insist that persons focus on enacting alternative economic or educational practices—and not political practices per se—in order to undermine prevailing unjust institutional practices. In consequence, it is the particular type of institution, that is, a strong centralized state, that Rustin identified as necessary (in order to alter social conditions and thus collective sentiments) that entailed a rejection of absolute pacifism.

In perhaps his most to the point statement about his reappraisal of pacifism, Rustin relates, "Whereas I used to believe that pacifism had a political value . . . I no longer believe that. I believe that pacifism is a personal witness to the truth as one sees it. I do not believe that pacifism can be politically organized."[42] He continues, "It is ridiculous, in my view, to talk only about peace. There is something which is more valuable to people than peace. And that is freedom. So we have to find a peaceful way to defend democratic freedom."[43] As I indicated earlier, there had long been tension in Rustin's thought between his absolute pacifism and his commitment to racial and economic justice. We can now see that Rustin resolved this tension by giving up his absolute pacifism. According to Rustin, because "people" value freedom more than peace, pacifism cannot be organized politically, which means that responsible political actors should concentrate on creating institutions that preserve "democratic freedom."

In *Parting the Waters*, historian Taylor Branch tells of a notable exchange between Rustin and King at the beginning of the Montgomery Bus Boycott. During an intense conversation about the dictates of Gandhian nonviolence, Rustin had "quibbled" with King's initial reservations about embracing absolute pacifism. King, then a mere 26 years old, confessed to Rustin that he was "trying to practice nonviolence but did not subscribe to Muste-style [radical] pacifism." From King's perspective, "no just society could exist without at least a police power."[44]

By 1965 Rustin and King had more or less traded places. By then, Rustin's radicalism had begun to congeal around his social democratic commitments, particularly his commitment to economic justice. On Rustin's view, the primary objective of social action should be the elimination of economic marginalization and exploitation (and the eradication of poverty). In particular, he presents economic equality as a goal that should orient social praxis. Leftists who propose substantive equality as the appropriate *immediate* goal of social action often prefer an interventionist state. So it was with Rustin, which helps make sense of his emphasis on the power of a centralized state. Given his explicit commitment to the employment of the power of the state, it is clear that Rustin was no longer committed to an ethic that called into question the existence of the territorial state or implied its elimination. He was thus no longer committed to an ethic that *implies* strong anarchism.

It should now be evident why anarchism is such a valuable analytical lens. Thinking through Rustin's commitments in relation to anarchism has helpfully brought into focus the implications of absolute pacifism. In many ways, so far this chapter has been an extended meditation on the radical implications of absolute pacifism in the contemporary sociopolitical context. I have maintained that Rustin was classifiable as a strong anarchist precisely because absolute pacifism, to my mind, implies a rejection of the modern territorial state.

But the analysis thus far has done more than make clear the radical character of absolute pacifism and Gandhian nonviolence. It has also made evident how difficult it is for persons committed to racial and economic justice to consistently embrace values that prohibit the use of violence and have as their end the rejection of the modern territorial state. Moreover, my analysis has made clear the fact that Rustin's shift in the 1960s was in part based on his recognition of the practical implications of a commitment to absolute pacifism and Gandhian nonviolence.

In the next section, I want to raise the stakes a bit. If the above analysis was in many respects an attempt to elucidate several critical political philosophical issues related to pacifism, then what follows constitutes an effort to clarify a bundle of questions that revolve around a thoroughgoing commitment to social justice that combines a commitment to using the state's power with an insistence that political disobedience is indispensable for effective social justice activism. In the "Introduction" and in Chapters 1 and 2, I suggested that *weak* anarchism allows for some support of the territorial state. In the final section of this chapter, I explain how this is so and suggest that weak anarchism is a conceptual category worth preserving in that it aptly captures the political philosophical commitments of numerous contemporaries, especially political radicals, such as Bayard Rustin. So what follows is contemplation of the question: Can one be an anarchist and at the same time maintain the necessity of the territorial state for the cause of social justice?

# VI

In emphasizing the necessity of a strong centralized state and government intervention, Rustin joins a long tradition of black political activists and social thinkers who are less fearful of state power than of concentrations of private power. Even the most "liberal" of black liberals, perhaps with the exception of conservative liberals such as Thomas Sowell or Clarence Thomas, tend to prefer a strong central state. A strong interventionist state is thought necessary as an instrument with which to discipline both capital and racist factions.

This view, of course, is undergirded by a particular interpretation of American political and social history. A distinctive feature of the experience of Africans in the Americas has been the way in which state action or inaction has determined the social and political status and welfare of the African American community and its members. This applies to enslavement and emancipation and Jim Crowism and the period after the citizenship rights movement of the mid-twentieth century. From the end of the American Civil

War through the New Deal era and the modern civil rights movement, many black social analysts have pointed to the positive functions of the national American government for African American persons. The use of force by the Union Army, of course, served as the means by which the Southern slave aristocracy was overthrown. And nearly a century later the federal government had to intervene in order to end Jim Crowism. These events are often interpreted as evidence of the necessity of a strong state for the protection of black persons in the American context. Such an interpretation of American history undoubtedly renders anarchism less attractive for African American social thinkers than it might otherwise be.

Nonetheless, I believe that careful reflection on various aspects of black social and political thought, particularly the values and principles that are prioritized, reveals that certain strands of black thought commend an attitude toward authority that is consistent with a particular variety of anarchism, namely weak anarchism. As is widely acknowledged, in addition to frequently commending the intervention of a strong state in society, many African American social thinkers have tended to proactively support political disobedience. In this respect African American social thought and praxis merely bears the imprint of its origins in a white supremacist social order: runaway slaves and freedom seekers in Jim Crow America lived in defiance of the state, its laws, and its agents. From Harriet Tubman and Frederick Douglass to Rosa Parks, Angela Davis, and Jessie Jackson, black social actors and thinkers have often denied the supremacy of the positive laws of the American state.

The commitments to state-centered social change and political disobedience, when taken together, constitute a distinctive dimension of African American political thought. According to Michael Dawson, the embrace of these two precepts marks the principal difference between what he refers to as "black liberalism" and the liberalism that he refers to as "the American Creed" (i.e. the mainstream liberalism adopted by a large class of white persons).[45] We can set aside the issue of whether black liberalism is the most appropriate label to attach to the political ideology in question and concentrate on the content of this ideology. We can also bracket the question as to whether all or even most African Americans accept the two principles in question. For our purposes, it is appropriate to focus on members of what, following Cedric J. Robinson, has been referred to as the *black radical tradition*.[46] Black radicals, I would like to suggest, do in fact embrace a commitment to (1) political disobedience (i.e. extraelectoral activism, protest, and agitation) and (2) state-centered social change.

Rustin was a member of this tradition par excellence, even in the phase during which he published his essay "From Protest to Politics." To understand how this is so, it is vital to appreciate that during the course of his advocating for a turn to electoral politics, Rustin presents *only* a practical claim about the importance of numbers (as power) for effectuating change;

his is not a claim about the importance of majority support as a basis for the moral legitimacy of a given political entity or political decision. That is to say, during the civil rights movement strategy-debate that I discussed above, Rustin embraced electoral politics as a part of a strategy for improving the economic situation of the economically marginalized. In criticizing protest, Rustin aimed only to persuade radicals to reconsider its proper place. Consistent with this, in early 1968, weeks before the planned start of the Poor People's Campaign and months before the famed Democratic convention in Chicago, he intimates:

> If our job is to get housing, schools, jobs and better medical care, then there is only one way to get them—and it is not by protest. Protest is not going to pressure Congress into doing things. We can protest but we can't make that the emphasis. The emphasis must be [formal] politics, because if we want billions of dollars from Congress then we've got to create the kind of Congress, which is prepared to vote that money.[47]

Rustin's above statement was an indirect criticism of King's effort to launch a protest movement for economic justice and a direct challenge to the new leftists who we discussed above. Again, to Rustin, the radicals of the 1960s, namely new leftists, were guilty of myopia. They adopted radicalism as a stance rather than as a strategy; they treated protest as an end when its rightful place is only as a means to an end.

Rustin urged activists to be more strategic or selective about their use of protest and more methodical in planning protests when it did in fact constitute the appropriate method. In general, he stressed three points: every direct action initiative needed to be linked to particular injustices or wrongs; direct action organizers needed to consider the probable effect of a given protest on potential allies; and direct action needed to be deployed only when it promised attaining material objectives. Rustin's exacting pragmatic bent is especially on display in a 1970 essay where he stresses the value of protest as means rather than an end. He complains that "black protest [has become] an end in itself and not a means toward social change." Such protest, says Rustin, "is an enormously expressive phenomenon which is releasing the pent-up resentments of generations of oppressed Negroes. But expressiveness that is oblivious to political reality and not structured by instrumental goals is mere bombast.[48]

Rustin's emphasis on the rational relationship between means and ends is notable because it directs our attention to the fact that, in his essays during the mid-to-late 1960s and early 1970s, he believes himself to be providing a "realistic strategy for achieving fundamental social change."[49] Especially notable for our purposes, Rustin was always open to employing nonviolent direct action and engaging in political disobedience. And he remained a radical activist in the most significant sense.

But why is being clear about the character of radicalism important in the first place? The short answer is the most relevant: the term radical is valuable as a descriptive marker. To an extent, to understand the characteristics of radicals is indispensable to our effort to understand the sociopolitical world that we inhabit. As simple as it might sound, being human amounts to little more than engaging in practical activity. We are constantly in the process of setting objectives, devising plans concerning how to realize them, and attempting to realize them in practice. Religious, political, and ethical life consist largely of (1) reflection on means and ends in relation to special values or ultimate values, which we call moral values or goods and (2) action in accord with the values or principles in question. The term "radical" helps us describe and interpret our experience. Specifically, in the political domain, the term radical is introduced in order to elucidate and differentiate between certain means, on the one hand, and certain ends on the other. Self-identifying radicals debate among themselves about both what qualifies as (1) a radical path to a given end and (2) what makes for a radical end. Others, of course, argue about whether the term radical is one of praise or ridicule. I mean neither to praise nor to ridicule at this point. Rather, I mean to mark off certain normative visions and the associated means so as to facilitate understanding of our sociopolitical milieu.

If Rustin is not always remembered as a radical, it is because sometimes too much emphasis is given to the means that he proposed on particular occasions without reference to the ends that he hoped to effectuate, and without meditation on the spirit in which the given means were proposed. In one of the more discerning analyses of Rustin's activism, Daniel Levine sheds important light on Rustin's conception of radicalism. In *Bayard Rustin and the Civil Rights Movement*, Levine explains:

> [For Rustin] the goal of political action was attainable progress. Things had to move, in fact, for the people he often referred to as "the masses of Negro people" (and he occasionally used the term "lumpen"). Sometimes this might mean action in the streets, defying laws (though always willing to suffer the legal consequences). Sometimes it might mean an entirely legal demonstration or march. Sometimes it might mean working within the political system, with Congress, the Department of Justice, or the president. The goal was to make a difference now, in this world, for the people now on earth. People who accuse Rustin of abandoning his radicalism do not realize that for him radicalism was instrumental, not a stance.[50]

I want to draw attention to Levine's evocative repetitive invocation of the terms "now" and "sometimes." Levine points us to the fact that Rustin combined an idealistic impulse with a deep commitment to making a concrete "difference now . . . for people now on earth." Rustin was something of a now-oriented radical, who would "sometimes" propose this course of action, "sometimes" that one. By Rustin's own account, he was quite impatient, deeply concerned with the consequences of social action, and remarkably adaptable, which bears on our analysis in significant ways.

Based on our analysis of Rustin in this chapter, and in the light of Levine's depiction, we might say that Rustin, particularly during the 1960s and 1970s, put a premium on what Barbara Epstein refers to as "the politics of immediate efficacy." According to Epstein, persons motivated by the politics of immediate efficacy are acutely concerned with the immediate consequences of any contemplated sociopolitical action. Epstein contrasts persons committed to the politics of immediate efficacy with persons committed to "the politics of experience and utopian vision." The latter type of activist is (1) eminently concerned with combating existential problems (particularly the sense of alienation), (2) typically devoted to living in accord with certain values, and (3) committed to the view that imagining and engaging in alternative lifestyles constitutes the key to adequate social change.[51]

To appreciate the way in which the idea of the politics of immediate efficacy accentuates important aspects of Rustin's sociopolitical thought during the 1960s and 1970s, we can once more compare Rustin with Dorothy Day. The pair held many values in common. The bases of their mutual affection were many, but the thing that they agreed on most was the ethical priority of the Sermon on the Mount. Further, they agreed that Christian love entailed being in solidarity with the oppressed. In the light of this, both Rustin and Day were committed to radical politics and emphasized the "fierce urgency of now," to borrow King's phrase. On the basis of these common commitments, they worked side-by-side on several social justice projects periodically throughout their respective careers. All of this notwithstanding, as we have seen, Day and Rustin parted ways on the question of centralization versus decentralization.

One way to make sense of their divergence on this matter is to understand how their contrasting dispositions led them to evaluate action(s) differently. I do not want to overstate Day's patience or exaggerate Rustin's concern with practical consequences. But it is safe to say that Day was more willing than Rustin to act on faith, *hoping* that the consequences of her actions would come into fruition at some point—perhaps distant point—in the future. Further, Day focused on a smaller scale than Rustin. She was not as concerned with each of her actions having an impact on the entire nation. Day's focus was on day-to-day concerns, ethical minutiae, an orientation structured by what we might call, after engaged Buddhist Thich Nhat Hahn, "mindful living" or the ethics of attentiveness. Day was concerned with what she ate, with the tone of voice that she employed with friends and strangers, with her dress—everyday virtuousness. Dorothy Day's politics of experience and utopian vision exhibits a sort of patience and comfort with the unknown that Rustin's politics lack in the 1960s and 1970s.

Rustin, of course, was dismissive of the politics of experience (what he refers to as expressiveness as "bombast") and the politics of utopian vision because to him such political orientations lead to action that is "not structured by instrumental goals." I would argue that Rustin's emphasis on the immediate efficacy of action informed his rejection of absolute pacifism, decentralization, and radical lifestyle experimentation, ideals that are central to *strong* anarchism in most of its contemporary emanations.

But Rustin's radical impatience is a coin with two sides. For, just as his emphasis on the immediate efficacy of sociopolitical action meant that in the end he was unable to commend absolute pacifism, communal living, or decentralist projects, Rustin was also unwilling to rely on the formal political process. The two sides of this coin, then, correlate with the black radical tradition's twofold commitment to political disobedience and state-centered social change.[52] As simple as it might sound, impatience with injustice and the concomitant commitment to social justice is what gives shape to the activism of the black radical tradition as a general matter.

Indeed, the political praxis of black radicals is *radical* owing precisely to the rigorous commitment to social justice that orients the actions of its members. The primacy that black radicals accord to social justice informs black radicals' social theory and praxis in two ways, as has already been suggested. To begin, the primacy that most black radicals accord to social justice motivates the acceptance of what can be referred to as an instrumental embrace of the state. (The state is valued as an instrument with which to positively alter social conditions.) On the surface this instrumental valuation of the state might be taken to entail a commitment to the view that one bears a *moral* obligation to obey the authorities or commands of that state. But an instrumental valuation of the state does not, as a practical matter or as a logical philosophical matter, require one to accept the legitimacy of the state or the idea of political obligation that is so often attached to claims about legitimate political authority.[53] And radical social activists, including members of the black radical tradition, certainly do not value the American state in a way that gives rise to the claim that there exists a *moral* duty to follow its laws and commands. An impatience with injustice or the primacy of social justice that undergirds the black radical ethos conditions how radicals relate to political authorities and the territorial state, so that, among black radicals, social justice is distinguished from and given primacy over values such as social order, obedience, civility, formal procedure, and so on.

Considering the general qualities and commitments of the social radical might make this point a bit clearer. On my view, radical social activists ordinarily have or possess three related values, beliefs, or qualities that set them apart from others. First, radical activists are typically persons who subscribe to and have determined to focus on a higher law of some sort, whether it is a set of moral principles derived from an interpretation of divine revelation, a prophet's message, a philosopher's treatise, or a revolutionary's manifesto. The higher law serves as the source of a radical's sociopolitical vision. This vision then inspires a critical perspective and a radical posture vis-à-vis standing political institutions. Second, with the stringent moral standard in mind, radical activists often contend that for the most part all existing territorial states are complicit in various types of exploitation, repression, and oppression that render them unjust *and* illegitimate from a moral vantage. Finally, because radicals tend to insist that vision and reality can and must be united via some kind of politically disobedient action, radicals are often disinclined to limit their praxis to the mechanisms and processes established and sanctioned by ruling political authorities. In fact, radicals typically insist that a commitment to social justice requires keeping open the means available in the pursuit for social justice.[54] Along these lines, in the essay "Resistance to Civil Government," where Thoreau explicitly rejects voting and lobbying, and relates that "As for adopting the ways which the State has provided for remedying the evil, I know not of such ways. They take too much time, and a man's life will be gone."[55] For John Brown, Karl Marx, Huey Newton, and others this means keeping revolutionary violence on the table. For Garrison, Tolstoy, Gandhi, Martin Luther King Jr, and others this means always being prepared to employ nonviolent direct action.

Consistent with the description above, we can say that members of the black radical tradition reject the idea that there is a general *moral* duty to obey the commands of political authorities; and so we can say that black radicals reject the idea that there are political obligations and deny the idea that political authorities have the right to issue commands that persons have a moral duty to obey. Finally, in consequence of the aspects of black radical thought discussed above, I contend that members of the black radical tradition exemplify what it means to reject the legitimacy of the territorial state *and* at the same time assert the necessity of the territorial state for desired social change.

This latter contention brings us to the central question of this section. How should we name or describe, as a political philosophical matter, persons who vehemently reject the idea that there are general moral duties to obey the law or territorial state commands and at the same time insist on the necessity of the state for liberation? I would argue that this is one of the more important questions for persons interested in descriptive ethics and in the study of social movement activism in general. On my view, we can wholly appreciate the character and implications of radical social theory and praxis only if we employ idiosyncratic conceptual terminology in our (interpretive) descriptions of it. Accordingly, I think that it is appropriate to categorize persons who commend perpetual political disobedience as *weak* anarchists.

Some theorists maintain that employing the term anarchism to describe persons who advocate for political disobedience without hoping to abolish or eliminate the territorial state is inappropriate. The term anarchism, it is suggested, ought to be preserved for persons who reject the state as such. Chaim Gans pursues this line of argumentation in his work, *Philosophical Anarchism and Political Disobedience*. Gans is primarily concerned with weak anarchists (or in his terms, "philosophical anarchists"), specifically professional philosophers, who assert that there is no general moral duty to obey the law, yet then give a host of moral reasons to account for why one should ordinarily obey the laws of most existing territorial states. Gans maintains, on the basis of his analysis of such anarchists, that weak anarchism is anarchism with "no bite." For him, the use of the term is misleading, since the behavior of many self-described weak anarchists is or will be indistinguishable from persons who maintain that there *is* a general moral duty to obey the law.[56]

One of the advantages of thinking about weak anarchism in relation to political radicals, as opposed to professional philosophers, is that it focuses our attention on activists who more or less engage in practices that are indistinguishable from strong anarchists as opposed to the professional philosophers that Gans has in mind when he questions the value of weak anarchism as an analytical construct. Accordingly, it is critical to acknowledge that the black radical tradition's members (and social movement activists generally speaking) take a stance vis-à-vis the state that is different from most persons residing in the American political territory. For, it seems undeniable that the person committed to perpetually employing political disobedience in order to contest unjust sociopolitical practices relates to political authority in ways that are substantially different from the majority of political agents. And unlike political liberals who regard the use of political disobedience as appropriate in exceptional cases or circumstances, radicals insist that disobedience is central to social justice activism. For radical social activists, formal political practices such as voting and lobbying take on a secondary importance at best. Further, while many political liberals take for granted the legitimacy of existing constitutional democratic governments, radicals proceed more or less from the assumption that existing territorial states are illegitimate.

In practice, these differences manifest in ways that are important for us to make sense of. And weak anarchism strikes me as an appropriate term for this purpose because of the fact that the radical social activist who advocates for and engages in political disobedience asserts in clear terms a central tenet of weak anarchism: there is no general moral duty to obey political authorities or the law in virtue of their social status or the source of the law.[57] The weak anarchists' position, then, is an important one to consider as we reflect on and endeavor to understand the history of political philosophy and social action.

As is often noted, the normative vision as to the individual person's proper relation to the state has undergone profound changes in recent centuries. Paul Goodman, the radical libertarian writer, suggested in the early 1970s that the West was on the brink of a New Reformation, by which he meant a rejection of the authority of the priesthood of the scientists and elite politicians and technocrats; others have argued at length that the 1960s and 1970s brought about the rejection of all forms of authority, including political authority. The significance of the late twentieth-century social movements, then, might be considered analogous to the Protestant Reformation. As the story of that sixteenth-century Reformation goes, the signs began during the Renaissance, with developments in the arts and astronomy, with the emergence of biblical criticism, or translations of the Bible into languages that large classes of the public could read, and criticisms of the moral probity of the clergy. These factors along with others slowly ushered in a rejection, by many, of the authority of the Roman Catholic Church. The Protestant Reformation itself then set in motion a more widespread rejection of the religious authority of clerics. Lutheranism spawned Anabaptism, and Congregationalist governance would soon rival Episcopalian polity.

Only time will reveal the full importance of modern social movements and revolutions. But what is clear is that there have been crucial changes. In his work *Democracy and Its Critics*, Robert Dahl offers an illuminating description of the way in which modern social developments have factored into altered conceptions of the individual person's moral duties vis-à-vis political institutions. According to Dahl,

> By the time anarchism was recast . . . in the nineteenth century, belief in the moral right to revolt against a bad regime was widely shared, certainly by most liberals and democrats. In the twentieth century the systematic terror, brutality, and oppression of totalitarian regimes converted what once might have been an arguable proposition into an almost uncontested assumption. Democrats, liberals, conservatives, radicals, revolutionaries, Christians, Jews, Muslims, atheists, and agnostics all agree [with anarchists] that no person has an obligation to support or obey an evil state.[58]

Dahl is not primarily interested in the commitments of black radicals, yet I submit that he articulates the way in which most contemporary radicals, including black radicals such as Bayard Rustin, relate to the territorial state or political authority.

It is with the above in mind that I would like to suggest that we should refer to Bayard Rustin as a certain type of anarchist, even after he abandoned his radical pacifism. Again, to refer to black radicals, including the later Rustin, as weak anarchists makes explicit an important development in radical sociopolitical thought during recent centuries: the widespread rejection of political authority in a traditional sense and a denial of the notion that there exists a moral obligation to obey political authorities in virtue of their formal social status, for a combination of principled and pragmatic reasons. The above point directs our attention to one of the distinctive features of radical social theory and praxis. Radicals tend to be pragmatic on principle. That is, a principled commitment to social justice inspires a pragmatic orientation. Black radicals can be properly described as persons who embrace weak anarchism in the light of a commitment to social justice and on the basis of a theory or assumption about the best way to liberate the oppressed and protect certain freedoms.

This book has in large part been an attempt to remember past radicalism. I have stressed the significance of conceptual clarity owing to my conviction that how we remember the past is largely a function of the terms that we invoke in order to make sense of it. And what we remember—that is, the stories that we tell about the past—nearly always exerts normative force in the present. For my part, I have given extensive attention to theorists of social change who put a premium on (right) action in accord with conscience or morally motivated political disobedience. In this chapter, particularly in this section, I take myself to be identifying the political philosophical description or categorization of black radicalism as a hard case and to be offering or at least inviting better or more helpful ways of describing certain types of action. Appropriately, I have suggested that we best capture Rustin's attitude toward political authority—the law and the state—if we characterize his political philosophy in terms of anarchism. But to be clear, I do not take myself to be settling this issue here. Rather, I am proposing a certain interpretation in part in order to provoke fruitful debate. For, one might want to take up this problem of classification or description only so as to say why I am incorrect to describe the theory and praxis of black radicals in the way that I have.

But even if one agrees with my classification, there are other important matters to take up. For example, one might concede that I am correct to describe the political philosophical commitments of black radicals in the way that I have, yet insist that persons committed to perpetual political disobedience and the occasional use of state power are in error from a moral vantage. Related to this, political theorists or philosophers might want to focus on tensions extant in the thought of a weak anarchist. For instance, one interested in the problem of double standards might ask, why should persons opposed to black radicals' political visions ever comply with any territorial state commands generated by black radical activism? Can a black radical provide moral reasons in order to justify his or her preferences with respect to the use of territorial state power? These are vital questions that are important to ask and answer, independent of how one comes down on them.

# VII

Gene Sharp, a leading nonviolent direct action theorist, provides perhaps the clearest articulation of precisely how attitudes toward authority relate to nonviolent social change in his work *Waging Nonviolent Struggle*. Sharp follows Thoreau, Tolstoy, and Gandhi in stressing the fact that the source of political power is and its maintenance depends on obedience and cooperation. These in turn hinge on a populaces' acceptance of authority. In Sharp's words,

> Authority is necessary for the existence and operation of any regime. All rulers require an acceptance of their authority: their right to rule, command, and be obeyed. . . . The weakening or collapse of authority inevitably tends to loosen the subjects' predisposition towards obedience. . . . The loss of authority sets in motion the disintegration of the rulers' power. Their power is reduced to the degree that their authority is repudiated.[59]

Rustin understood Sharp's point quite well, as have most black radicals. With a nonviolent theory of social change in mind, and history as his tutor, Rustin once proclaimed, "We need in every community a group of angelic troublemakers. Our power is in our ability to make things unworkable. All we have is our bodies. We need to tuck them, tuck them, in places so that the wheels don't turn."[60]

Anyone concerned about the situation of the world's dispossessed and oppressed, including America's poor, whether brown, white, or black, whether suburbanites, urbanites, or country folk, probably appreciates that every community needs a few angelic troublemakers. No less than in the 1960s, poor persons in America lack power. Fifty years after passage of the Voting Rights Act, the condition of the black underclass has been only modestly altered. By some measures its size and scope has expanded. In such a context, it is crucial for American critical theorists and radical activists to grapple with the normative visions articulated by black radicals and others during the mid-1960s. In particular, we should reflect on the rationale for and the consequences of the calls, during the mid-to-late 1960s and after, for the normalization of social action and for the replacement of nonviolent direct action with formal political action and advocacy.

Rustin's activist career is especially important, as he was at the center of a debate about the meaning of social justice and the means necessary for attaining it that continues up to the present moment. In this chapter, I have endeavored to give an account of Rustin's shift from protest to politics and have attempted to demonstrate that what was at issue in his running debate with King and Carmichael was the anticipated effectiveness of rival strategies for social change and not the question as to the moral acceptability of political disobedience. Rustin rightly contended that civil rights were null in the absence of certain social and economic conditions. Formal legal equality was not enough because wholly exercising civil rights hinges on achieving a certain social and economic status. Moreover, Rustin's criticisms of decentralist projects were a salutary intervention on the American left. Rustin was correct to worry that abandoning the American state, or efforts to shape its practices, would put the welfare of African Americans in jeopardy, given the role that the federal government has played in African American life since the Great Depression, or even the American Civil War. While I have less faith in the American territorial state than Rustin did and find myself more and more attracted to the decentralists that Rustin so often criticized, Rustin's point is well taken and his intervention presents an important challenge to strong anarchists who argue for a redirection of energies away from the territorial state and electoral politics.

Yet as important as Rustin's thought might be for strong anarchists, it strikes me as though his legacy poses the greatest challenge to political liberals, republicans, and card-carrying Democrats. As a member of the black radical tradition, Rustin insisted on making a concrete difference for people now on earth. He internalized the black radical mantra announced by Frederick Douglass: there can be no justice or progress without struggle and without sacrifice. Rustin demanded a return on action. For radical activists who reject strong anarchism and embrace state-centered theories of social change, the most important question is how to make state institutions respond to the needs of the working class and unemployed.

Reflecting on Rustin's thought invites a reconsideration of the direction that social activism has moved in recent decades. On some levels, with little to show for it, an entire generation of activists has stayed on a path similar to the one that Rustin laid out in his most famous essay. Since the late 1960s, liberals and leftists—whether black, white, yellow, or brown—have relied mostly on formal political action. Rustin's understanding of the inadequacy of civil rights legislation was prescient. Yet, at the same time, in retrospect, it is clear that Rustin placed undue faith in the formal electoral process. From our vantage, it is all too apparent that the Democratic Party cannot be the vehicle of revolution that Rustin envisioned in the 1960s and that formal electoral politics in general cannot deliver the goods that Rustin hoped for.

Realizing and being faithful to Bayard Rustin's sociopolitical vision will probably be possible only if social justice theorists, organizers, and activists invert his thesis and move from politics to protest. As it is, extrajudicial means have almost always been necessary in order to radically transform social structures and redistribute power. And the time that has elapsed since Rustin wrote his famous essay has only confirmed the fact that social justice comes only after struggle. To that end, if we are to be and become the kinds of persons that act in ways that lead to a world that better accords with our visions, we will probably have to adopt Rustin's *attitude* toward political authority. That is, the practical viability of realizing the needed social action will likely hinge on the degree to which we are able to embody the anarchist's spirit or attitude, which is precisely why we must remember the visions, sacrifices, and heritage of angelic troublemakers.

# Conclusion:
# "The Awakening to Come"

*I am wiser than the founding fathers.*
WENDELL PHILIPS

*Our government has certainly not measured up to expectations.*
WALTER LIPPMANN, "The Taboo"

*Our inherited freedom is spent.*
HENRY DAVID THOREAU

*Let's get free.*
DEAD PREZ

As anarchist historian George Woodcock elegantly intimates, "the heritage that anarchism has left to the modern world is to be found in a few inspiring lives of self-sacrifice and devotion . . . [and] most of all in the incitement to return to a moral and natural view of society which we find in the writings of Godwin and Tolstoy." According to Woodcock, "The great anarchists call on us to stand on our own moral feet like a generation of princes, to become aware of justice as an inner fire." The great anarchists insist that "freedom and moral self-realization are interdependent, and one cannot live without the other."[1]

Through an analysis of the religious-ethical visions espoused by Henry David Thoreau, Dorothy Day, and Bayard Rustin, I have sought to elucidate the elements of anarchism that Woodcock identifies. Proceeding as I have has allowed me to illustrate the way in which Thoreau, Day, and Rustin were angelic troublemakers, possessed with the spirit of anarchism, which reveals that instead of being antithetical to anarchism as some assume, theism can actually motivate an anarchist ethic.

Although their religious-ethical commitments were not identical, Thoreau, Day, and Rustin agreed that God endowed human persons with the capacity to discern the moral truth and the capacity to fulfill the moral law in practice. In view of their respective theological assumptions and religious-ethical beliefs, Thoreau, Day, and Rustin each endeavored to live in accord with the moral truth as they understood it, which involved encouraging others to answer the call of the divinity within and to stand on their own moral feet. Notably, the three all regarded individual assertions of moral autonomy as indispensable to any effective social justice movement or social reform activism. Indeed, Thoreau, Day, and Rustin, at different points in their activist careers, all posited rigorous ethical reflection and fidelity to God as the most auspicious means by which to usher in a more just social order; and they suggested that religious fidelity requires being proactively and assiduously engaged in the sociopolitical realm, as durable conditions of justice will become a possibility only if individual persons *incessantly seek* to be morally good or perfect and thus *always refuse* to comply with or participate in unjust practices.

In order to register the far-reaching sociopolitical implications of Thoreau's, Day's, and Rustin's respective religious-ethical visions, I have argued they each emphasize individual moral responsibility in a way that entails adopting a posture vis-à-vis modern territorial states that is constitutive of anarchism or an anarchist attitude toward political authority. More specifically, my analysis of Thoreau, Day, and Rustin has demonstrated how a commitment to social justice, an emphasis on moral responsibility (for oppression and social suffering), and an ethic of noncomplicity (Thoreau) or noncooperation (Day and Rustin) with unjust social practices can commend an anarchist posture or attitude. It should come as no surprise that one can derive a radical normative political vision from a given conception of God, the person, and moral truth. Yet, by making this fact explicit, I have shed important light on the commitments and values that informed Thoreau, Day, and Rustin as they endeavored to be morally good and illustrated the way in which certain religious commitments seem to point in inevitably and profoundly radical sociopolitical directions.

As most would agree, a commitment to always acting in accord with conscience or the higher law entails a refusal to take a given territorial state authority's command as a determinative reason for action. So a person who is committed to the idea of moral responsibility or autonomy, as I have described it, essentially denies that there is ever a reason to act strictly based on reasons provided by modern territorial state authorities. The significance of this denial comes to the fore in the light of the fact that a person can be said to follow the dictates of an authoritative figure only to the extent that the person bases his or her decision to perform or not perform a given act on an authoritative figure's dictate. When a person acts in a certain way based *solely* on the command of a given figure of authority, then the authoritative figure in that case represents the source of the reason on which the person acts. The figure in that case actually constitutes an authoritative figure. Modern state officials (political authorities), of course, claim to have a right to issue commands that others have the duty to obey. Anarchists reject this assertion of authority; or, better, they deny that state officials possess *legitimate* authority. This denial, I have said, is constitutive of *weak* anarchism.

Stating the matter as I have points to the fact that many moral theories share an affinity with *weak* anarchism. This owes to several related developments in contemporary ethical discourse. To begin, individual conscience and an idea of moral autonomy have assumed a central place in modern ethical thought. Further, many ethicists and activists specify at least some absolute prohibitions and differentiate between social practices and a higher moral law of some sort. In practice, for such persons, when the moral law and a social practice are in conflict, the upstanding moral subject is charged with acting in accord with the moral law or conscience against the social practice or legal norm. Thus, if a state requires a person to perform immoral acts, then an individual has a moral duty to defy or disobey commands or laws issued by territorial state authorities. In this way, many moral theorists maintain that as a moral matter the positive law is subordinate to the dictates of individual conscience. (On my view, to emphasize moral autonomy in the way that many contemporary theorists do, invites a consideration of the relationship between moral autonomy and varieties of anarchism.)

It is crucial to appreciate that whether a government or political organization actually calls for its subjects to commit immoral or morally prohibited acts is an empirical question. And the more concerned one is by the fact of social injustice and the more seriously one takes one's ethical commitments, the more pressing one is going to find this kind of question. (These matters are especially urgent for religionists such as Mennonites, Quakers, Buddhists, Sufis, and others who maintain that their religious commitments prohibit participation in the organized practice of killing.) When persons conclude that a particular territorial state or political entity systematically requires persons to perform immoral acts, then the anarchist impulse will become more pronounced, which is what we would expect and is undoubtedly why anarchism gained so many adherents during the American-Vietnamese war of the 1960s and 1970s. Thoreau, Day, and Rustin, for their part, argued that territorial states, as a practical matter, are given to coercing persons into participating in unjust social practices, which is a claim that I am inclined to agree with, based upon the territorial states that have existed since Thoreau published *Walden*.

The question as to whether we should comply with the commands of a given territorial state is no less urgent today than it was during the eighteenth century, the nineteenth century, or the 1950s, 1960s, and 1970s. (The age of revolution has not ended.) That so many are convinced otherwise only underscores how complicated the structure of modern society is and the degree to which we assume that it is impossible to avoid complicity in oppressive social practices. But it is precisely this complicatedness that makes it so critical for us to reflect on what individual persons must do and who we must become if we are to be decent. Perhaps the only option for a morally conscious agent at this point in history is perpetual political disobedience or revolutionary withdrawal. Anarchism as a moral tradition poses these kinds of questions, which is why it is essential to know something about the tradition and to reflect on the anarchist challenge.

As I suggested in the introduction, because anarchism is frequently associated with or reduced to terrorism, nihilism, and antireligious atheism, many are reticent to take anarchist activists and thinkers seriously. Since in the modern world, especially the American context, religious awakening and sociopolitical revolution have gone hand-in-hand, anarchists do a disservice to their revolutionary cause by neglecting religiously motivated anarchism, in that this neglect facilitates the common misunderstanding of anarchism. In other words, the neglect of certain varieties of the general anarchist tradition reinforces problematic assumptions about anarchism and makes it more difficult than it needs to be to make anarchism an attractive option for large segments of the population. By focusing on religiously motivated expressions of nonviolent anarchism, I hope that I have made a case for dispensing with at least a few of the reductive understandings of anarchism. Such reductions or caricatures obscure the character of our normative political philosophical options and thus impede constructive normative exchange and debate about possible viable action in the face of an unsatisfactory and unjust status quo.

As more attention is given to anarchist thought, I anticipate that not only will the many caricatures likely be dispensed with. Several of the bases on which theorists tend to reject anarchism will also be called into question. For example, it is common for liberal and republican political theorists to reject anarchism based on a claim about the need for social order. But as far as I am concerned, such rejections often fall short on account of their being predicated on two debatable assumptions or claims about the modern territorial state and a related mistaken belief about anarchism itself. To examine anarchist theory necessarily entails reassessing these kinds of assumptions and beliefs.

With respect to the first assumption about the state, many persons maintain that the territorial state is desirable or necessary. Many if not most persons who proceed from this assumption about the state's necessity tend to downplay the territorial state's role as an oppressive and repressive entity and thus neglect the major criticism of the state forwarded by anarchist social critics. As I have already intimated, Thoreau, Day, and Rustin (especially during his radical pacifist phase) contended that territorial states actually foster nationalism and racism, mostly in service of capitalism, in order to make persons into instruments of oppression and repression. Ruling elites employ the state apparatus in order to transform subjects into objects. This objectification (process) is extended indefinitely: one set of tools (police or soldiers) is employed by ruling elites in order to oppress and repress another set of tools (workers and dissidents). The territorial state, as a type or form of political organization, is problematic from a moral perspective because of the way in which it systematically interferes in the lives of persons in order to force persons to be or become agents of domination. (Again, it is the fact that the state operates in this fashion that makes principled noncooperation or disobedience an effective means by which to interrupt the workings of the unjust machine, as Thoreau puts it.)

It is undoubtedly possible to argue for the necessity of the territorial state and also acknowledge the way in which territorial states function as entities that protect the interests of ruling elites (with violence or the threat of violence). Persons who take up this stance sometimes regard the territorial state as a necessary evil, which brings us to the second problematic assumption about the state that often buttresses criticisms or the rejection of anarchism. Ordinarily, theorists who acknowledge the state's role in sustaining unjust conditions and nonetheless reject anarchism do so based on the (implicit) assumption that the modern territorial state is the only viable type of political organization.

It is easy to appreciate why persons might assume this, given how pervasive modern states are in the affairs of most societies, how much they affect the lives of most persons, and the degree to which we presently depend on goods that state agencies produce. Nonetheless, as a practical and theoretical matter, the territorial state is not the only feasible type of political or governmental organization. More to the point, as simple or as obvious as it might seem, it is imperative to explicitly acknowledge that the territorial state is not the only possible source of law and order, even if we concede—which strong anarchists do not—that territorial states contribute to just social conditions rather than perpetuate a multiplicity of injustices. To assume that the state is the only viable type of political organization is to unnecessarily constrain our imagination and it is therefore an assumption that must be challenged.

It is also an assumption that connects directly to the common misconception about anarchism that I mentioned earlier. In this work, I have presented what probably strikes some as a problematic conception of anarchism. Distinguishing between strong anarchists and weak anarchists, I have indicated that in practice most consistent strong anarchists advocate for the establishment of decentralized and nonviolent or noncoercive (or at least minimally violent or coercive) political organizations or institutional practices. As I have noted already, the fact that this is the case deserves greater attention than it has received, since it calls attention to the fact that anarchism is not best thought of as a rejection of political organization or government per se. Articulating the matter somewhat ironically, I have insisted that anarchism can actually be thought of as a type of political organization or a norm with which to evaluate and identify morally acceptable forms of organization. Because few critics of anarchism acknowledge this fact, much criticism of anarchism actually fails to respond to what I take to be the fundamental contentions or aspirations presented by most anarchists.

There is a dialectical and paradoxical relationship between the neglect, misunderstanding, and mischaracterization of anarchist theory and the neglect or portrayal of anarchist experimentation and disobedience. So, it is not simply that persons misunderstand anarchist theory, or more particularly, anarchist ideas as they are presented in writing. Persons also fail to appreciate the character of anarchist sociopolitical experiments. For, many of the theoretically informed anarchist experiments underway across the globe are neither given the attention that they deserve nor accurately portrayed when they are discussed.

There are several factors that might help explain this neglect and misunderstanding. Part of it has to do with the fact that many persons simply take no interest in anarchism and base their views on secondary accounts of anarchism. But this does not explain why the caricatures and reductions exist in the first place. My sense is that one must take into consideration how our predispositions and biases inform our neglect and misunderstandings. To understand why anarchism has been interpreted and described as it has been, one must recognize that many persons, particularly in America, are predisposed to suppose that there are no practically viable alternatives to existing institutional arrangements. For better or worse, our notions of what is possible are shaped by dominant narratives that reinforce our sense that the status quo is either inevitable or nearly the best that we should or can hope for in good faith.

Critical theorists since Marx have referred to these dominant narratives, that is, conceptions of reality, as ruling ideologies. These ideologies shape consciousness or lead to what we might refer to as a particular frame of mind. In our era, the predominant frame of mind leads people to conceptualize the earth's terrain in the light of the political geographical boundaries accepted by the political leaders of the political units with the most advanced and organized military forces. But not only do territorial states claim a monopoly on the earth's territory, they claim a monopoly on justice on the earth. As most would agree, in popular thought and political theory, the existence of the territorial state, particularly in its representational democratic form, is taken for granted. And among most contemporary political theorists, justice, to invoke Alain Badiou, is posited as a relation to the state.

Anarchist theory and praxis, of course, challenges the territorial state order on exactly these points. To begin, at a basic level, anarchist experimentation and disobedience, such as Thoreau's and Day's principled withdrawal or quasisecession, challenge the territorial state's claim to a monopoly on the earth's terrain. In addition to challenging the state's monopoly on the earth's soil, anarchist experiments and disobedience represent a challenge to the territorial state's claim to a monopoly on justice on planet earth (just as the Black Panthers and Zapatistas challenge the state's claim to a monopoly on organized violence).

As I alluded to earlier, the predominant way of thinking about geography, justice, and social reality generally speaking undermines our capacity to wholly appreciate the character and significance of anarchist experimentation and disobedience in that the predominant way of thinking shapes how anarchist experimentation and disobedience are described. Persons who are committed to alternative social practices, such as founding anarchist communities or communes, are routinely and even predictably described (or dismissed) as "unrealistic," "naïve," "other-worldly," "freaks," "utopian," and so on. So, when anarchists are not simply ignored, they are mocked or subjected to name-calling. In truth, many anarchists take these labels as compliments, and so the point here is not to condemn mockery. Rather it is to draw attention to the way in which this kind of name-calling functions to shape discourse and thus our orientation toward certain social agents and objects of inquiry. Name-calling of this sort is meant to preclude conversation rather than initiate it. It is a stand-in for analysis rather than an invitation for analysis. Ironically, name-callers of the kind that I have in mind are often name-callers precisely because they hope to avoid (perhaps unconsciously) confronting certain facts about reality, namely social injustice and our complicity in it.

In the end, the general response to anarchists is probably the response that we should expect from persons who are conditioned (as we to some extent all are) to assume that no just political thing can exist that does not exist in relation to the territorial state, since existing territorial states have laid claim to the entire earth and to justice on earth. This basic assumption might be described as a facet of *cartographical hegemony*. It is an idea or ideal that stems from certain social practices and in turn plays a role in perpetuating the social practices in question. To the extent that we play a role in perpetuating cartographical hegemony, we impede the realization of alternative social practices by discouraging imagination and experimentation. It is a role that radical activists and intellectuals in the coming years must refuse to play and must discourage others from playing.

Although anarchist thought is not a panacea and has its gaps, tensions, and perhaps even contradictions, as is true of all theoretical orientations, since anarchism is so little understood, it is at present difficult to have a fruitful debate about the strengths and weaknesses of anarchist thought. Such a debate is probably a long way off and will become possible only once anarchism as a normative political philosophy is better understood. Once a larger number of theorists adequately understand the varieties of anarchism, the door will open for discussions about substantive disagreements and more constructive comparisons of anarchist thinkers with critics of anarchism or persons who do not explicitly accept anarchism, and more sober evaluations of anarchist praxis. In fact, comparative analysis is one path to the improved understanding that I contend is needed.

With this in mind, going forward, it will behoove anarchist theorists to identify nonanarchist theorists, philosophies, or traditions that share commonalities with anarchism. Comparative analysis of this sort will involve both explicating anarchism in terms that reveal how much anarchism shares in common with ostensibly rival theories and interpreting the given rival theories in a way that brings to the fore elements of those theories that complement or are compatible with anarchism. There are at least three ways in which an anarchist theorist or student of anarchism might approach these ostensibly competing theories. First, one might make a strong claim and assert that, given a particular theorist's normative commitments, the theorist can actually be said to put forward a vision that is consistent with certain brands of anarchism. Alternatively, one might make a weaker claim and simply suggest that the given theorist presents a vision and develops concepts in a way that might facilitate the refinement of arguments for an anarchist ethic or the evaluation of anarchist praxis. Finally, one might, of course, attempt to combine the two above approaches.

For an abbreviated yet concrete example of how such an argument or reflection might go, I can briefly discuss Hannah Arendt's political philosophy in a way that illustrates why it might be an especially fecund place for anarchists to turn. Based on Arendt's criticisms of Thoreau that were canvassed in Chapter 1, one might imagine that Arendt and anarchists conceive of social life in ways that are irreconcilable. Yet, I think that an anarchist theorist might offer an interpretation of Arendt that shows that Arendt's normative vision is closer to certain expressions of anarchism than one might at first suppose. Wholly appreciating this, of course, is possible only insofar as one proceeds with the conception of anarchism that I have endeavored to explicate in this text.

The promise of Arendt's conception of politics for anarchist theorists is especially evident in her reflection in *On Revolution*, where she spells out her normative political vision through an interpretation of the American Revolution or the events surrounding it. Resisting the tendency among political philosophers and social theorists in the mid-twentieth century to conflate violence, power, and politics, Arendt insisted that politics properly understood transcends violence. She predicated this claim on a particular understanding of the difference between violence and power. To Arendt, the denial of this distinction has led and leads many theorists to misunderstand the character of revolutions and to miss the meaning of politics per se. (Consistent with this, on one level, Arendt's reflection on the American Revolution is meant to demonstrate how power and authority are distinct from one another and from violence and to show how the former two can be lost without violence; thereby a revolution itself, properly understood, does not require violence even if revolutionary situations are often accompanied by it.) It is not a stretch to say that one of Arendt's principal contributions to twentieth-century political thought was the way in which she held fast to the distinction between power and violence, which is one of the reasons why her thought is pertinent for anarchists.[2]

Arendt's conceptions of the political realm and power are tied to her understanding of freedom. In *On Revolution*, as elsewhere, Arendt asserts that freedom is the freedom to participate in the political realm. Participation in the political realm entails getting together and making and keeping promises that pertain to the common good. Power is the fruit of participation. In consequence, for Arendt, political freedom is expressed when people get together and make and keep mutual promises that have to do with public goods.

Bona fide political action, then, presupposes reciprocity and mutuality—equality. It is precisely this, if Arendt is correct, that American revolutionaries seemed to realize. Three long quotes bring together why Arendt finds this so significant and points to how considering Arendt's thought might be edifying for anarchist theorists. According to Arendt,

> The unique and all-decisive distinction between the settlements of North America and all other colonial enterprises was that only the British emigrants had insisted, from the very beginning, that they constitute themselves into "civil bodies politic." These bodies, moreover, were not conceived as governments, strictly speaking; they did not imply rule and the division of people into rulers and ruled. . . . These new bodies politic were "political societies," and their great importance for the future lay in the formation of a political realm that enjoyed power and was entitled to claim rights without possessing or claiming sovereignty.[3]

Moreover, Arendt suggests that American revolutionaries recognized and maintained that

> Power comes into being only if and when men join themselves together for the purpose of action, and it will disappear when, for whatever reason, they disperse and desert one another. Hence, binding and promising, combining and covenanting are the means by which power is kept in existence.[4]

For the American revolutionaries,

> Power [that] rested on reciprocity and mutuality . . . was real power and legitimate, whereas the so-called power of kings or princes or aristocrats, because it did not spring from mutuality but, at best, rested only on consent, was spurious and usurped.[5]

All of this is of note for our purposes in that Arendt echoes self-described anarchist theorists on fundamental points. As a practical matter, there is little difference between what Arendt refers to as "political societies" and the political entities that most strong anarchists are interested in bringing into fruition. In fact, Arendt can be taken to provide support for strong anarchists who hope to build or found political associations on the basis of universal mutual consent (and thus disperse power and authority so as to do away with a distinctive ruling class), since, as should be clear, in what Arendt calls "political societies," persons' political obligations are derived from promises that they have made.[6] In sum, Arendt suggests that only mutual consent can create fully legitimate political power and obligations.[7]

Arendt makes this explicit with her invocation of the idea of a "horizontal social contract," which she contrasts with "vertical social contracts." Arendt complains that with a vertical social contract, the type proposed by Thomas Hobbes, a person surrenders his or her "rights and powers to either government or the community" and resigns his or her "power to some higher authority and consents to be ruled in exchange for a reasonable protection of his life and property."[8] Vertical social contracts, Arendt tells us, are antithetical to action qua *mutual* promising. Vertical contracts might ensure physical security. But vertical contracts comprise exchanges that undermine the possibility of freedom or veritable political action.

For the above reasons, Arendt prefers horizontal contracting. According to Arendt, American revolutionaries, namely New Englanders, did too. They entered into horizontal contracts as opposed to vertical contracts on account of a commitment to mutuality and reciprocity. They preferred mutual promises because they appreciated that, with mutual promises, the contracting parties' powers are mutually multiplied and amplified rather than restricted. Describing horizontal contracts and mutual promising, Arendt intimates, "As far as the individual person is concerned, it is obvious that he gains as much power by the system of mutual promises as he loses by his consent to a monopoly of power in the ruler."[9] So, the horizontal contract presupposes and implements a vision of equality, whereas vertical contracting undermines equality by institutionalizing rulership, that is, the division between the ruler and the ruled.

Insofar as we recognize that anarchism does not entail the rejection of government or political organization per se, it should be evident how anarchism relates to or might be related to visions spelled out by ostensibly antianarchist or nonanarchist philosophers and theorists such as Hannah Arendt. I would certainly have to say more than I have in order to make wholly clear how this is the case. But, at the very least, it should be apparent that an anarchist might interpret and develop Arendt's normative vision in ways that would enrich anarchist theory and perhaps make anarchism more attractive to certain contingents than it might otherwise be. As one of

CONCLUSION: "THE AWAKENING TO COME"        165

the twentieth century's leading champions of political imagination, Arendt sought to transform our perception of sociopolitical reality by altering our understanding of what certain terms mean. By calling into question how we communicate about human interaction, Arendt prods us to imagine the past and present anew, which liberates us to think differently about future possibilities. In the words of Jonathan Schell, Arendt's approach was to "boldly take sides in debates on the meanings of certain words."[10] After clarifying or fixing the meaning of certain terms she would offer "a new interpretation of historical events" and thus a new understanding of the present and what it requires of us.[11]

Arendt not only reconsiders the meaning of revolution in order to provide an account of how revolutions can be effectuated without employing violent means. She also suggests, by melding her idea of mutual promising with the idea of the horizontal contract, a fresh way for theorists to think about the concrete form that anarchist sociopolitical practices might take. Through her creative interpretation of American history, Arendt aspired to provoke a reconsideration of our presuppositions about what the political represents and how we might attain political freedom. One of the enduring messages that Arendt communicates in *On Revolution* is that in practice it is profoundly difficult to preserve the kind freedom and equality realized among certain early Americans. If Arendt turned to the American revolutionaries in part to celebrate their wise preference for the horizontal contract, she also turned to them in order to bemoan their failure to create political institutions that facilitate the kind of active participation that is necessary to preserve the freedom and power of the people.

To Arendt, the American Revolution was only halfway successful in that the emergence of representational constitutionalism undermined the political participation of the demos. That is, in postrevolutionary America—the United States of America—"the people" were largely excluded from participating in the political sphere. Much of Arendt's writing throughout the 1960s in one way or another touched on the question of how to spur the kind of active (participatory political) life that she deemed necessary for the realization of freedom—and even the full expression of human personality—that she believed the American revolutionaries had envisioned and temporarily embodied.[12]

For any future people to realize freedom, Arendt thought that they would have to understand what it means to be free. Arendt explicates the meaning of freedom by juxtaposing it with liberation. To confuse liberation with freedom is one way to undermine the viability of any revolutionary praxis. Liberation from oppression, Arendt tells us, is not the same thing as freedom. Liberation is related to freedom, yet the state of being liberated is not identical with the state of being free. According to Arendt, for oppressed and repressed peoples liberation is a precondition to the realization of freedom. Once realized, freedom (as power) becomes the thing that keeps repression and oppression at bay. To be free, persons must be willing to be constantly active. This is because, for Arendt, the only way to secure freedom is by generating and sustaining power. Because political power is the effect of mutual promises, and since mutual promising brings persons together and this togetherness is constitutive of power, we must continuously make and keep promises. In other words, to be free, we must (voluntarily) remain (active) together. In the end, Arendt draws her many distinctions primarily so as to highlight her sense of the demanding character of the authentic political life. It is perhaps on this point that Arendt most agrees with contemporary anarchists and has the most to teach us.

In this book, I have concerned myself with making sense of the religious-ethical visions of three American radicals who insist that there is no rest for those who would be free or for those who would be just. Neither freedom nor justice can be inherited, say these radicals. And even if freedom can be inherited, from where we stand, it is difficult to disagree with Thoreau. "We have used up all our inherited freedom. If we would save our lives, we must fight for them."[13]

Religious radicals in the anarchist tradition insist that the first line of struggle is the struggle with (in) ourselves. We cannot change the world without changing ourselves, including how we describe our social milieu. For Thoreau, Day, and Rustin, to describe reality, including God, the self, and social institutions, is to make or remake it or at least fundamentally transform how we experience reality. In other words, the struggle for freedom is one that begins with self-examination and self-reformation. The self-struggle must be accompanied by an awakening to the value of other human persons as individuals.

One wellspring of social justice movement and authentically revolutionary praxis is properly valuing oneself and others. It is persons awakened to the value of *all* individual human persons, then, who will usher in an age in which justice has been extended by at least one step. This is because it is such persons who will find the status quo unacceptable. In Thoreauvian terms, we might say that a new (more just) world will be a discovery of *conscience*. Conscience prompts our empathetic impulse and provokes visions and dreams of a freer world—freedom dreams, as Robin Kelley and Eddie Glaude Jr have put it. And as Thoreau put it, a step in the direction of a more desirable world is to announce the kind of world that would command our respect. We must share our freedom dreams before we can realize them.

It might be difficult to imagine taking any revolutionary steps given the present state of our world. Although we have failed to be awake, we should hope that we are living in the end of an ice age—an age of callous hearts and political apathy. Indeed, as Cornel West notes, "Some awaking is taking place. People are becoming more alert. The sleepwalkers are beginning to wake just a little bit. Any such awakening is like falling in love: you care so much that you can't help yourself." What we need now, says West, is "leaders—namely, each one of us—to fall awake in this way."[14] As we fall awake, which is nothing other than falling in love with the right things, we will experience a blossoming of conscience, faith, and imagination. *Let us be awake.*

# NOTES

## Introduction

1  Guenther Roth and Claus Wittich, eds, *Max Weber: Economy and Society: An Outline of Interpretive Sociology* (Berkeley: University of California Press, 1978), 54.

2  Robert Paul Wolff, *In Defense of Anarchism* (Berkeley: University of California, 1998), 4.

3  To be clear, the ideal of voluntarism—the fact of consent—can be accepted as a theoretical or logical matter yet rejected as either a description of actual political life or a claim about what is practically possible in present political life.

4  Anarchists who reject all forms of government or political organization typically extend the voluntarist principle along two lines that rule out the possibility of just political authority. First, such anarchists insist that there is a moral duty to exercise autonomy and understand this duty to entail a strict prohibition against the practice of issuing promises, as promising is said to constitute a surrendering of moral autonomy. Second, they contend that all coercion (or violence) is wrong. In consequence, they hold that contractual agreements, including political pacts and contracts, are inherently problematic. I should also note that I recognize that one might reject all forms of government and at the same time (1) assert the possibility of morally acceptable promise making and (2) allow for the possibility of just coercive or violent action. However, once one concedes the acceptability of promise making, it is difficult to provide compelling reasons for considering unanimous or consensus decision-making procedures morally problematic, especially if one allows for just coercive or violent action. Therefore, it would seem that in order to defend what I am calling an absolute anarchist position, one would probably have to endorse a prohibition against promise making. At the very least, one who defends the two prohibitions in question is likely to present the most philosophically defensible version of the extreme version of anarchism that I have identified. I direct our attention to this strand of anarchism mostly for the sake of contrast and to highlight the falsity of the common assumption that embracing anarchism requires rejecting all forms of government.

5  Interestingly, while unanimous or consensus democracy may lend legitimacy to a given political entity, it is unclear whether the idea of political rule is applicable to cases in which decision making and the passage of legislation

require unanimity or consensus. Hence, it is not clear how the idea of authority would itself be applicable in the case of unanimous or consensus democracy.

6  As we move along, we must acknowledge the distinction between government proper and the modern territorial state as such. The modern territorial state emerges after the Westphalian Treaty (Phillip Bobbitt); it asserts the right to rule over a geographic area and the right to rule is the right to tax, execute, jail, command, conscript; and via standing armies, police bureaus, surveillance, and clandestine agencies territorial states rule over human persons and claim a monopoly on organized violence (Max Weber), which includes the reservation of the right to establish who is an enemy, who is a friend (Carl Schmitt), and thus the right to determine who is an eligible object of attack—subject to be killed via the violent means that the state has at its disposal. One can concede that the state solves coordination problems through the implementation of regulatory schemes (after John Finnis) without believing that this is the distinctive feature of the modern territorial state. On my view, the modern state, which is widely thought to have emerged after Westphalia, is a political entity that is territorial, bureaucratic, centralized, and militarized. I will refer to the modern state as the *territorial* state given how important rule over territory is for the modern political units that we refer to as states.

7  Rigorous moral theories, whether religiously or nonreligiously motivated, often underwrite anarchism precisely because of the fact that the rigorous moralist is often unwilling to cede authority to a majority from which the moralist is herself excluded.

8  Legal and political philosophers, with this issue in mind, draw a distinction between anarchists who argue that persons have a moral duty to withdraw support from the state and those who do not by invoking varying terminology. Probably most common is to discuss this distinction in terms of *philosophical* anarchism and *political* anarchism. This distinction between philosophical and political anarchism is helpfully explicated by philosopher A. John Simmons in his analysis of variant types of anarchism. *Political* anarchists, as Simmons describes the lot, are persons who conclude that the modern territorial state lacks moral legitimacy and further assert that persons have "an immediate requirement of opposition to illegitimate states." *Philosophical* anarchists, on the other hand, do not draw such a conclusion on the basis of the state's lack of moral legitimacy. Rather, "philosophical anarchists hold that there may be good moral reasons not to oppose or disrupt at least some kinds of illegitimate states, reasons that outweigh any right or obligation of opposition" (A. John Simmons, *Justification and Legitimacy: Essays on Rights and Obligation* (New York: Cambridge University Press, 2001), 107–9). I will draw extensively from Simmons, yet for the sake of clarity will discuss the distinction in question in terms of strong anarchism and weak anarchism. For an additional and helpful account of philosophical anarchism see chapter 2 of David Miller's *Anarchism*.

9  This is something of a formal definition of anarchism. Perhaps, it is important to differentiate between the various orientations to the law in a way that I have not. We might maintain that merely arguing against a general duty to obey the law is a necessary but insufficient basis on which to attribute a commitment of weak anarchism to a particular moral agent. I give some

attention to this issue in Chapter 3, where I reflect on the relationship of a commitment of political disobedience to weak anarchism.

10  Crucially, as we proceed, I will take opposition to include both active resistance, that is, obstructive or disruptive action, and the withdrawal of cooperation.

11  I borrow this language from A. John Simmons. See Simmons, *Justification and Legitimacy*, 109. A couple of challenges emerge here. How should we characterize the practices or commitments of a person who believes that the state ought to be eliminated yet does not proactively oppose the state? And how do we best capture or describe the posture of a person who is skeptical as to whether the state can be transformed or abolished yet insists that a person bears a moral duty to resist the immoral dictates of the state? I am inclined to say that one who argues that there is a duty to disobey state commands, laws, or policies and denounces a reliance on formal democratic procedure should be classified as a strong anarchist. We should also acknowledge that to be a gradualist does not mean that one is not an anarchist. Anarchism addresses both means and the ultimate end. A gradualist can seek the same end as those preferring a more immediate realization of the ultimate objective. One can propose to *gradually* eliminate the state without contradiction. The state can be thought of as a primary color. Slowly adding another primary color to the mix over time will result in a new color. The gradualist might recommend voting or disobedience as a means by which to transform the state. The strong anarchist will simply hope that, over time, the state is transformed so much so that eventually it is not the same entity. This speaks to the importance of regarding the modern territorial state as a contingent social fact. Most anarchists insist on this point. Were the United States to cease holding two million people in prison; were it to refrain from employing military force to realize its interests; were it to refrain from perpetuating hierarchical socioeconomic arrangements; were it to eliminate its standing army and abolish the draft; were the United States to do these things, then it would no longer be worth referring to it as a modern territorial state. Again, we must avoid conflating politics and government with the modern territorial state.

12  Lawrence Buell, *The Environmental Imagination: Thoreau, Nature Writing, and the Formation of American Culture* (Cambridge: Harvard University Press, 1995), 327.

13  Alan D. Hodder, *Thoreau's Ecstatic Witness* (New Haven: Yale University Press, 2001), 20.

14  As Leigh Kathryn Jenco makes clear in her insightful essay on Thoreau, "Thoreau's act of state resistance is not a celebration of liberal democracy, but rather one part of an ongoing process of challenging, and giving new definitions to, those terms usually employed to justify it." In general, I join Jenco in suggesting that we resist situating Thoreau as a democratic individualist whose normative ethical vision is consistent with representational constitutional democracy.

15  Dorothy Day, *The Long Loneliness: The Autobiography of Dorothy Day* (New York: HarperOne, 1997), 62.

16  Day relates, "The Church is infallible when it deals with truth of the faith such as the dogma of the Immaculate Conception and the Assumption of

the Blessed Virgin Mary. When it comes to concerns of the temporal order—capital versus labor, for example—on all these matters the Church has not spoken infallibly. Here there is room for wide differences of opinion." Dorothy Day, *Loaves and Fishes. The Inspiring Story of the Catholic Worker Movement* (Maryknoll, NY: Orbis Books, 1997), 122.

# Chapter 1

1  Lewis Perry, *Radical Abolitionism: Anarchy and the Government of God and Antislavery Thought* (Knoxville: University of Tennessee Press, 1995), 44.
2  Hodder uses the term or phrase "Immanence of the divine principle" to describe the phenomenon. Hodder, *Thoreau's Ecstatic Witness*, 57. Perry, *Radical Abolitionism*, 44.
3  Transcendentalists worked out a metaphysical view that had perhaps been most clearly articulated by George Fox and the Society of Friends (Quakers), who maintained that there is in every person an inner light that is one with God.
4  William E. Cain, *A Historical Guide to Henry David Thoreau* (Oxford: Oxford University Press, 2000), 17.
5  Lawrence Buell, *Literary Transcendentalism: Style and Vision in the American Renaissance* (Ithaca: Cornell University Press, 1979), 45.
6  Helena Adell Snyder, *Thoreau's Philosophy of Life. With Special Consideration of the Influence of Hindoo Philosophy* (Whitefish, MT: Kessinger Publishing, 2010), 17.
7  Henry David Thoreau, "Monday," *The Higher Law: Thoreau on Civil Disobedience and Reform*, ed. Wendell Glick (Princeton: Princeton University Press, 2004), 140.
8  Henry David Thoreau, "*Walden*," *A Week in Concord Merrimack Rivers, Walden, The Main Woods, Cape Cod*, ed. Robert Sayre (New York: Library of Americas, 1998), 429.
9  This theological view probably aligns best with what mid-to-late-twentieth-century theorists refer to as panentheism.
10  For Ralph Emerson's clear statement to this effect, see his essay "The American Scholar," *The Oxford Authors*, ed. Richard Poirier (New York: Oxford University Press, 1990), 38, 41. And in an address in September 1838, entitled "Self-Culture," William Ellery Channing relates a similar view in "Self-Culture" (Boston, September 1838).
11  Henry David Thoreau, *A Week in Concord Merrimack Rivers, Walden, The Main Woods, Cape Cod*, ed. Robert Sayre (New York: Library of Americas, 1998), 182.
12  After English romantics such as Coleridge and Blake, and Germans such as Schiller and Fitche, and his mentor Emerson, and against Locke's idea of a tabula rasa, Thoreau believed that sense experience and innate capacity, consisting of a priori knowledge, interacted to make moral and empirical knowledge possible.
13  Thoreau, "Monday," 108.
14  Thoreau, "Monday," 103.

15 Stanley Cavell, *The Senses of Walden* (Chicago: University of Chicago Press, 1992), 79.
16 Thoreau, *Walden*, 389.
17 Thoreau, *Walden*, 394.
18 Thoreau, *Walden*, 335.
19 Thoreau, *Walden*, 394.
20 Thoreau, *Walden*, 466.
21 Thoreau, *Walden*, 549.
22 Thoreau does not routinely employ the term alienation, yet the idea of alienation is an appropriate term for the phenomenon that Thoreau takes to have been instigated by technological or production-related innovations during the eighteenth and nineteenth centuries. See Thoreau, *Walden*, 344, 352, and 396.
23 Thoreau, *Walden*, 329.
24 Thoreau, *Walden*, 330.
25 Thoreau, *Walden*, 329.
26 Thoreau, *Walden*, 332.
27 Thoreau, *Walden*, 352.
28 Thoreau, *Walden*, 396.
29 Thoreau, *Walden*, 350.
30 Thoreau, *Walden*, 493.
31 Thoreau, *Walden*, 334.
32 Thoreau, *Walden*, 334.
33 Thoreau, *Walden*, 338.
34 Thoreau, *Walden*, 387.
35 Slaveholders and ship makers, of course, exemplified interest and complicity in the slave trade and slave economy.
36 Thoreau, *Walden*, 497.
37 This trend or tendency in one way or another can be seen in the work of a diverse lot that includes theorists and philosophers Michel Foucault, Charles Taylor, Alasdair McIntyre, Michael Sandel, Romand Coles, and Martha Nussbaum.
38 John Thomas, "Romantic Reform in America, 1815–1865," *American Quarterly* 17, no. 4, 1965: 671.
39 Political resistance, in the context of the modern territorial state, is a precondition for awakening; and paradoxically, awakening is a precondition for political resistance.
40 Isaiah Berlin, *Russian Thinkers* (New York: Viking Press, 1978), 79.
41 Thoreau, *Walden*, 389.
42 Henry David Thoreau, "Resistance to Civil Government," *The Higher Law: Thoreau on Civil Disobedience and Reform*, ed. Wendell Glick (Princeton: Princeton University Press, 2004), 65.
43 Thoreau, "Resistance to Civil Government," 66.
44 Thoreau, "Resistance to Civil Government," 64.
45 Thoreau, "Monday," 105–6.
46 Thoreau, "Monday," 105–6.
47 Thoreau, *Walden*, 459.

48 Henry David Thoreau, "Slavery in Massachusetts," *The Higher Law: Thoreau on Civil Disobedience and Reform*, ed. Wendell Glick (Princeton: Princeton University Press, 2004), 92.

49 Thoreau, "Slavery in Massachusetts," 94.

50 Thoreau, "Slavery in Massachusetts," 105.

51 Thoreau, "Resistance to Civil Government," 71–2.

52 Thoreau, "Resistance to Civil Government," 71.

53 For an instructive analysis of come-outerism, see Perry, *Radical Abolitionism*, especially pages 65–77 and 92–102; see also John R. McKivigan, *The War against Proslavery Religion: Abolitionism and the Northern Churches, 1830–1865* (Ithaca: Cornell University Press, 1984).

54 Alcott, for instance, published a piece in *Non-Resistant* in which he announced, "I look upon the Non-Resistance society as an assertion of the right of self-government. Why should I employ a church to write my creed or a state to govern me? Why not write my own creed? Why not govern myself?" (Alcott quoted in Perry's *Radical Abolitionism*, 83–4).

55 Staughton Lynd, *Intellectual Origins of American Radicalism* (Cambridge: Cambridge University Press, 2009), 101, 123; See also, Perry, *Radical Abolitionism*, 163–7.

56 Thoreau, "Resistance to Civil Government," 65.

57 Thoreau, "Resistance to Civil Government," 84.

58 Thoreau, "Resistance to Civil Government," 63.

59 Thoreau, "Resistance to Civil Government," 67.

60 Thoreau, "Resistance to Civil Government," 64.

61 The idea that anarchism does not rule out government is certainly a minority view, but I am not alone in holding it. David DeLeon, for example, supports the claim in *The American as Anarchist* (Baltimore: Johns Hopkins University Press, 1978) where he notes that for certain anarchists the ideal social order would be based on "government by consent" in which the "necessary functions of society could be accomplished by voluntary associations" (78).

62 Thoreau, "Resistance to Civil Government," 86.

63 Thoreau, "Resistance to Civil Government," 86.

64 To this end, Thoreau imagines "a State at last which can afford to be just to all men, and to treat the individual with respect as a neighbor. . . . A State which bore this kind of fruit, and suffered it to drop off as fast as it ripened, would prepare the way for a still more perfect and glorious State, which also I have imagined, but not yet anywhere seen." Thoreau, "Resistance to Civil Government," 90.

65 In many respects, it is the bringing together of these assertions that gives rise to an anarchist ethic. Anarchists typically maintain that unjust decision-making procedures themselves render a state illegitimate, so that persons have no moral duties to comply with its commands on the basis of the source of the commands in question.

66 One reason that it strikes me as instructive to discuss Thoreau's political commitments in terms of anarchism is because of what Thoreau rejects. He rejects majoritarian democracy. The will of the majority cannot generate norms that individual persons have duties to comply with in virtue of the source of the law. Some have thought of this form of democracy as pure democracy.

Thoreau also rejects constitutionally restricted majoritarian democracy. In addition, Thoreau rejects as legitimating the various devices celebrated by liberal democratic theorists: periodic elections of representatives, that is, he explicitly rejects representation as appropriate; denies that one can be taxed without consent; this is not even to address Thoreau's criticisms of the judiciary, prisons, and militaries of territorial states.

67  David Miller, *Anarchism* (London: J.M. Dent and Sons, 1984), 15.

68  Miller, *Anarchism*, 16.

69  I suspect that Miller attributes passivity to Thoreau in part because he is not thinking about Thoreau's oeuvre as a whole or reflecting on Thoreau's religious and political writing and action in relation to mid-nineteenth-century New England social activism, including abolitionism and anti-imperialism.

70  Hannah Arendt, "Civil Disobedience," in *Crises of the Republic* (San Diego: Harvest Book Harcourt Brace & Company, 1972), 60.

71  Arendt, *Crises of the Republic*, 64.

72  This line of analysis will also reveal precisely how Thoreau's moral theory diverges from the democratic individualism that George Kateb commends. In his work *Hannah Arendt*, Kateb defends the majority-principle and representational democracy by noting the positive effects that he attributes to democratic culture, including periodic elections. But, in the essay "Resistance to Civil Government," Thoreau explicitly rejects the idea that the institutions that Kateb has in mind are in fact praiseworthy.

73  One can reject theological-metaphysical bases for conscience and avoid subjectivism. For, the advance of social theoretical accounts of moral development in the light of reflection on moral pluralism has led to more complicated understandings of the derivation of moral sensibility. That there *is* a source is more important than *the* source: it is possible to assert that one's conscience can be God's creation or the product of social practices or moral education.

74  Barbara Packer, *Transcendentalism* (Athens: University of Georgia, 2007), 97.

75  Thoreau, *The Higher Law*, 73.

76  Thoreau, *The Higher Law*, 72.

77  Thoreau, "Resistance to Civil Government," 75.

78  Thoreau, "Resistance to Civil Government," 76.

79  So Thoreau asks, "Must the citizen ever for a moment, or in the least degree, resign his conscience to the legislator? Why has every man a conscience, then? I think that we should be men first, and subjects afterward." Few things are as manifestly contrary to Thoreau's ethics as a theory that commends procedural justice or some majority-principle over and against an insistence on substantive justice.

80  Thoreau, "Slavery in Massachusetts," 103.

81  As Edward Andrew says, "For the radical thinkers, conscience was the voice of dissent from consensus that the inequalities of commercial societies are inevitable; it was also the voice of certainty . . . that oppression is wrong." *Conscience and Its Critics: Protestant Conscience, Modern Enlightenment Reason, and Modern Subjectivity* (Toronto: University of Toronto Press, 2001), 5.

82  Thomas, "Romantic Reform in America, 1815–1865," 674.

83  Leo Tolstoy, *The Kingdom of God Is Within* (New York: Barnes and Noble, 2005), 325.

84  Thoreau, *The Higher Law*, 195.

85  Thoreau therefore asserts that "It is not so important that many should be as good as you, as that there be some absolute goodness somewhere; for that will leaven the whole lump" (*The Higher Law*, 69).

86  Thoreau, *Walden*, 389.

87  Thoreau, *Walden*, 486.

88  Thoreau, *The Higher Law*, 120.

89  Thoreau, *The Higher Law*, 137.

90  Thoreau, "Slavery in Massachusetts," 104.

91  Thoreau, *The Higher Law*, 45–6.

92  Mohandas Gandhi, actually, is among the many twentieth-century activists who interpreted Thoreau's ethics in anarchist terms. For instance, in his 1939 essay, "Enlightened Anarchy: A Political Ideal," Gandhi writes, "Political power, in my opinion cannot be our ultimate aim. . . . In an ideal State there will be no political institution and therefore no political power. That is why Thoreau has said in his classic statement that that government is the best which governs the least" (*Collected Writing of Mohandas Gandhi*, 68:265; quoted in Leela Gandhi, *Affective Communities: Anticolonial Thought, Fin-de-Siecle Radicalism, and the Politics of Friendship* (Duke University: Durham, 2006)).

# Chapter 2

1   William James, *The Varieties of Religious Experience: A Study in Human Nature* (New York: Random House, 1902), 192.

2   Dorothy Day, *From Union Square to Rome* (Maryknoll, NY: Orbis Books, 2006), 18.

3   Day, *Loaves and Fishes*, 75.

4   Day, *Loaves and Fishes*, 43.

5   Day, *From Union Square to Rome*, 153.

6   Day, *The Long Loneliness*, 29.

7   Day, *The Long Loneliness*, 141.

8   Day, *The Long Loneliness*, 229.

9   Day, *The Long Loneliness*, 243.

10  Day, *The Long Loneliness*, 286.

11  Day, *The Long Loneliness*, 285.

12  Dorothy Day, *On Pilgrimage* (Grand Rapids, MI: William B. Eerdmans, 1999), 162.

13  Among academic ethicists and theologians, it is probably Paul Tillich who espouses a theory of love most similar to Day's. In *Love, Power, and Justice: Ontological Analyses and Ethical Applications*, Tillich announces that "Love is the drive towards the unity of the separated. Reunion presupposes separation of that which belongs essentially together. . . . Love manifests its greatest power there where it overcomes the greatest separation" (New York: Oxford University Press, 1954), 25.

14  Dorothy Day, *House of Hospitality* (New York: Sheed and Ward, 1939), 254–6.

15  Day does not explain how the fact of the unity of humanity relates to the fact of separation or disunion that she posits as a problem to be surmounted. Yet this difficult theological question does not need to be dealt with here, as it is not my task to vindicate Day's theology or theological professions. We need only to understand it and appreciate how it relates to Day's religious-ethical commitments and normative political philosophy.

16  Galatians 3.28 is also sometimes read as a way to understand the doctrine. In that biblical text, Paul intimates, "All you who have been baptized in Christ have put on Christ. There is neither Jew nor Greek, slave nor free, male nor female, for you are all one in Christ Jesus." This equalizing sentiment is not expressed as a universal statement. Notice that its reach is limited to the baptized. Day, obviously, does not build this limitation into her expression of the doctrine of the Mystical Body of Christ.

17  For a comparison of Day's interpretation of the Mystical Body of Christ doctrine with other Catholics, see William T. Cavanaugh's "Dorothy Day and the Mystical Body of Christ in the Second World War," in *Dorothy Day and the Catholic Worker Movement: Centenary Essays*, especially pages 463–4. To see how an official Catholic statement on the doctrine relates to Day's stance, see Eugenio Pacelli's (Pope Pius XII) 1943 encyclical, *Mystici Corporis Christi*.

18  Dorothy Day, "Liturgy and Sociology," *Catholic Worker* (January 1936), 5.

19  Day, *From Union Square to Rome*, 13.

20  Mel Piehl, *Breaking Bread: The Catholic Worker and the Origin of Catholic Radicalism in America* (Tuscaloosa: University of Alabama Press, 2006), 85.

21  Day, *On Pilgrimage*, 224.

22  Day, *From Union Square to Rome*, 8.

23  For Day's reservations about the Catholic Church see, *The Long Loneliness*, 150.

24  In *Pedagogy of the Oppressed* (New York: Continuum, 1986), Paulo Freire, eloquently captures this idea: when "the oppressed to struggle against those who made them so . . . the oppressed must not, in seeking to regain their humanity (which is a way to create it), become in turn oppressors of the oppressors, but rather restorers of the humanity of both" (44).

25  Day, *The Long Loneliness*, 78.

26  For an analysis of Day's personalism, see *The Catholic Worker Movement: Intellectual and Spiritual Origins* (New York: Paulist Press, 2005) by Mark and Louise Zwick, especially chapters 5 and 6. For personalist essays that influenced Day, see Emmanuel Mounier's *The Personalist Manifesto* (New York: Longmans, Green and Company, 1938) and Jacques Maritain's *The Person and the Common Good* (New York: C. Scribner's Sons, 1947).

27  Zwick and Zwick, *The Catholic Worker Movement*, 76–7.

28  The relevant text in 1 John (4.40) states: "If any man say, I love God, and hateth his brother he is a liar. For he that loveth not his brother, whom he seeth, how can he love God, whom he seeth not?" Maria Vidale and Rosa Adela O. Sierra use the term "anthropological experience of God" in "The Spirituality of the Brazilian Base Communities," in *Spirituality of the Third World*, ed. K. C. Abraham and Bernadette Mbuy-Beya (Maryknoll, NY: Orbis Books, 1994), 42. Day, *From Union Square to Rome*, 152.

29  John Rawls uses the term "enabling right" in *A Theory of Justice* (Cambridge: Belknap Press of Harvard University Press, 1971), 213.

30  This is because self-actualization requires taking responsibility, which presupposes and requires the opportunity, that is, the material freedom, to do so.

31  For a study on this tradition see Ernst Troeltsch, *The Social Teachings of the Christian Churches* (London: George Allen, 1931); Ronald G. Musto's *The Catholic Peace Tradition* (New York: Peace Books, 2002); Thomas Merton's *The Wisdom of the Desert* (New York: New Directions Publishing, 1970), especially pages 3–26; and Piehl's *Breaking Bread*, especially chapters 2 and 5.

32  *House of Hospitality*, 274–5. Day's running debate with priests and theologians about the general and universal applicability of the counsels of perfection raises questions that I will not take up here. For a review of this debate, see pages 185–200 in William Miller's *A Harsh and Dreadful Love: Dorothy Day and the Catholic Worker Movement*, 2nd edition (Milwaukee: Marquette University Press, 2005).

33  Day quoted in Robert Coles, *Dorothy Day: A Radical Devotion* (New York: Da Capo Press, 1987), 21.

34  Dorothy Day, "Spring Appeal," *Catholic Worker* (April 1958).

35  Day, *From Union Square to Rome* 155.

36  To be clear, while Day stresses human agency, she adds that God's grace facilitates loving agency. Day, *The Long Loneliness*, 178.

37  Day, *The Long Loneliness*, 176.

38  Moral perfectionists assert that the moral life entails aspiring to attain and promote certain kinds of excellences. In Stanley Cavell's words, "Perfectionism is the dimension of moral thought directed less to restraining the bad than releasing the good" (*Conditions Handsome and Unhandsome* (Chicago: University of Chicago Press, 1991), 18). To be clear though, while perfectionism is oriented toward the good, goodness is not regarded as prior to rightness by all perfectionists. For three contrasting treatments of moral perfectionism see John Rawls, *A Theory of Justice*, especially 324–31; Cavell, *Conditions Handsome and Unhandsome*, especially chapters 1 and 2; Jeffrey Stout, *Democracy and Tradition* (Princeton: Princeton University Press, 2004).

39  While many follow Kant and insist that categorical imperatives are duties that persons have independent of interests and materiality, it is possible to understand categorical imperatives independently from Kant's controversial metaphysical assertions. Specifically, there can be empirically conditioned moral imperatives. To that end, Charles Larmore relates, "Kant's exorbitant notion of freedom forms no necessary part of an imperative [i.e. categorical imperative] conception of morality." Charles Larmore, *The Morals of Modernity* (New York: Cambridge University Press, 1996), 33.

40  Day, *The Long Loneliness*, 265.

41  Day, *House of Hospitality*, 254–6. Day has this idea in mind when she announces, "This work of ours toward a new heaven and a new earth shows a correlation between the material and the spiritual, and, of course, recognizes the primacy of the spiritual" (*House of Hospitality*, 274–5).

42  Piehl, *Breaking Bread*, 137.

43  Zwick and Zwick, *The Catholic Worker Movement*, 92.

44  Day, *The Long Loneliness*, 169.

45  Piehl, *Breaking Bread*, 25.

46  Day, *Loaves and Fishes*, 205.

47  Day, *Loaves and Fishes*, 198.

48  Day, *Loaves and Fishes*, 190.

49  Day, *Loaves and Fishes*, 190.

50  Dorothy Day, "The Pope and Peace," *Catholic Worker* (February 1954), 1, 7.

51  Day, "The Pope and Peace," 1, 7.

52  Day, "The Pope and Peace," 1, 7.

53  Day, "Catholic Worker Positions," *Catholic Worker* (May 1972).

54  Dorothy Day, "The Scandal of the Works of Mercy," *Commonweal* (November 4, 1949), 99–102.

55  Pope Pius XI, *Quadragesmio Anno* (1931), 79.

56  While the doctrine of subsidiarity was important for Day, it did not serve as a building block for her anarchism in the same way that love served as a building block for her pacifism. Instead, she was probably attracted to the idea of subsidiarity as a result of her interest in localism and decentralization. We might say then, following Fred Boehrer, that the idea of subsidiarity provided Day with a "bridge between Roman Catholicism and anarchism." Fred Boehrer. "Diversity, Plurality, and Ambiguity: Anarchism in the Catholic Worker Movement," in *Dorothy Day and the Catholic Worker Movement: Centenary Essays*, ed. William Thorn, Phillip Runkel, and Susan Mountin (Marquette University Press: Milwaukee, 2001), 95–127, 98.

57  Day assumed that the centralized territorial state would have to operate both on the basis of representation, and by extension, on some version of the majority-principle. Day quotes Robert Ludlow in order to relate that all modern territorial states, both democratic and nondemocratic, are "government by representation" and to suggest that "there is no reason why Catholic must believe that people must be governed by representatives" (*The Long Loneliness*, 268).

58  Craig L. Carr puts this in terms similar to the ones that I have used here. "Coercion and Freedom," *American Philosophical Quarterly* 25, no. 1 (1988): 59–67.

59  There are notable silences in Day's commentary on coercion. For instance, Day does not state specifically how parental authority would be altered by her normative vision. But it is safe to say that Day recognized that parents or even adults would exercise some degree of authority over children. But even in the realm of parenthood, Day did not endorse the use of corporeal punishment or the threat of violence to enforce household rules, and so on.

60  For the sake of my analysis of Day's political philosophical commitments, I assume that morally autonomous action, in a non-Kantian sense, is in fact possible. Related, I also assume that it is actually possible for one to be coerced and therefore deprived of moral freedom or autonomy broadly speaking.

61  That is, Day maintains that persons (perhaps it is important to say "adult" persons) only have moral duties or obligations to obey rules or laws of organizations when they have voluntarily joined the organizations in question.

62  Thomas Aquinas, *Summa Theological of St. Thomas Aquinas*, 2nd and revised edition, translated by Fathers of the English Dominican Province (1920 [1273] I Q82 A1).

63  One must be cautious about asserting too much in favor of a particular interpretation of Aquinas' work. However, I have presented an uncontroversial interpretation of Aquinas' respective conceptions of violence, coercion, and voluntary action. Moreover, the fact that Aquinas places emphasis on voluntary action without endorsing voluntarism elucidates the degree to which Day's religious-ethical commitments diverge from many Catholics on crucial points. This is a rather banal point, but it is too often assumed that, once we know that a person is a Catholic, we know all that we need to know about the person's moral or political commitments.

64  Accordingly, in an article on obedience, Day says, "Obedience is a matter of love which makes it voluntary, not compelled by fear or force" ("Reflections during Advent, Part Four: Obedience," *Ava Maria* (December 17, 1966), 20–3).

65  Dorothy Day, "The Case of Father Duffy," *Catholic Worker* (December 1949), 1, 4.

66  Day, "Reflections during Advent, Part Four: Obedience," 20–3. See also Michael Riccards, *Vicars of Christ: Popes, Power, and Politics in the Modern World* (New York: Crossroad, 1998), for a helpful history of the Catholic Church and its claims of authority from the mid-nineteenth century through the signing of the Lateran Treaty.

67  In fact, Day quotes Catholic Worker Robert Ludlow making a similar claim about anarchism in general: "When you analyze what anarchists advocate . . . it really boils down to the advocacy of decentralized self-governing bodies. It is a form of government." *The Long Loneliness*, 268.

68  Paradoxically, my emphasis on the centrality of voluntarism and moral autonomy for Day's anarchism is in part meant to reveal how anarchists such as Day take for granted the necessity of community, cooperation, and organization and simultaneously make explicit the criteria that such anarchists apply in order to evaluate the relevant social practices.

69  Day, *Loaves and Fishes*, 73.

70  Day, *Loaves and Fishes*, 74.

71  Day, *From Union Square to Rome*, 15.

72  Day, *Loaves and Fishes*, 86.

73  In *A Preface to Democratic Theory*, Dahl argued that, in America, there is no dominant class, with any unified class interests, in control of the state. According to Dahl, there are multiple elite classes competing for control of the state apparatus, but never actually capturing it for an extended enough duration to impose its will on society. To my knowledge, Day never directly commented on R. A. Dahl's "democratic pluralist thesis," yet she definitely held a contrary view.

74  Day, "The Pope and Peace," 1, 7.

75  Day positively cites the *American Encyclopedia* in order to define anarchism: "Anarchism is a vaguely defined doctrine which would abolish the state and other established social and economic institutions and establish a new order based on *free* and spontaneous cooperation among individuals, groups, regions, and nations" (*The Long Loneliness*, 54 (emphasis mine)).

76 "Catholic Worker Positions," *Catholic Worker* (May 1972).

77 David Graeber, *Direct Action: An Ethnography* (Oakland: AK Press, 2009), 211.

78 Murry Bookchin, *Post-Scarcity Anarchism* (London: Wildwood House, 1974), 104.

79 Day, "Catholic Worker Positions."

80 Tolstoy states the importance of refusal in *The Kingdom of God Is Within*. According to Tolstoy: "Everything depends on the strength of Christian truths in each individual. And therefore we consider it the duty of every man who thinks war inconsistent with Christianity, meekly but firmly refuse to serve in the army. . . . The destiny of humanity in the world depends, so far as it depends on men at all, on their fidelity to their religion" (20).

81 Day, *Loaves and Fishes*, 86.

82 Day, *Loaves and Fishes*, 86.

83 I should note, Day did not think that it was possible under mid-twentieth-century conditions for one to wholly extricate oneself from the system. The modern social structure is quite complex, which makes it difficult to withdraw, even if one refuses to earn wages, pay taxes, vote, serve in the military or as an officer of the state. Yet still, the difficulties notwithstanding, the upstanding moral agent must minimize her complicity by refusing to cooperate with or contribute to certain social practices. To that end, Day announces that she and the *Catholic Worker* believe "in a withdrawal from the capitalist system *so far as each one is able to do so*" (May 1972) (emphasis mine).

84 Day, *House of Hospitality*, chapter 8. Day was quick to point out that her "insistence on worker-ownership, on the right to private property, on the need to de-proletarize the worker" are "all points which had been emphasized by the Popes in their social encyclicals" (*The Long Loneliness*, 188). Day is here thinking especially of Pope Pius XI's encyclical *Quadragesmio Anno*.

85 *The Long Loneliness*, 185.

86 It is important to understand Day's subtle reference to the social distribution of goods in the light of the differences between "collectivists" and "communists." Contra anarchist communists, anarchist collectivists have maintained that it is unnecessary to abolish the wage system, monetary exchange, private property, or merit-based worker's compensation of workers based on relative productivity, time, or contribution. In the end, Day is unclear about the extent to which she sides with the communists or the collectivists in this debate, but most of what she says suggests that she rejects representation and thus sides with the former group. That being said, it is important that Day, following Catholic social teaching, leaves room for private property. For an account of the differences between anarchist collectivism and anarchist communism, see Peter Kropotkin's "The Collectivist Wage System," in *The Conquest of Bread* (1892).

87 *The Long Loneliness*, 220; Day, "Catholic Worker Positions."

88 Day, "Catholic Worker Positions."

89 Murray Rothbard, *The Betrayal of the American Right* (Auburn, AL: Ludwig von Mises Institute, 2007), 2.

90 Rothbard, *The Betrayal of the American Right*, 165. For a representative statement on the Old Right, see Frank Chodorov's *The Economics of Society,*

*Government and State* (New York: Analysis Associates, 1946) and especially *Taxation Is Robbery* (Chicago: Human Events Associates, 1947).

91  Frank Chodorov, Letter to *National Review* 2, no. 20 (October 6, 1956).

92  That libertarians, especially right-libertarians, are often uniformly regarded as conservatives has numerous other causes. First, many American conservatives, including pre-1960 Democrats and post-Lyndon B. Johnson Republicans, have invoked libertarian themes in order to oppose Civil Rights and New Deal legislation, judicial opinions, and executive policies. Also important, in recent decades, certain libertarian principles and themes have probably been articulated most clearly by economists (such as Milton Friedman) affiliated with the Republican Party and opposed to Keynesian economic theories. These factors combine to make it quite difficult to make sense of the American political-ideological landscape.

93  Roderick T. Long, "Market Anarchism as Constitutionalism," in *Anarchism/ Monarchism: Is Government Part of a Free Country*, ed. Roderick T. Long and Tibor R. Machan (Burlington, VT: Ashgate, 2008), 138.

94  That said, Franz Oppenheimer's theory of the origin and social function of the modern state, in the book *The State* (1908), has been influential for many right-libertarians, including Murray Rothbard and Roderick T. Long. Oppenheimer regarded the state as a product of war and conquest, and regarded capitalism as a system of exploitation that depends on the power of the modern state. Importantly, right-libertarians (qua anarcho-capitalists) maintain that capitalism as we know it is not in fact a free-market economy. Rather, existing capitalist economies consist of state-subsidized corporate monopolies. Assumptions such as these inform Long's account of the role of the territorial state (government). Long argues, "The power of the wealthy might pose a danger to liberty in a market anarchist society. But the notion that the danger of plutocracy is less under a government is hard to believe. On the contrary, government magnifies the power of the rich" (Long, "Market Anarchism as Constitutionalism," 137). This conception of the function or role of the state, while quite basic, hardly differs from Day's. Also see "Libertarian Anarchism: Responses to Ten Objections" (August 19, 2004) for an example of this kind of argument. This last essay is available at www.lewrockwell.com/long/long11.html

95  Indeed, taking a remarkably different position from Day, right-libertarian Walter Block maintains that voluntarily slavery is morally permissible ("Towards a Libertarian Theory of Inalienability: A Critique of Rothbard, Barnett, Smith, Kinsella, Gordon, and Epstein," *Journal of Libertarian Studies* 17, no. 2 (2003), see especially pages 44–8).

96  Cornel West, *Prophetic Fragments* (Grand Rapids, MI: William B. Eerdmans, 1993), 130.

97  To endorse decentralization, says West, would be to ignore crucial facts about contemporary social reality: "Centralization, hierarchy, and markets are inescapable economic realities for modern social existence" (*Prophetic Fragments*, 135). And so, "the crucial question is how various forms of centralization, hierarchy, and markets are to be understood, conceived and judged in light of Christian commitments to democracy and individuality" (135).

98   Dorothy Day, for her part, never cast a vote in a local or national election, as
     she was as pessimistic about reforming the state as Cornel West tends to be
     about the possibility of moving beyond it. As Day wrote, "No political party,
     no political action, but only revolutionary personalist direct action on the
     part of workers (and non-violent action which entails the most discipline and
     suffering) is going to get anywhere" ("The Case of Father Duffy," *Catholic
     Worker* (December 1949), 1, 4).

99   Day, *House of Hospitality*, 240.

100  Coles, *Dorothy Day*, 96.

101  Day, *The Long Loneliness*, 247.

102  Day, *Loaves and Fishes*, 111.

103  Day quoted in Coles, *Dorothy Day*, 109.

104  David Graeber, "The New Anarchists," *New Left Review* 13, January–
     February 2002. George Lakey has also contributed to the reconceptualization
     of revolution. In particular, Lakey reimagines (nonviolent) revolution as
     "continual creation and elaboration of new institutions based on new,
     non-alienating modes of interaction—institutions that could be considered
     prefigurative" (George Lakey, *Strategy for a Living Revolution* (Ann Arbor:
     University of Michigan Press, 1973), as discussed by Graeber in *Direct
     Action: An Ethnography*).

105  *From Union Square to Rome*, 154.

106  Day, *Loaves and Fishes*, 50.

# Chapter 3

1   Charles DeBenedetti, *The Peace Reform in American History* (Bloomington:
    Indiana University Press, 1980). Charles Chatfield, *The American Peace
    Movement: Ideals and Activism* (New York: Twayne, 1992).

2   Scott H. Bennett, *Radical Pacifism: The War Resisters League and Gandhian
    Nonviolence in America, 1915–1963* (Syracuse: Syracuse University Press,
    2003), xii.

3   See Adam Fairclough, *To Redeem the Soul of America: The Southern Christian
    Leadership Conference and Martin Luther King, Jr.* (Athens: University of
    Georgia Press, 1987); Clayborne Carson, *In Struggle: SNCC and the Black
    Awakening of the 1960s* (Cambridge: Harvard University Press, 1995).

4   James R. Tracy, *Direct Action: Radical Pacifism from the Union Eight to the
    Chicago Seven* (Chicago: University of Chicago Press, 1997), 29.

5   John D'Emilio, *Lost Prophet: The Life and Times of Bayard Rustin* (Chicago:
    University of Chicago Press, 2003), 50.

6   For analyses of Gandhi's social philosophy and theory of social change that
    influenced Rustin, see Richard Gregg, *The Power of Non-Violence* (1934);
    Bart de Ligt, *The Conquest of Violence* (1938); Krishnalal Shridharani, *War
    Without Violence* (1938); and Joan V. Bondurant, *Conquest of Violence: The
    Gandhian Philosophy of Conflict* (1958).

7   Rustin, "The Negro and Nonviolence," 9.

8   Bayard Rustin to Dear Friend, 8/15/1942; D'Emilio, *Lost Prophet*, 48.

9   Rustin's Quaker faith, at least the detailed character of it, is difficult to
    speak of, since he kept no journal, seldom spoke publicly in concrete ways
    about his religious beliefs, and did not regularly participate in a religious
    congregation. Yet from the fervency of his activism, his work with the Friends,
    FOR, and his advising of A. J. Muste it is clear that Rustin had a profoundly
    spiritual or religious orientation. Indeed, he interpreted his experiences in
    the light of his religious beliefs and put great emphasis in the Sermon on the
    Mount. Importantly, Rustin noted that his Quaker upbringing constituted the
    greatest influence on his social activism. Jervis Anderson, in the biography
    *Bayard Rustin: The Troubles I've Seen*, quotes Rustin: "My activism did not
    spring from being black. Rather, it is rooted fundamentally in my Quaker
    upbringing and the values instilled in me by [my] grandparents" (New York:
    HaperCollins, 1997), 7.
10  See *United States* v. *Kauten* (2d Cir. 1943) for a helpful historical summary of
    US conscript-exemption law.
11  Clarence Marsh Case identifies four prototypical mid-twentieth-century
    American conscientious objectors or war resisters: (1) Socialist resisters
    who believed that war reinforced divisions that impeded the overthrow of
    capitalism. (2) Radical individualists, the rare rebels who based resistance
    not on the wrongness of war but on account of a deep independent streak.
    (3) Nonreligious humanitarians who insisted on the sanctity of life and
    repudiated national identification. (4) Religionists who asserted that the state's
    conscription law and practice of war-making contradicted a religious calling or
    God's law. Clarence Marsh Case, *Non-Violent Coercion: A Study in Methods
    of Social Pressure* (New York: Century, 1923), 259–65.
12  Bayard Rustin, *Time on Two Crosses: The Collected Writings of Bayard
    Rustin*, ed. Devon W. Carbado and Donald Weise (San Francisco: Cleis Press,
    2003), 11.
13  Rustin, *Time on Two Crosses*, 12.
14  Rustin, *Time on Two Crosses*, 12.
15  Rustin, *Time on Two Crosses*, 12.
16  As the above quotations attest, Rustin's loyalty is to God and God's law as
    it is reflected in the moral order. It is the contradiction between God's law/
    will and the state's conscription law that motivates Rustin's disobedience.
    He does not invoke the term conscience, yet it is implicit in his explanation
    of his disobedience. So with respect to the source of the moral rule that
    Rustin is adhering to we can say that he is at one with Martin Luther, whose
    declaration is well known: "My conscience is captive to the Word of God: I
    cannot and will not retract anything, since it is neither safe nor right to go
    against conscience. I cannot do otherwise, here I stand, may God help me,
    Amen." It is notable that Luther departed from a tradition of Pauline thinkers
    who have based their understanding of political obligation on Paul's Epistle
    to the Romans (13.1–2) where Paul asserts: "For there is no authority except
    from God, and those that exist have been instituted by God. Therefore he who
    resists the authorities resists what God has appointed, and those who resist
    will incur judgment." There's debate about the most appropriate interpretation
    of this declaration. Yet my interest is not in the relative persuasiveness of

competing exegetes. Here the interest lies in the implications of the competing biblical interpretations for an account of moral duties that one owes to the state. Rustin would clearly have difficulty basing his disobedience on Romans 13. Rejecting this Pauline claim about temporal authorities paves the way for the anarchist ethos that we are interested in. Political authorities, once recognized as secular, are subject to criticism, refusal, and disposal. This is the legacy of the Reformation, the Enlightenment, and the American and French revolutions.

17  Evan Thomas quoted in Clarence Marsh Case, *Non-Violent Coercion*, 278.

18  To be clear, our interest at this stage is the issue of moral motivation: What motivates action? Is it the *source* of the positive law or the *content* of the positive law?

19  *Democracy and Tradition*, 198.

20  Paul W. Kahn, *Sacred Violence: Torture, Terror, and Sovereignty* (Ann Arbor: University of Michigan Press, 2008), 106.

21  D'Emilio, *Lost Prophet*, 50–63.

22  Bayard Rustin, "Civil Disobedience, Jim Crow, and the Armed Forces" (1948), *Time on Two Crosses*, ed. Devon W. Carbado and Donald Weise (San Francisco: Cleis Press, 2003), 29–30.

23  Bayard Rustin, "New South . . . Old Politics" (1956), *Time on Two Crosses*, ed. Devon W. Carbado and Donald Weise (San Francisco: Cleis Press, 2003), 100–1.

24  There are additional assumptions informing my analysis that it might help to make explicit. As I have suggested already, I assume here that modern territorial states would no longer be the same entities if states dissolved standing armies and ceased to engage in war. I also assume that the modern territorial state would not necessarily have to be abolished in its present form if it became an instrument of economic justice for the working class, underclass, or lower income professionals; a new class would have to seize control of the territorial state; while as a practical matter it is presently unlikely that this will occur in the American context, it is not theoretically impossible.

25  Bayard Rustin, "The Blacks and the Unions" (1971), *Time on Two Crosses*, ed. Devon W. Carbado and Donald Weise (San Francisco: Cleis Press, 2003), 255.

26  Rustin, "The Blacks and the Unions," 262.

27  Farmer quoted in Rustin's *The New York Times* obituary. Eric Pace, "Bayard Rustin Is Dead at 75; Pacifist and a Rights Activist" (*New York Times* August 25, 1987).

28  Bayard Rustin, "From Protest to Politics," *Time on Two Crosses*, ed. Devon W. Carbado and Donald Weise (San Francisco: Cleis Press, 2003), 117.

29  Rustin, "From Protest to Politics," 121.

30  Rustin, "From Protest to Politics," 119.

31  Rustin, "From Protest to Politics," 123.

32  Barbara Epstein, *Political Protest & Cultural Revolution: Nonviolent Direct Action in the 1970s and 1980s* (Berkeley: University of California Press, 1991), 38.

33 Bayard Rustin, "The Failure of Black Separatism," *Time on Two Crosses*, ed. Devon W. Carbado and Donald Weise (San Francisco: Cleis Press, 2003), 232.

34 Rustin, "The Failure of Black Separatism," 232–3.

35 Martin Luther King, *Where Do We Go from Here* (Boston: Beacon Press, 1967), 30–1.

36 Rustin, "From Protest to Politics," 125.

37 Bayard Rustin, "The Total Vision of A. Philip Randolph," *Time on Two Crosses*, ed. Devon W. Carbado and Donald Weise (San Francisco: Cleis Press, 2003), 201.

38 Rustin, "The Blacks and the Unions," 251.

39 Rustin, "From Protest to Politics," 123.

40 Bayard Rustin, "Black and Gay in the Civil Rights Movement," *Time on Two Crosses*, ed. Devon W. Carbado and Donald Weise (San Francisco: Cleis Press, 2003), 291.

41 Interestingly, King agreed with Rustin that it was important to change institutions and also argued that such changes would affect the formation of individual character. Nonetheless, King adhered to the Gandhian emphasis on "hearts" until the end. This fact actually reveals a tension at the heart of King's social thought.

42 Rustin in Anderson, *Bayard Rustin: Troubles I've Seen*, 292.

43 Anderson, *Bayard Rustin: Troubles I've Seen*, 292.

44 Taylor Branch, *Parting the Waters: America in the King Years 1954–1963* (New York: Simon & Schuster Adult Publishing Group, 1989), 179.

45 See Michael C. Dawson, *Black Visions: The Roots of Contemporary African-American Political Ideologies* (Chicago: Chicago University Press, 2001), 260–70.

46 It is common for this tradition to also be referred to as the black protest tradition. The radical activists that I have in mind would be persons belonging to the radical wing of the protest tradition and persons who regard social justice activism as a vocation.

47 Convocation Address, Clark College, March 5, 1968 quoted in Jerald Podair *Bayard Rustin: American Dreamer* (Lanham, MD: Rowman & Littlefield, 2009), 143.

48 Rustin, "The Failure of Black Separatism," 230.

49 Rustin, "From Protest to Politics," 122.

50 Daniel Levine, *Bayard Rustin and the Civil Rights Movement* (New Brunswick: Rutgers University Press, 2000), 250.

51 See Epstein's *Political Protest & Cultural Revolution: Nonviolent Direct Action in the 1970s and 1980s* for her delineation of these different sociopolitical orientations, especially pages 48–51.

52 Which of the two elements receives priority or emphasis has varied over time and among individual members, but subscribing to the former of these two elements circumscribes any conception of political obligation that members of the black radical tradition will accept.

53 The instrumental value of the state must be differentiated from the instrumental value of consent. One who argues for the instrumental value of consent might claim that compliance must be pervasive if a state is to persist. Yet if one denies this premise, then one may further posit the separateness,

logical and practical, of political authority and political obligation, meaning
that the latter is not a condition of the possibility of the emergence and
sustenance of the former. See Leslie Green, *Authority of the State* (Oxford:
Oxford University Press, 1988), especially pages 180–3 for an analysis of
the differences between an instrumental justification of the state and an
instrumental justification of consent.

54 Thoreau, *The Higher Law*, 74.

55 This analysis brings to the surface the fact that one can reject the idea that
there is a moral duty to obey political commands and laws for principled
reasons, pragmatic reasons, or both. The reasons discussed in this section
might be construed as strictly pragmatic. I have suggested that radicals argue
against a general moral duty to follow political commands on the basis of a
view about the positive practical value of political disobedience. Yet this, of
course, is not the only basis on which to reject the duty in question. Rather, in
some cases the commitment to disobedience will be motivated by reasons that
relate exclusively to a moral assessment of the command or law in question;
and some radicals maintain that one should not posit that there is a general
moral duty to follow the law because to obey a given command might entail
performing an immoral action. Finally, one might assert the interconnectedness
of principled reasons and pragmatic reasons. Thoreau, Tolstoy, Gandhi,
Day, and the early Rustin are examples of radicals who make this latter
kind of assertion; as we have seen, they maintain that noncomplicity or
noncooperation with unjust practices is precisely the way in which to initiate a
revolution.

56 See Chaim Gans's *Philosophical Anarchism and Political Disobedience*
(Cambridge: Cambridge University Press, 1992).

57 While I am here limiting my attribution of weak anarchism to radicals
who propose perpetual political disobedience, I am inclined to say that all
proponents of political disobedience are committed to a strand of weak
anarchism. Many proponents of political disobedience have attempted to
demonstrate why *civil* disobedience should be permitted in a liberal democratic
society by rendering a certain description of moral action and by providing
a certain interpretation of the principles underlying certain types of political
disobedience, namely *civilly* disobedient action. In short, such proponents
(or perhaps apologists) of civil disobedience have endeavored to demonstrate
how civilly disobedient actors might violate the law and nonetheless remain
in fidelity to the law. I presume that Martin Luther King's justification of
political disobedience falls into this category, specifically in his "Letter from a
Birmingham Jail." The same is true of John Rawls, who in *A Theory of Justice*
devotes nearly an entire chapter to the question of what moral obligations
persons have to obey the law in cases where certain laws themselves violate
basic principles of justice. Most defenses of civil disobedience rely on an idea
similar to prima facie duties. In ethical theory, in general, the concept of prima
facie duties is invoked in order to describe and explain how a rule can be
binding in most but not all cases. In the realm of political philosophy the idea
of prima facie duties is often invoked in a parallel fashion in order to explain
how one can have a conditional moral duty to obey the law and to provide an
explanation as to how one can violate the law and remain committed to the

law as such. Since the idea of prima facie duties is so important in the effort to reconcile (civil) disobedience with a moral duty to obey the law, a complete defense of the claim that civil disobedience entails weak anarchism would require a consideration of whether civil disobedience can be reconciled with a theory that imposes the duty to obey the law by way of the idea of prima facie duties. My sense is that the idea of prima facie duties is insufficient as a way to avoid weak anarchism. But making a case for this position would take me into technical philosophical debates that I have attempted to bracket for the purposes of my analysis. In this chapter, especially this note, I have raised an important question that I will devote attention to in future work.

58  Robert Dahl, *Democracy and Its Critics* (New Haven: Yale University Press, 1989), 40.

59  Joshua Paulson and Gene Sharp, *Waging Nonviolent Struggle: 20th Century Practice and 21st Century Potential* (Manchester: Extending Horizons Books, 2005), 31.

60  *Brother Outsider: The Life of Bayard Rustin*, DVD, Director, Bennett Singer (Passion River, 2008).

# Conclusion

1  George Woodcock, *Anarchism: A History of Libertarian Ideas and Movements* (Harmondsworth: Penguin, 1963), 8.

2  Arendt was well aware of the reality of the relationship between violence and politics as it is generally understood. She did after all devote two decades to contemplating political evil and analyzing totalitarianism. Yet she did not think that violence is what separates the political from other social practices. She deliberately contrasts her conception of the political with the conceptions proposed by theorists such as Carl Schmitt, Max Weber, and certain Marxists who insist on the logical or necessary relationship between politics and violence.

3  Hannah Arendt, *On Revolution* (New York: Penguin Books, 2006), 159.

4  Arendt, *On Revolution*, 166–7.

5  Arendt, *On Revolution*, 173.

6  Interestingly enough, with some variation, there are thousands of persons across the earth actually living in a manner similar to the early modern New Englanders who Hannah Arendt celebrated. There are in various parts of the world, group of persons who have founded anarchist political organizations or other organizations that make decisions in a way that is consistent with anarchist values. Many of these groups are comprised of persons who insist that they are not members of the states that claim control over the territory that these anarchists inhabit, just as many early European settlers in the Americas denied that they were subjects of the various European countries that they had fled. Although Arendt might not have endorsed such communities, we might say, after Arendt, that even now hundreds of little eighteenth-century New England-style "political societies" are scattered across the globe. From Italy and Spain to America and India, persons have created what Hakim Bay, Cindy Milstein, Richard Day, David Graeber, and others refer to as

"autonomous zones," zones that operate mostly outside the structure of the capitalistic territorial state social order. Future study might compare these contemporary political communities to the New England communities that Arendt concentrated on in *On Revolution*. To appreciate all of this, anarchists who turn to Arendt will probably need to give up Arendt's proclivity for invoking the this-world/other-world dichotomy. Just as it led Arendt to misinterpret Thoreau's religious-ethical vision, the "other-world" idea functions to reinforce the status quo by discounting the value of many of the radical social experiments currently underway across the globe.

7   The relationship that Arendt suggests obtains between "people getting together," "power," "promising," "mutuality," and "legitimacy" is profoundly important. These concepts play the same role in the vision of many anarchists and it will be instructive going forward for anarchists to at least contemplate the significance of Arendt's vision for anarchist thought. This is perhaps most clear in another essay, where Arendt suggests that legitimate authority is only possible where there has been mutual consent. In particular, she maintains that the moral content of mutual or reciprocal consent "is like the moral content of all agreements and contracts; it consists in the obligation to keep them. This obligation is inherent in all promises." So she intimates that we might say that the only obligation that a person has, in her capacity as citizen, is "to make and to keep promises" (*Crises of the Republic*, 92).

8   Arendt, *On Revolution*, 160.

9   Arendt, *On Revolution*, 162.

10   Jonathan Schell, *The Unconquerable World: Power, Nonviolence, and the Will of the People* (New York: Holt Paperbacks, 2003), 218.

11   Schell, *The Unconquerable World*, 218.

12   I will not here discuss the various means that she proposed or address the potential problems with her interpretation of American history. For our purposes, what is important is to appreciate Arendt's normative vision and understand how it complements or contradicts norms posited by certain anarchists.

13   *The Higher Law*, 108.

14   In a preface to *Against the Wall: Poor, Young, Black, and Male*, ed. Elijah Anderson (Philadelphia: University of Pennsylvania, 2008), xv.

# SELECTED BIBLIOGRAPHY

Abraham, K. C. and Bernadette Mbuy-Beya, eds. *Spirituality of the Third World*. Maryknoll, NY: Orbis Books, 1994.

Anderson, Jervis. *Bayard Rustin: Troubles I've Seen*. New York: Harper Collins, 1997.

Andrew, Edward. *Conscience and Its Critics: Protestant Conscience, Modern Enlightenment Reason, and Modern Subjectivity*. Toronto: University of Toronto Press, 2001.

Arendt, Hannah. *Between Past and Future: Eight Exercises on Political Thought*. New York: Penguin Classics, Penguin Books, 2006.

—. *Crises of the Republic: Civil Disobedience*. San Diego: Harvest Book Harcourt Brace & Company, 1972.

—. *Eichmann in Jerusalem: A Report on the Banality of Evil*. New York: Penguin Books, 2006.

—. *The Human Condition*. Chicago: University of Chicago Press, 1998.

—. *On Revolution*. New York: Penguin Books, 2006.

—. *The Origins of Totalitarianism*. San Diego: Harvest Book Harcourt, 1994.

Badiou, Alain. *Metapolitics*. New York: Verso, 2005.

Bedau, Hugo A. "On Civil Disobedience," *Journal of Philosophy* 58, no. 21, 1961: 653–61.

Benhabib, Seyla. *The Reluctant Modernism of Hannah Arendt*. Lanham, MD: Rowman & Littlefield, 2000.

Bennett, Scott H. *Radical pacifism: The War Resister League and Gandhian Nonviolence in America, 1915–1963*. Syracuse: Syracuse University Press, 2003.

Berlin, Isaiah. *Russian Thinkers*. New York: Viking Press, 1978.

Boehrer, Fred. "Diversity, Plurality and Ambiguity: Anarchism in the Catholic Worker Movement." *Dorothy Day and the Catholic Worker Movement: Centennial Essays*. Ed. William Thorn, Phillip Runkel, and Susan Mountin. Milwaukee: Marquette University Press, 2001.

Bondurant, Joan V. *Conquest of Violence: The Gandhian Philosophy of Conflict*. Princeton: Princeton University Press, 1988.

Bookchin, Murray. *Post-Scarcity Anarchism*. London: Wildwood House, 1974.

Branch, Taylor. *At Canaan's Edge: America in the King Years 1965–68*. New York: Simon & Schuster, 2006.

—. *Parting the Waters: America in the King Years 1954–1963*. New York: Simon & Schuster Adult Publishing Group, 1989.

Buell, Lawrence. *Literary Transcendentalism: Style and Vision in the American Renaissance*. Ithaca: Cornell University Press, 1979.

Cain, William E. *A Historical Guide to Henry David Thoreau.* Oxford: Oxford University Press, 2000.

Camus, Albert. *The Plague.* New York: Vintage Books, 1991.

Carmichael, Stokely and Charles Hamilton. *Black Power: A Politics of Liberation in America.* New York: Vintage, 1992.

Carson, Clayborne. *In Struggle: SNCC and the Black Awakening of the 1960s.* Cambridge: Harvard University Press, 1995.

Carter, April. *The Political Theory of Anarchism.* New York: Harper Collins, 1971.

Case, Clarence Marsh. *Non-Violent Coercion: A Study in Methods of Social Pressure.* New York: Century, 1923.

Catholic Church. *Catechism of the Catholic Church.* Citta del Vaticano: Libreria Editrice Vaticana, 1993.

Cavell, Stanley. *The Senses of Walden.* Chicago: University of Chicago Press, 1992.

Chaitanya Yati, Nita. *Marxism and Humanist Monarchy.* Kerala, India: Mangala Press, East-West University of Brahmavidya, 1980.

Channing, William Ellery. "Self-Culture: An Address" Introductory to the Franklin Lectures. Boston, London: Palmer and Clayton, 1838.

Chatfield, Charles. *The American Peace Movement: Ideals and Activism.* New York: Twayne, 1992.

Chomsky, Noam. *Chomsky Anarchism.* Edinburgh, Oakland, and West Virginia: AK Press, 2005.

Coles, Robert. *Dorothy Day: A Radical Devotion.* New York: Da Capo Press, 1987.

Cone, James H. *Martin & Malcolm & America: A Dream or a Nightmare.* Maryknoll, NY: Orbis Books, 1991.

Cook, Anthony E. *The Least of These: Race, Law, and Religion in American Culture.* New York: Routledge, 1997.

Crowder, George. *Classical Anarchism: The Political Thought of Godwin, Proudhon, Bukunin, and Kropotkin.* Oxford: Clarendon Press, 1991.

Cruse, Harold. *The Crisis of the Negro Intellectual.* New York: New York Review of Books, 2005.

Dahl, Robert A. *Democracy and Its Critics.* New Haven: Yale University Press, 1989.

Dawson, Michael C. *Black Visions: The Roots of Contemporary African-American Political Ideologies.* Chicago: Chicago University Press, 2001.

Day, Dorothy. *Loaves and Fishes: The Inspiring Story of the Catholic Worker Movement.* Maryknoll, NY: Orbis Books, 1997.

—. *The Long Loneliness: The Autobiography of the Legendary Catholic Social Activist.* New York: HarperOne, 1997.

Day, Richard J. F. *Gramsci Is Dead: Anarchist Currents in the Newest Social Movements.* Ann Arbor: Pluto Press, 2005.

DeBenedetti, Charles. *The Peace Reform in American History.* Bloomington: Indiana University Press, 1980.

D'Emilio, John. *Lost Prophet: The Life and Times of Bayard Rustin.* Chicago: University of Chicago Press, 2003.

Dyson, Michael Eric. *I May Not Get There with You: The True Martin Luther King, Jr.* New York: Touchstone, 2000.

Edwards, Steward, ed. *Selected Writings of Pierre-Joseph Proudhon.* London: Macmillan, 1969.

Eller, Vernard. *Christian Anarchy: Jesus' Primacy over the Powers.* Grand Rapids, MI: Eerdmans, 1987.

Ellul, Jacques. *Anarchy and Christianity.* Grand Rapids, MI: William B. Eerdmans, 1991.

Elshtain, Jean Bethke, ed. *The Jane Addams Reader.* New York: Basic Books, 2002.

Emerson, Ralph Waldo. "The American Scholar." *The Oxford Authors.* Ed. Richard Poirier. New York: Oxford University Press, 1990.

Epstein, Barbara. *Political Protest & Cultural Revolution: Nonviolent Direct Action in the 1970s and 1980s.* Berkeley: University of California Press, 1991.

Fairclough, Adam. *To Redeem the Soul of America: The Southern Christian Leadership Conference and Martin Luther King, Jr.* Athens: University of Georgia Press, 1987.

Fanon, Franz. *The Wretched of the Earth.* New York: Grove Press, 2004.

Forest, Jim. *Love Is the Measure: A Biography of Dorothy Day, Founder of the Catholic Worker.* Revised edition. Maryknoll, NY: Orbis Books, 2006.

Francis, Richard. *Fruitlands: The Alcott Family and Their Search for Utopia.* New Haven: Yale University Press, 2010.

—. *Transcendental Utopias: Individual and Community at Brook Farm, Fruitlands, and Walden.* Ithaca: Cornell University Press, 1997.

Freire, Paulo. *Pedagogy of the Oppressed.* New York: Continuum, 1986.

Gandhi, Leela. *Affective Communities: Anticolonial Thought, Fin-de Siecle Radicalism, and the Politics of Friendship.* Durham: Duke University Press, 2006.

Gandhi, M. K. *Hind Swaraj or Indian Home Rule.* Ahmedabad, India: Navajivan Publishing House, 1938.

Gans, Chaim. *Philosophical Anarchism and Political Disobedience.* Cambridge: Cambridge University Press, 1992.

Garrow, David J. *Bearing the Cross.* New York: Williams Marrow and Company, 1986.

Goldman, Emma. "Anarchism: What It Really Stands For." *Anarchism and Other Essays.* New York: Mother Earth Publishing, 1917.

Goodman, Paul. *People or Personnel.* New York: Random House, 1965.

Goodman, R. B. *American Philosophy and the Romantic Tradition.* Cambridge: Cambridge University Press, 1990.

Goodwin, Barbara, ed. *The Philosophy of Utopia.* Portland: Frank Cass, 2001.

Gougeon, L. *Virtue's Hero: Emerson, Antislavery, and Reform.* Athens: University of Georgia Press, 1990.

Graeber, David. *Direct Action: An Ethnography.* Oakland: AK Press, 2009.

—. *Fragments of an Anarchist Anthropology.* Chicago: Prickly Paradigm Press, 2004.

—. *Possibilities: Essays on Hierarchy, Rebellion and Desire.* Edinburgh: AK Press, 2007.

Green, Leslie. *The Authority of the State.* New York: Oxford University Press, 1988.

Groff, R. *Thoreau and the Prophetic Tradition.* Los Angeles: Manas Publishing, 1961.

Guérin, Daniel. *Anarchism.* New York: Monthly Review Press, 1970.

Hansen, O. *Aesthetic Individualism and Practical Intellect: American Allegory in Emerson, Thoreau, Adams, and James.* Princeton: Princeton University Press, 1990.

Harding, Vincent. "The Religion of Black Power." *African American Religious Thought: An Anthology*. Ed. Cornel West and Eddie Glaude Jr. Louisville: John Knox Press, 2003.

Hauerwas, Stanley. *The Peaceable Kingdom: A Primer in Christian Ethics*. Notre Dame: University of Notre Dame, 1983.

Hayek, F. A. *Road to Serfdom*. Chicago: University of Chicago Press, 2007.

Hentoff, Nat, ed. *The Essays of A. J. Muste*. Indianapolis: Bobbs-Merrill, 1967.

Hixson, Walter. *The Myth of American Diplomacy*. New Haven: Yale University Press, 2008.

Hodder, Alan D. *Thoreau's Ecstatic Witness*. New Haven: Yale University Press, 2001.

Holmes, Robert L. *On War and Morality*. Princeton: Princeton University Press, 1989.

Iyer, Raghavan, ed. *The Essential Writing of Mahatma Gandhi*. New York: Oxford University Press, 2007.

James, William. *The Varieties of Religious Experience: A Study in Human Nature*. New York: Random House, 1902.

Jenco, Leigh Kathyrn. "Thoreau's Critique of Democracy." *A Political Companion to Henry David Thoreau*. Ed. Jack Turner. Lexington: University Press of Kentucky, 2009.

Jordan, Patrick, ed. *Dorothy Day: Writing from Commonweal*. Collegeville, MN: Liturgical Press, 1980.

Joseph, Peniel E. *Waiting 'til the Midnight Hour: A Narrative History of Black Power in America*. New York: Henry Holt and Company, 2006.

Kahn, Paul W. *Sacred Violence: Torture, Terror, and Sovereignty*. Ann Arbor: University of Michigan Press, 2008.

Kateb, George. *Hannah Arendt: Politics, Conscience, Evil*. Totowa, New Jersey: Rowman & Allanheld, 1983.

—. *The Inner Ocean: Individualism and Democratic Culture*. Ithaca: Cornell University Press, 1992.

Kelley, Donald R. and Bonnie G. Smith, eds. *Proudhon: What Is Property?* Cambridge: Cambridge University Press, 2007.

King, Martin Luther, Jr. *Where Do We Go from Here: Chaos or Community?* Boston: Beacon Press, 1967.

Kropotkin, Peter. *Revolutionary Pamphlets*. Ayer Co. Publication, 1968.

Krutch, J. W. *Henry David Thoreau*. New York: William Sloan Associates, 1948.

Larmore, Charles. *The Morals of Modernity*. New York: Cambridge Press, 1996.

Levine, Daniel. *Bayard Rustin and the Civil Rights Movement*. New Brunswick: Rutgers University Press, 2000.

Lynd, Staughton. *Intellectual Origins of the American Radicalism*. Cambridge: University Press, 2009.

MacIntyre, Alasdair. *After Virtue*. Notre Dame: University of Notre Dame, 1984.

Maritain, Jacques. *The Person and the Common Good*. New York: C. Scribner's Sons, 1947.

Marshall, Megan. *The Peabody Sisters: Three Women Who Ignited American Romanticism*. Boston: Houghton Mifflin, 2005.

Maude, Aylmer. *The Life of Tolstoy: The Later Years*. London: Oxford University, 1930.

Mayer, Henry. *All On Fire: William Lloyd Garrison and the Abolition of Slavery*. New York: St. Martin's Press, 1998.

McKivigan, John R. *The War against Proslavery Religion: Abolitionism and the Northern Churches, 1830–1865*. Ithaca: Cornell University Press, 1984.

McLaughlin, Paul. *Anarchism and Authority: A Philosophical Introduction to Classical Anarchism*. Burlington, VT: Ashgate, 2007.

Merton, Thomas. *The Wisdom of the Desert*. New York: New Directions Publishing, 1970.

Michnik, Adam. *Letters from Prison and Other Essays*. Berkeley: University of California Press, 1987.

Milder, R. *Reimagining Thoreau*. Cambridge: Cambridge University Press, 1995.

Miller, David. *Anarchism*. London: J.M. Dent and Sons, 1984.

Miller, William D. *Dorothy Day: A Biography*. New York: Harper & Row, 1982.

—. *A Harsh and Dreadful Love: Dorothy Day and the Catholic Worker Movement*. Milwaukee: Marquette University Press, 2005.

More, Thomas. *Utopia*. New York: Penguin Books, 1965.

Morris, Aldon D. *The Origins of the Civil Rights Movement: Black Communities Organizing for Change*. New York: Free Press, 1984.

Morris, Brian. *Bakunin: The Philosophy of Freedom*. New York: Black Rose Books, 1993.

Mounier, Emmanuel. *The Personalist Manifesto*. New York: Longmans, Green and Company, 1938.

Musto, Ronald G. *The Catholic Peace Tradition*. New York: Peace Books, 2002.

Myerson, Joel, ed. *Cambridge Companion to Henry David Thoreau*. Cambridge: Cambridge University Press, 1995.

Nozick, Robert. *Anarchy, State, Utopia*. United States: Basic Books, 1974.

Pace, Eric. "Bayard Rustin Is Dead at 75: Pacifist and a Rights Activist." *New York Times* August 25, 1987. www.nytimes.com/1987/08/25/obituaries/bayard-rustin-is-dead-at-75-pacifist-and-a-rights-activist.html

Packer, Barbara. *Transcendentalism*. Athens: University of Georgia, 2007.

Pennock, J. Roland and John W. Chapman, eds. *Anarchism: Nomos XIX*. New York: New York University Press, 1978.

Perry, Lewis. *Radical Abolitionism: Anarchy and the Government of God and Antislavery Thought*. Knoxville: University of Tennessee, 1995.

Phillips, Kevin. *Wealth and Democracy: Political History of the American Rich*. New York: Broadway Books, 2003.

Piehl, Mel. *Breaking Bread: The* Catholic Worker *and the Origin of Catholic Radicalism in America*. Tuscaloosa: University of Alabama Press, 2006.

Piven, Frances Fox and Richard A. Cloward. *Poor People's Movements: Why They Succeed, How They Fail*. New York: Vintage Books, 1979.

Podair, Jerald. *Bayard Rustin: American Dreamer*. Lanham, MD: Rowman & Littlefield, 2009.

Porte, J. *Emerson and Thoreau: Transcendentalists in Conflict*. Middletown: Wesleyan University Press, 1966.

Rawls, John. *A Theory of Justice*. Cambridge: Belknap Press of Harvard University Press, 1971.

Raz, Joseph. *Practical Reason and Norms*. London: Hutchinson, 1975.

—. "Obligation to Obey: Revision and Tradition," *Notre Dame Journal of Law, Ethics and Public Policy* 1, 1984–5: 140.

Reiman, Jeffrey H. *In Defense of Political Philosophy: A Reply to Robert Paul Wolff's* In Defense of Anarchism. New York: Harper & Row, 1972.

Riasanovsky, Nicholas. *A History of Russia.* New York: Oxford University Press, 1963.

Richardson, Robert D. *Emerson: The Mind on Fire.* Berkeley: University of California Press, 1995.

—. *Henry David Thoreau: A Life of the Mind.* Berkeley: University of California Press, 1992.

Roberts, Nancy. *Dorothy Day and the Catholic Worker.* Albany: State University of New York Press, 1984.

Robinson, Cedric J. *Black Marxism: The Making of the Black Radical Tradition.* Chapel Hill: University of North Carolina Press, 2000.

Rosenblum, Nancy L. "Thoreau's Militant Conscience," *Political Theory* 9, no. 1, 1981: 81–110.

Ross, William David. *The Right and the Good.* Oxford: Clarendon Press, 1930.

Roth, Guenther and Claus Wittich, eds. *Max Weber: Economy and Society: An Outline of Interpretive Sociology.* Berkeley: University of California Press, 1978.

Rucker, Robert C., ed. *The Marx-Engels Reader.* 2nd edition. New York: W. W. Norton, 1978.

Rustin, Bayard. *Time on Two Crosses: The Collected Writings of Bayard Rustin.* Ed. Devon W. Carbado and Donald Weise. San Francisco: Cleis Press, 2003.

Schell, Jonathan. *The Unconquerable World: Power, Nonviolence, and the Will of the People.* New York: Holt Paperbacks, 2003.

Schmitt, Carl. *The Concept of the Political.* Chicago: University of Chicago Press, 1997.

Sharp, Gene and Joshua Paulson. *Waging Nonviolent Struggle: 20th Century Practice and 21st Century Potential.* Manchester: Extending Horizons Books, 2005.

Shatz, Marshall. *Bakunin: Statism and Anarchy.* Cambridge: Cambridge University Press, 2005.

Shelby, Tommie. *We Who Are Dark: The Philosophical Foundations of Black Solidarity.* Cambridge: Belknap Press of Harvard University Press, 2005.

Simmons, A. John. *Justification and Legitimacy: Essays on Rights and Obligation.* New York: Cambridge University Press, 2001.

—. *Moral Principles and Political Obligations.* Princeton: Princeton University, 1979.

Simon, Myron. "Thoreau and Anarchism," *Michigan Quarterly Review* 23, no. 3, Summer 1984: 360–84.

Singer, Director Bennett. *Brother Outsider: The Life of Bayard Rustin,* DVD, Passion River, 2008.

Smith, M. B. E. "Is There a Prima Facie Obligation to Obey the Law?" *Yale Law Journal* 82, 1973: 950–76.

Snyder, Helena Adell. *Thoreau's Philosophy of Life: With Special Consideration of the Influence of Hindoo Philosophy.* Whitefish, MT: Kessinger Publishing, 2010.

Stringham, Edward, ed. *Anarchy, State and Pubic Choice.* Northampton, MA: Edward Elgar, 2005.

Tarrow, Sidney. *Power in Movement: Social Movements and Contentious Politics.* 2nd edition. Cambridge: Cambridge University Press, 2008.

Tauber, Alfred. *Henry David Thoreau and the Moral Agency of Knowing.* Berkeley: University of California Press, 2001.

Taylor, B. P. *America's Bachelor Uncle: Thoreau and the American Polity.* Lawrence: University Press of Kansas, 1996.

Taylor, Cynthia. *A. Philip Randolph: The Religious Journey of an African American Labor Leader.* New York: New York University Press, 2006.

Thomas, John. "Romantic Reform in America, 1815–1865," *America Quarterly* 17, no. 4, 1965: 656–81.

Thoreau, Henry David. *The Higher Law: Thoreau on Civil Disobedience and Reform.* Princeton: Princeton University Press, 2004.

—. *A Week in Concord Merrimack Rivers, Walden, The Main Woods, Cape Cod.* Ed. Robert Sayre. New York: Library of Americas, 1998.

Tolstoy, Leo. *The Kingdom of God Is Within.* New York: Barnes and Noble, 2005.

Toure, Kwame and Charles Hamilton. *Black Power: The Politics of Liberation in America.* New York: Vintage, 1992.

Tracy, James R. *Direct Action: Radical Pacifism from the Union Eight to the Chicago Seven.* Chicago: University of Chicago Press, 1997.

Troeltsch, Ernst. *The Social Teachings of the Christian Churches.* London: George Allen, 1931.

Turner, Jack, ed. *A Political Companion to Henry David Thoreau.* Lexington: University Press of Kentucky, 2009.

Unger, Roberto Mangabeira. *Law in Modern Society: Toward a Criticism of Social theory.* New York: Free Press, 1976.

—. *The Self Awakened.* Cambridge: Harvard University Press, 2007.

—. *What Should Legal Analysis Become?* New York: Verso, 1996.

Van Deburg, William L. *New Day in Babylon: The Black Power Movement and American Culture, 1965–1975.* Chicago: University of Chicago Press, 1992.

Walzer, Michael. *Interpretation and Social Criticism.* Cambridge: Harvard University Press, 1987.

—. *Obligations: Essays on Disobedience, War, and Citizenship.* Cambridge: Harvard University Press, 1970.

West, Cornel. *Democracy Matters.* New York: Penguin Press, 2004.

—. *Prophesy Deliverance!: An Afro-American Revolutionary Christianity.* Philadelphia: Westminster Press, 1982.

Wilson, A. N. *Tolstoy.* New York: W.W. Norton, 1988.

Wilson, William Julius. *The Declining Significance of Race: Blacks and Changing American Institutions.* 2nd edition. Chicago: University of Chicago Press, 1980.

Wolff, Robert Paul. *In Defense of Anarchism.* Berkeley: University of California, 1998.

Wolpert, Stanley. *Gandhi's Passion: The Life and Legacy of Mahatma Gandhi.* New York: Oxford University Press, 2001.

Woodcock, George. *Anarchism: A History of Libertarian Ideas and Movements.* Harmondsworth: Penguin, 1963.

York, Trip. *Living on Hope while Living in Babylon: The Christian Anarchists of the 20th Century.* Eugene: Wipf and Stock, 2009.

Zwick, Louise and Mark Zwick. *The Catholic Worker Movement: Intellectual and Spiritual Origins.* New York: Paulist Press, 2005.

# INDEX

false necessity 9, 27–31, 38, 48, 50
Farmer, James 108, 111, 132
Faulkner, William 57
Federal Bureau of Investigation 91
federalism 37, 99
Fellowship of Reconciliation 10, 76, 108, 112
Fourierists 50
Francis of Assisi 71
freedom viii, 25, 31, 34, 38, 43, 44, 45, 48, 49, 70, 71, 76, 79, 84, 87, 88, 97, 99, 104, 105, 113, 127, 138, 141, 143, 151, 155, 163–6, 178, 179
French personalist, French personalism 62, 63, 69, 82, 84
French Revolution 6
"From Protest to Politics" 132, 133, 135, 137, 139, 143, 185, 186
From Union Square to Rome 56, 58, 60, 66, 67, 72, 104
Fugitive Slave Act of 1850 30
Fuller, Margaret 17

Gandhi, Mohandas 42, 47, 65, 73, 95, 111, 112, 148, 152, 176n. 9, 187n. 55
Gandhian ethics 112, 113
Gandhian nonviolence 2, 109, 111, 113, 122, 138, 139, 141, 142
Gandhian philosophy 67, 69, 112, 113, 183n. 6
Gandhian theories 12, 112, 139, 139
Gans, Chaim 149
Garrison, William Lloyd ix, 17, 33, 35, 75, 94, 111, 121, 148
God 7–10, 16, 17–20, 25, 34, 38, 38, 46, 49, 50, 58–63, 65–72, 74, 75, 81, 89, 93, 101, 115, 116, 117, 122, 123, 155, 156, 166, 172n. 3, 175n. 73, 177n. 28, 178n. 36, 184nn. 11,16
God's law 20, 123, 184n. 11
Goldman, Emma 54, 114
Goldwater, Barry 98
Goodman, Paul 3, 54, 80, 150
Gospel 71, 72, 74, 77, 83, 112
government 11, 29, 31, 33, 34, 35, 36, 44, 50, 51, 55, 81, 85, 88, 91,
98, 99–101, 104, 109, 114, 115, 122, 123, 124, 125, 133, 134, 137, 143, 149, 153, 155, 157, 163, 164, 170n. 6, 171n. 11, 174n. 61, 176n. 92, 179n. 57, 182n. 94
form of government 3, 8, 37–41, 89, 124, 169n. 4, 180n. 67
grace 60, 67, 69, 73, 102, 178n. 36
Graeber, David 94, 104, 183n. 104, 188n. 6
Great Depression 77, 112, 133, 153
Greenwich Village 57

Harrington, Michael 100, 101, 108
Hayek, F. A. 98
heart 17, 25, 28, 55, 57–60, 63, 66, 74, 112, 128, 130, 138–40, 166, 186n. 41
Hedge, Frederick Henry 17
hell 63
higher law 123, 124, 148, 156
Hodder, Alan D. 7, 172n. 2
Holmes, John Haynes 115
Hopedale 33
Houser, George 108
Hughan, Jessie Wallace 110
human dignity 80, 89, 90
human nature 17, 31, 49
human rights 38

imperialism 48, 53, 98, 122, 175n. 69
Indian Appropriations Act of 1871 53
Indian wars 53
Industrial Workers of the World 58
industrialization 135
injustice ii, 4, 8, 11, 15, 25, 28, 31–3, 38, 42–6, 50, 53, 56, 57, 67, 68, 94, 96, 111, 122, 123, 125, 126, 132, 135, 138, 140, 144, 147, 157, 159, 161
institutional practices 24, 26, 32

jail 30, 45, 48, 65–8, 115, 122, 187n. 6
James, William 105
Jenco, Kathryn 171n. 14
Jews 92, 150
Jim Crow 109, 123, 143
Johnson, Lyndon B. 78, 101, 127, 128, 130, 182n. 92